Japan on the Jesuit Stage

BLOOMSBURY NEO-LATIN SERIES

Series editors: William M. Barton, Stephen Harrison, Gesine Manuwald and Bobby Xinyue

Early Modern Texts and Anthologies
Edited by Stephen Harrison and Gesine Manuwald

Volume 4

The 'Early Modern Texts and Anthologies' strand of the *Bloomsbury Neo-Latin Series* presents editions of texts with English translations, introductions and notes. Volumes include complete editions of longer single texts and themed anthologies bringing together texts from particular genres, periods or countries and the like.

These editions are primarily aimed at students and scholars and intended to be suitable for use in university teaching, with introductions that give authoritative but not exhaustive accounts of the relevant texts and authors, and commentaries that provide sufficient help for the modern reader in noting links with classical Latin texts and bringing out the cultural context of writing.

Alongside the series' 'Studies in Early Modern Latin Literature' strand, it is hoped that these editions will help to bring important and interesting NeoLatin texts of the period from 1350 to 1800 to greater prominence in study and scholarship, and make them available for a wider range of academic disciplines as well as for the rapidly growing study of Neo-Latin itself.

Japan on the Jesuit Stage

*Two 17th-Century Latin Plays
with Translation and Commentary*

Akihiko Watanabe

BLOOMSBURY ACADEMIC
LONDON • NEW YORK • OXFORD • NEW DELHI • SYDNEY

BLOOMSBURY ACADEMIC
Bloomsbury Publishing Plc
50 Bedford Square, London, WC1B 3DP, UK
1385 Broadway, New York, NY 10018, USA
29 Earlsfort Terrace, Dublin 2, Ireland

BLOOMSBURY, BLOOMSBURY ACADEMIC and the Diana logo are
trademarks of Bloomsbury Publishing Plc

First published in Great Britain 2023

Cover design: Terry Woodley
Cover image © Illustration by Nicolas Trigault (1623). Historic Images / Alamy
Stock Photo

A catalogue record for this book is available from the British Library.

A catalog record for this book is available from the Library of Congress.

ISBN: HB: 978-1-3502-1720-1
       PB: 978-1-3502-1719-5
       ePDF: 978-1-3502-1721-8
       eBook: 978-1-3502-1722-5

Series: Bloomsbury Neo-Latin Series: Early Modern Texts and Anthologies

Typeset by RefineCatch Limited, Bungay, Suffolk
Printed and bound in Great Britain

To find out more about our authors and books visit www.bloomsbury.com
and sign up for our newsletters.

Contents

Names

- Japanese proper names are transcribed according to the Hepburn romanization system. *macra* are omitted for common geographical names (e.g. Tokyo rather than Tōkyō).
- Modern personal names are written in the order of personal name first and surname second (e.g. Akihiko Watanabe), but the order is reversed for early modern ones (e.g. Toyotomi Hideyoshi). After the first mention, surnames are typically used (e.g. Watanabe) except when surnames are dynastic (e.g. Hideyoshi rather than Toyotomi).
- Early modern Jesuit versions of Japanese personal names (usually contemporary Latin transcriptions of native court titles or nicknames, or Western baptismal names) are used as a rule when literary incarnations rather than actual historical figures are meant (e.g. Taico(sama) rather than Hideyoshi, Safioye rather than Hasegawa Fujihiro/Sahyōe, and Thomas rather than Honda Heibyōe).
- Act/part and scene numbers are indicated by capital Roman numerals and Arabic numerals, respectively; e.g. I.1=Act/Part one, Scene one.

Figures

Acknowledgements

Martyrium Iapones, Theodisci drama dederunt;
accipe, posteritas, hoc pietatis opus.

A.W.

This book owes its existence to fortuitous meetings with many experts. It is impossible to enumerate them all and the following are just a few that come to mind.

I met Oba Haruka in Kyoto in 2016, and since then she has always generously shared her unparalleled knowledge of early modern European reception of Japanese Catholic missionary history. Among other things, our cooperation led to a joint Austro-Japanese research project ('Japan on the Jesuit Stage', 2016–18, FWF-JSPS), of which the Austrian PI was Florian Schaffenrath. Florian's apparently limitless dedication to Neo-Latin research has been the object of my admiration ever since our first meeting in Lexington, KY in 2015. Other members of the project were Patrick Schwemmer and Maria Maciejewska. Maria together with Florian read and commented on the preliminary transcript and translation of *VJ*, while Patrick has often corrected my rudimentary understanding of the history of my own country.

While we were wrapping up this joint project, I attended the 2018 IANLS triennial conference in Albacete, Spain. During one of its excursions I was truly fortunate to sit next to James Parente on a bus, for during our conversation it turned out that we shared among other things an interest in Neo-Latin drama (though my travel companion's expertise was obviously much deeper and wider than mine), and James further recalled having seen some manuscripts of a play about Japan in Koblenz. In subsequent days I had some hurried email exchanges which eventually led to the examination of manuscript images kindly obtained from the LHA by Florian and Maria and shared with the author. The upshot of all of this was the discovery of *JM*'s script.

The first Austro-Japanese project was followed by another one in 2019, Haruka being the Japanese PI and Arno Strohmeyer the Austrian counterpart. During its seminar in Kyoto I got to know the other participants including Doris Gruber, Marion Romberg and Michael Hüttler who kindly shared with me their tips not only on early modern central Europe but also on Vienna as I was planning for a Sabbatical in that beautiful city for AY 2020.

The *annus terribilis* of 2020 turned out to be vastly different from what not only I but the majority of the world had doubtlessly expected. But due to the generosity and flexibility of colleagues and administrators at Otsuma Women's University I was in the end able to spend seven months in Austria and Germany during AY 2020, a stay which was truly indispensable for the preparation of this volume. My unexpectedly solitary sojourn in Europe at this time also meant not a small amount of privation to my spouse and two children as well as perhaps our dog who all missed out on an opportunity to experience some Viennese life.

Considering the challenging and extraordinary circumstances I recall with all the more gratitude the generous help I received from many friends and colleagues during my stay. Not only Arno, who kindly agreed to be my Viennese supervisor, but Doris and Marion continued to give me numerous suggestions and tips. From conversations with other OeAD colleagues such as Yasir Yilmaz, Ilya Berkovich, William Godsey and Zsuzsanna Cziraki I also received much-needed enlightenment concerning the variegated ethnicities that have historically made up the truly precious tapestry of central Europe. Elisabeth Klecker and Hartmut Wulfram generously facilitated my use of the University of Vienna Classics Department Library. Elisabeth also opened doors to many other contacts, among them Matthias Pernerstorfer and Dorothea Weber.

Dorothea and Matthias (who both gave me many other essential tips on the research behind this volume) are connected to the Holy Grail of Japan-themed Jesuit plays, the papers of Margret Dietrich (1920–2004). Dietrich is someone I never had the chance to meet in real life but to whom I feel that I also owe much debt of gratitude as a scholar, with due recognition of her problematic political past.. During my stay in Vienna, Franz Fillafer, to whom Matthias introduced me, first allowed me to locate the Dietrich papers which I subsequently was allowed to look into in greater detail thanks to their custodians (and Dietrich's former students) Elisabeth Grossegger and Andrea Sommer-Mathis.

I had heard about the papers as early as 2008 from Kurt Smolak and had seen them briefly with Haruka ten years later, but their renewed examination in 2020–21 was truly inspirational. Although Dietrich and her associates (to my relief actually, as far as I could determine) had never looked at *JM* or *VJ*, the immense amount of data accumulated by them on similar plays (which I hope will some day see the light of day in a deserving manner; see <https://www.oeaw.ac.at/en/ikt/research/theatre-and-theatricality/archiving-project-of-the-estate-of-margret-dietrich-1920-2004> (accessed 11 March 2022)) perhaps finds a dim reflection in this volume's Introduction.

The late Fidel Rädle (1935–2021) kindly received me at his Göttingen home as I was returning from Koblenz to Vienna in the summer of 2020 and gave me numerous suggestions concerning both *JM* and *VJ* (especially, but not limited to, the biblical and classical parallels therein). From another continent but equally learned, Mark Riley also carefully read my transcripts and translations of the two plays and offered countless comments. Brad Walton, from whom I learned Latin verse composition many years ago, generously and immediately answered from the University of Toronto Libraries my plea for help regarding hard-to-get references this time. Salvador Bartera helped me with information on Stefonio, while Makoto Harris Takao kindly and expertly clarified some musical notations in *JM*.

When I had nagging questions about Koblenz and plucked up the courage to email Karl-Heinz Zuber, whose guidebook is listed under Bibliography 4, I was delighted to receive an immediate, polite and helpful response. Through him I got in touch with Johannes Dillinger, who pointed out a crucial piece of the puzzle surrounding *JM* as is explained in Introduction 2.2. In another great blessing I met Antonia von Karaisl in Munich who came to assist my research at critical moments when (especially after my return to Japan in early 2021) visits to European archives and libraries became next to impossible. Aside from uncovering important information regarding *JM*'s text which will be discussed in Introduction 2.3 and pointing out some rough spots in my manuscript, Antonia also contacted Peter Kefes to whom I owe a biographical detail connected to *VJ* (see Introduction 3.2).

Last but not least, Beatrice Bodart-Bailey, my erstwhile colleague and mentor at Otsuma Women's University, has never been stinting in her advice regarding Japanese history, and among many other things suggested the illustration for Daifu/Ieyasu for use in this volume (Figure 1). Any errors that have remained in spite of all the generous help I received from these experts are my own.

In my research, other than the archives mentioned under Bibliography 2, I have also been much obliged to the excellent services of the Austrian National Library, the various libraries of the Austrian Academy of Sciences and the University of Vienna, the National Diet Library of Japan, and above all the Kirishitan Bunko Library of Sophia University. Work for this volume has received financial support from research funds provided by Tokyo University, Otsuma Women's University, JSPS (project no. 19K00503), JSPS-FWF, and OeAD (Richard Plaschka Fellowship).

Finally I would like to dedicate this book to my spouse Kanan and my children Rio and Yoritaka, who have helped me in ways that are beyond imagining.

Introduction

Japan on the Neo-Latin Jesuit Stage

Missionary background and transmission of information from Japan to Europe

Although traces of Christian activity in East Asia have been detected from as early as the seventh century,[1] direct contact between Japan and the Christian West, as far as is known, did not start until the early modern period. Francis Xavier (1506–52), the first documented Christian missionary to come to Japan, landed on the southern island of Kagoshima on 15 August 1549. This day, other than being the feast day of the Assumption of Mary, was also the fifteenth anniversary of the celebrated meeting between Ignatius Loyola (1491–1556) and his six companions including Xavier in the Paris crypt (1534) which eventually led to the founding of the Society of Jesus (1540). The Illustrious Seven who met in Paris were all university students (including Loyola, who was forty-two years old at that time), and a distinctively academic streak was to be a lasting mark of this order.[2] The Society which emerged from this meeting in the university town not only went on to found countless academies around the world but also ushered in the so-called Christian Century (i.e. the mid-sixteenth to early-seventeenth century) of Japan[3] and played a major part in collecting, relaying and disseminating information about the East in early modern Europe.

When Xavier reached Japan in 1549, the country was in a state of endemic civil strife which had lingered on in wake of the catastrophic Ōnin civil war (1467–77). The dual rule by the emperor, whose role by then had become mostly ceremonial, and the so-called *shogun* (supreme military commander), who was in charge of military and secular affairs, had all but broken down and much of the country was being governed by quasi-independent warlords (the so-called *daimyō*). In this fractured and conflict-laden environment, Xavier and other Jesuits who followed him attracted listeners and converts not only among commoners but also within the warrior class (the so-called *samurai*). The most famous among those whom Xavier met was the *daimyō* Ōtomo Yoshishige (1530–87), also known as Sōrin, who was baptised much later in

1578 and came to be known in Jesuit literature as *Franciscus rex Bungi* ('Franciscus king of Bungo').[4] To those like him, who came to be called *kirishitan*[5] *daimyō* once they were baptised, the newly arrived foreign religion not only offered a spiritual alternative to traditional Buddhist teachings (which had reached Japan via China and Korea in the sixth century), but the prospect of smoother trade relations with Portuguese merchants who were in close contact with the Jesuits, twin benefits of obvious value in these unstable times.[6]

Ōmura Sumitada (1533–87), the first *daimyō* to become a *kirishitan*, received baptism in 1563. Around this year he also opened in his own domain the port of Nagasaki, which soon became not only a busy hub in the growing Luso-Asian trade network but also the centre of Jesuit missionary enterprise in Japan. His elder brother and neighbouring *daimyō* Arima Yoshisada (1521–77) followed him to the baptismal font in 1576. The latter's homonymous domain of Arima (present-day Minamishimabara city), like the neighbouring port of Nagasaki, came to house a large concentration of Catholics and became home to the Jesuit seminary where not only religious doctrine but also Western art and languages including Latin were taught.[7] The first play in our collection dramatizes a martyrdom that took place early in the next century in this same domain when the tide of evangelization was being reversed.

A grand event that marked the zenith of Jesuit activity in Japan was the so-called Tenshō embassy (1582–90). Four teenage Japanese boys, all recent graduates of the Jesuit seminary and ostensibly representatives of the 'kings of Japan', i.e. the *kirishitan daimyō* of Nagasaki and several surrounding areas, were sent to pay homage to the supreme pontiff in Rome and feted by members of southern European royalty, clergy and nobility everywhere they passed through.[8] The embassy, aside from causing a brief PR sensation in Europe, also gave rise to documented cases of Japanese reception of Western culture, including classical Graeco-Roman and humanistic elements. To give a couple of examples, the ambassadors were shown Latin dialogues and plays in European Jesuit academies, and their reports back home likely inspired the performance of a Neo-Latin play in the Japanese seminary during the Christmas celebration of 1592.[9] The embassy also carried on their way back the first Western-style movable-type printing press in the Far East which was subsequently used to produce Latin as well as Japanese books for both seminarians and lay converts.[10] The embassy however was also symptomatic of a serious disconnect between realities on the ground and an over-optimistic outlook on the future of the Japanese mission which members of the regional Jesuit leadership such as Alessandro Valignano (1539–1606), the Italian Visitor of the Indies, advertised to the European public.[11] Most importantly, the 'kings of Japan', whose representatives these boys ostensibly were, were nothing more than local dynasts whose powers, including the freedom to be baptised and to protect Catholics in their own domains, were about to be radically curtailed as the period of internal warfare was coming to an end and centralized governance was gradually but surely being restored.

One likely impetus behind the Tenshō embassy was a 1580 meeting between Valignano and the powerful *daimyō* and then de-facto national hegemon Oda Nobunaga (1534–82), known as Nombunanga in Jesuit accounts. Nobunaga appeared favourably disposed to Catholicism and granted them a number of privileges such as the right to build a Jesuit house and seminary close to his own castle, although he may have done so more to dent the prestige of his Buddhist enemies than from any deep-seated pro-Christian sentiment.[12] Nobunaga in any case was unexpectedly assassinated by his lieutenant Akechi Mitsuhide[13] (1526–1582) just after the Tenshō embassy left Japan and the hegemony devolved to his subordinate Toyotomi Hideyoshi (1537–98) (called Taico or Taicosama[14] in Jesuit accounts), who, after a period of initial ambivalence, turned hostile to the Catholics. Hideyoshi/Taicosama eventually initiated the persecution of 1596–97 which culminated in the so-called Martyrdom of Twenty-Six Saints (1597) that forms the background of the second play in this volume.

One of the major triggers to this incident, in which twenty-six believers ranging from missionary priests to recent converts were marched from the ancient capital of Kyoto to Nagasaki and crucified in full view of the still heavily Catholic city, was an unguarded remark by a pilot of a stranded Spanish ship to the effect that Catholic missionaries were in the front line of the rapidly expanding global Iberian empire.[15] The idea that Catholic evangelization is a preparation for military invasion and that its suppression therefore is a matter of national security resurfaces in the first play in this volume.

This oft-repeated suspicion of collusion between Catholic missionaries and Spanish *conquistadores* ('conquerors'), whether historically justified or not,[16] is related to another problem that the Jesuits in Japan were facing at this time, namely interference from their less locally experienced colleagues, mostly Franciscans but later Augustinians and Dominicans as well, who had begun to trickle in from the newly established colony of the Philippines. The arrival of the Philippines-based missionaries starting in the 1590s was quite possibly in response to a genuine need felt by Japanese converts for more priests and was facilitated by burgeoning trade between Luzon and Nagasaki,[17] but the Jesuit attitude to these newcomers was often less than fraternal. In addition to differences in cultures and chains of command between the orders, to the already acclimatised Jesuits the Hispanic mendicants often seemed brash and insensitive to local conditions, while the latter accused their Macao-based colleagues of lacking in proper fortitude and being excessively accommodating toward Eastern pagans.[18]

But if the animosity between the Jesuits and the mendicant orders was troublesome, the spill-over from the ferocious contemporary European conflict between Protestants and Catholics turned out to be catastrophic. In the final years of the sixteenth century, Dutch ships, soon followed by the British, began to appear in the East Indies in the hopes of undermining Catholic Iberian trade monopoly. Meanwhile Hideyoshi passed away in 1598, leaving an heir who was widely perceived to be weak, and another *daimyō* by the name of Tokugawa Ieyasu (1543–1616) (Figure 1) began his manoeuvre to take over as the national hegemon. Known as Daifu or Daifusama[19] in Jesuit accounts, Ieyasu not only succeeded in becoming the next hegemon but founded a dynasty that went on to rule Japan until the mid-nineteenth century. This astute politician Ieyasu/Daifu looms large in our first play as will be discussed below.

In 1600, a storm-battered Dutch ship limped into a port in Japan and two survivors from the crew, including one Englishman by the name of William Adams (1564–1620), were brought to Ieyasu's court. When the Jesuits heard of this arrival, they sent an envoy demanding their immediate execution as pirates illegally disrupting Portuguese maritime trade. Ieyasu however refused and instead groomed the castaways to become his personal advisors. From these grateful Westerners as well as the Dutch East India Company which they represented, Ieyasu learned that Europe, contrary to what the Jesuits had been telling the Japanese, was not united in peace under a single pope,[20] and that Protestant nations, far from being puny and soon-to-be vanquished pockets of rebellion, had the ambition and capacity to supplant the Iberians and furnish Japan with the necessary trade relations with the West.[21]

At this point, Protestant presence in the East Pacific and Ieyasu's prospect for lasting hegemony were still both tenuous. But as they both solidified in the coming decades, it was only logical that Catholic prospects in Japan would wane in proportion. A major landmark in the intensifying persecution was the anti-Christian decree of 1614 and mass expulsion of Catholic missionaries and the *kirishitan*, including the famous *daimyō* Iustus Takayama Ukon (1552–1615) who became a hero of several Jesuit plays[22] and makes a cameo appearance in our second play. The first piece in our collection is based on a martyrdom that took place in 1613 as Ieyasu and his agents were setting the stage for this major assault on Catholicism in Japan.

In the 1620s and 30s, Catholic priests still ministered quietly and in hiding in Japan. But a final blow was dealt following the ferocious Shimabara rebellion (1637–8), in which mostly *kirishitan* farmers and former *samurai* fought and lost in southern Japan against forces gathered by the Tokugawa

Figure 1 Tokugawa Ieyasu, a.k.a. Daifu, Kunōzan Tōshōgū Museum, Edo period (*Tōshō Daigongen* picture).

dynasty. The rebellion resulted amongst other things in the eradication of the remaining *kirishitan* in Arima, and more importantly it convinced the Tokugawa dynasty that Christianity, if allowed to continue in any social stratum, would be an existential threat to the feudal social order, the bedrock of its rule. Even though the Catholic church never gave official approval to this armed insurrection, the *kirishitan* became an avowed public enemy in the eyes of the central government since the majority of the rebels self-identified as such.[23] In 1639 all ties with Macao were severed and the Dutch, who promised never to mix faith with finances, became the only Western party allowed to do business in the country (and even then, under severe local restrictions). It is thought that the last ordained Catholic priest to minister to the remaining *kirishitan*, a Japanese Jesuit by the name of Konishi Mancio (1600–44) who may have been a grandson of the famous *kirishitan daimyō* Konishi Yukinaga (1555–1600) and had studied in the Collegio Romano, was discovered and executed in the mid-1640s.[24]

The Jesuits were prolific letter-writers, and information from Japan during their period of activity sketched above reached Europe through two distinct epistolary channels. First there were the annual letters, called *litterae annuae* in Latin. These were official communications that climbed up the Jesuit chain of command from all regions or 'provinces' (as the Jesuits called them) of the world to reach the centre in Rome. The letters were not only read within the Society to shore up morale but were also often collected, edited and printed in different languages, including Latin, to garner popular support. Secondly, less formal epistolary narratives were also exchanged within or with those outside the Society to supplement the official accounts. These letters, annual or otherwise, were often further collected and redacted into annalistic accounts of regions, or sometimes large-scale histories of the entire Jesuit order or even of the Catholic church or of the Christian world.[25] One must keep in mind that on all levels, from their origin in Japan to the many redactions on their way to and in Europe, these accounts were composed, collated and edited by Catholics, mostly Jesuits, who were not professional journalists or historians in the modern sense but were consciously working for the greater glory of their church and God.

Japanese information presented in Jesuit plays, as far as can be determined, comes from these printed editions of various letters or annals based thereupon, rather than first-hand oral or handwritten testimonies. We would accordingly be well advised not to take these pieces featuring starry-eyed Japanese converts, nefarious bonzes (Buddhist priests), and raging persecutors as a true-to-life reflection of historical events in Japan but rather as Catholic Counter-Reformation propaganda based on sources which were themselves propagandistic. In this sense, it may make sense to see these Jesuit plays as a mirror-image of the rabid anti-*kirishitan* literature that proliferated in seventeenth- and eighteenth-century Japan which depicted the missionaries as diabolical agents working at the behest of foreign powers to subvert the divine nation of the Rising Sun.[26]

It would however be equally misleading to dismiss the accounts from Japan on which the plays are based and indeed the plays themselves as fantasy, pure and simple. Works composed by Jesuit and other early modern Catholic missionaries concerning the Japanese language, literature, customs and history reveal authentic first-hand knowledge and are duly recognized as invaluable sources for linguists, literary scholars and cultural historians today.[27] There is no doubt that these frontline missionaries interacted directly with the Japanese populace on all social levels, from commoners to members of the *samurai* class all the way to some *daimyō* and occasionally national hegemons like Ieyasu. If their venture eventually failed, the failure should not be imputed to their ignorance of local language or culture but rather to wider historical vicissitudes sketched above, which produced numerous losers (so to speak) within Japan other than the Catholics. Many of the martyr accounts can be corroborated with non-Catholic (both Japanese and foreign, including Protestant) reports. There is a large body of surviving material evidence as well, both archaeological finds such as local *kirishitan* graves and relics of martyrs that were smuggled abroad during the Christian century, which all testify to the rapid spread of Catholicism in early modern Japan and the ferocious persecution that drove it underground.[28] The Jesuit plays on Japan may justifiably be presented as a genuine outcome of a chain reaction that reverberated from the Far East to Europe, even with all the propagandistic 'noise' (which to be sure also deserves scholarly attention).

The first mention of Japan in a Jesuit Neo-Latin school text seems to be in Juan Bonifacio (1538–1606)'s collection of anecdotes modelled on Valerius Maximus (active 1 c.), the *Christiani Pueri Institutio* printed in Salamanca in 1575.[29] Incidental appearances of Japan as an allegorical figure or occasional Japanese characters are known to have occurred in European academic spectacles in the 1580s, as mentioned in connection with the Tenshō embassy above. The earliest known plays set in Japan (as opposed to those simply having occasional Japanese characters) were produced in Genoa and Graz in 1607,[30] but future research may uncover older examples in Iberian academies which had more direct missionary contact with the East. The first piece in our collection, the 1625 Koblenz play, is the earliest known Neo-Latin drama of this kind whose script is extant.

Estimates differ, but at least a few hundred plays primarily concerned with Japan are known to have been produced in Europe in the seventeenth to nineteenth century.[31] Since there are still many dark spots in current Neo-

Latin theatrical research (especially with regard to the vast majority of texts that were not printed),[32] future investigation is likely to uncover other pieces of this kind, including possibly those produced in Western-controlled territories outside Europe.[33] Furthermore, Japanese themes are also often found in orations, dialogues, epic and shorter poetry, meditative texts and other Neo-Latin genres.[34] Neo-Latin as a whole may still be a sunken continent that is rising only slowly[35] and the present volume only offers a *Stichprobe* ('spot check') of the reception of Japan therein.

Early modern Jesuit education and classical humanism

The Jesuit order as mentioned above had its genesis in the early modern European academia, and profound respect bordering on sacralization of the classical Graeco-Roman heritage was one element that it inherited therefrom.[36] The Jesuits however simultaneously presented themselves as the most loyal frontline soldiers of Catholicism and ostensibly embraced all the traditions of the church, not only the Judeo-Christian foundations but also patristic, scholastic and baroque theology. Their literature therefore, as can be seen in the texts in this volume, may present such (to modern sensibilities) bizarre and contradictory combinations as Jupiter and Neptune appearing on the same stage alongside Jesus Christ, the angels, and personifications of the church and cardinal virtues. As if this were not enough, the Jesuits were also enthusiastic and active agents in contemporary social, political and scientific scenes across the globe and did not shy away from advertising their internationalism and interdisciplinarity, with the result that in our plays Buddhist deities, historical Japanese figures, and contemporary cosmological observations are all thrown into the mix. As adequate discussion of all these different strands would fill at least several volumes,[37] the following brief sketch concentrates on just one element therein, namely classical humanism, arguably the oldest pillar in this variegated academic colonnade.

Intense linguistic grounding in Latin, followed by a somewhat lighter one in Greek and occasionally Hebrew, was the staple and *sine qua non* of the Jesuit college (also called gymnasium, especially in the German context) in which boys (girls were not admitted) usually in their early teens spent about six years of schooling. The rough equivalent today in terms of age is secondary education, and the comparison is also apt since this was the preparatory stage before pupils went on to study more specialised fields such as law, medicine, natural philosophy, theology or combinations thereof in universities.[38] In terms of the intensity and level of linguistic training in the classical languages however, classroom experience in the Jesuit college or gymnasium must have easily been the equivalent of, if not more intense than, what takes place in tertiary or quaternary education today.[39] Early modern Jesuit students not only had to read but also write and speak Latin in their schools and could be penalized for using the vernacular at unguarded moments.[40]

The inculcated linguistic norm was humanistic Latin that recognized and aspired toward the classical model of Cicero (106–43 BCE) and Virgil (70–19 BCE) but did not exclude eclectic elements taken from later Roman authors such as Seneca the Younger (*c.* 4 BCE–65 CE) and approved late antique to early modern authors such as Jerome (*c.* 342/7–429) and Justus Lipsius (1547–1606).[41] As the famous *Ratio Studiorum,* the Jesuit manual of education, makes clear, the aim of this early stage of education was to teach students to become eloquent communicators and not classical philologists in the modern sense.[42] Under the direction of their teachers and elder peers, boys in Jesuit colleges assiduously read and composed classicizing humanistic Latin prose and verse. Public plays, carefully prepared throughout the school year to be performed in front of a large audience that could include their own parents as well as local political and ecclesiastical dignitaries, were a culmination in this early stage of education. A few, but by no means all, students were expected to eventually enter ecclesiastical careers including those in the Jesuit order. The rest were to follow secular career paths generally in line with their social origins, enhanced by skills and connections forged in these schools.[43]

While one cannot deny the spiritual originality of Ignatius Loyola and his early followers, in respect to humanistic education, the Jesuits' contribution may be characterized rather as fastening onto an already existing early modern European academic trend and universalizing it. They became an enthusiastic part of the learned and philologically aware, but at the same time productive, Neo-Latin (as we term the phenomenon) Republic of Letters and took their deep attachment to the language and culture of the Romans far beyond Europe. To come back to Japan for a moment, while early modern Jesuits operating in East Asia often resorted in their day-to-day administration to Romance vernaculars (Portuguese, Spanish and occasionally Italian),[44] there is abundant evidence that in their Japanese seminary, which was modelled on the order's colleges in Europe, serious efforts were made to turn local boys into fluent users of humanistic Latin. From the 1590s to the 1610s, Jesuit teachers prepared a Latin grammar with Japanese notes, a Latin-Portuguese-Japanese dictionary, and linguistic primers including selections from Cicero, dialogues on the Tenshō embassy, and an anthology of classical-patristic adages in order help their Japanese students develop facility in the target language. Due to the relatively short duration of Jesuit education in early modern Japan and the loss of most of the student material produced therein, it is difficult to make an estimate of how successful this Neo-Latin education was. But about a dozen Latin texts produced by the Jesuit-educated Japanese, mostly handwritten letters but also one printed oration and another printed Ovidian epigram, are extant and they do suggest that at least some of the alumni reached a level of linguistic expertise on par with that of their European contemporaries.[45]

To return to Europe and specifically to Koblenz and Munich, in order to properly appreciate the two plays presented in this volume, it is vital to understand that they too were produced within this educational milieu which aimed to fashion pious and learned citizens well-grounded in the linguistic, literary and cultural norms of classical humanism and simultaneously wide open to contemporary world events. This broadly humanistic and rhetorical education was meant to prepare them to become all things for all men according to the Pauline ideal,[46] indeed the same ideal which motivated the Jesuit missionaries to travel to the far ends of the world and learn an astounding range of local languages and cultures. The picture that we get of seventeenth-century German students impersonating the martyrs, Buddhist priests and rulers of far-away Japan using the language and format of ancient Roman drama can and should be understood against this uniquely variegated and integrative educational background suffused with the spirit of early modern European humanism.[47]

Japanese Martyrs (Koblenz 1625)

Origin and transmission: From Arima in 1613 to Europe in the 1620s

The Koblenz play of 1625 (the *Martyres Iaponenses* ('*Japanese Martyrs*'), henceforth *JM*)[48] is centred on an event that occurred in Arima in January 1613, at a time when the central government under Ieyasu was gearing up toward the anti-Christian edict of 1614 (see 1.1). While, as usual in Jesuit plays, it presents a radically simplified and propagandistic version of the story that is only loosely based on a printed missionary report, it deserves attention as a dramatic representation of a historically attested Japanese event to a European audience barely ten years after it occurred and at a time when Catholic missionaries were still active in the country.

The protagonists of *JM* are modelled on a *kirishitan samurai* by the name of Honda Heibyōe (1571/2–1613), whose baptismal name was Thomas, his brother Matthias (1584/5–1613), and Thomas's two children Iustus (1601/2 –13) and Iacobus (1603/4–13). Thomas's wife Iusta (active 1600s) may have also appeared on stage as a silent character. The Honda family seems to have been of mid- to high-ranking *samurai* class, and Thomas may have previously served two prominent *kirishitan daimyō*, Ukon and Yukinaga (see 1.1).[49]

After the latter's defeat and execution in 1600, Thomas found a new master in Arima Harunobu (1567–1612), the famous Jesuit patron of Jesuits also known by his baptismal name Protasio, the son of Arima Yoshisada and one of the 'kings' who ostensibly dispatched the Tenshō embassy (see 1.1). By 1612, Thomas had become a well-known resident and church member in the still heavily Catholic domain of Arima.[50]

JM's foremost antagonist, Safioye, is the dramatic incarnation of Hasegawa Fujihiro (1568–1617), also known by his Japanese nickname Sahyōe (hence Safioye, Safioie etc. in contemporary Western accounts). In Jesuit reports he is said to have been of a humble origin, a former woodworker or carpenter,[51] but Japanese sources suggest that he came from a family of nobility that had fallen on hard times.[52] Around 1597, Fujihiro's younger sister by the name of Natsu (1581–1660) became a favourite concubine of the aged ruler Ieyasu and he took advantage of this family connection to climb up the ladder of feudal bureaucracy, eventually becoming the third Tokugawa-appointed governor or *bugyō* of Nagasaki (1606). The *bugyō* at this time were mid- to high-ranking administrators under the command of the regional *daimyō* or of the central government (as in this case).[53]

The office of the Nagasaki governor, instituted by Ieyasu in 1603, was tasked from the beginning with containing local Catholic power. Eventually, its duty was to extend to the detection and eradication of all *kirishitan* in this area as well as strict checks on flows of merchandise and information through this sole port of entry into Japan for most of the Edo period (1603–1868). Japanese historians credit Fujihiro with a great deal of bureaucratic diligence and political acumen that enabled him to successfully consolidate this multi-faceted administrative office in its early years and reverse the growth of Catholicism in Nagasaki and surrounding territories,[54] although his tenure ended in 1614 before the most intense phase of persecution began. His successes in this regard also made him a great villain in Jesuit eyes, as we can see in *JM*.

The conviction and death of Arima Harunobu in 1612 in consequence of a murky affair involving bribery between him and a prominent Nagasaki-based *kirishitan* as well as an alleged attempt by this *kirishitan daimyō* to assassinate Fujihiro provided another opportunity to the ambitious Nagasaki governor to extend his control and counteract Catholic influence. The hegemon Ieyasu allowed the disgraced Harunobu to be succeeded by his son Naozumi (1586–1641), who had been baptised under the name Michael but had subsequently apostatized. Naozumi had also divorced his *kirishitan* wife and married Ieyasu's relative and foster-daughter in 1610. Thus, when the young apostate became lord of Arima in 1612, it was only natural that he should be put under Fujihiro's tutelage as they ruled over neighbouring territories and were both proteges and favoured agents of Ieyasu in his increasingly anti-Catholic agenda. The Fujihiro-Naozumi alliance immediately began to urge prominent *kirishitan* residents of Arima to apostatize and to humiliate or in extreme cases execute those who refused, and the Honda family fell victim to this wave of persecution.[55]

According to Jesuit reports, Naozumi was initially reluctant to execute Thomas and Matthias as he recognized them as loyal subjects who had served his family with distinction, and when he finally gave in to the urgings of Fujihiro and his own anti-*kirishitan* spouse, he resorted to the following unusual ruse to entrap the victims. Naozumi had his local henchman invite Thomas to a banquet, during which the host brought a newly acquired sword to be admired by the guest. Thomas, sensing the treachery, nevertheless handled the weapon and complimented it as required by etiquette. When he politely handed back the blade to his host, the latter promptly swung it to dispatch the martyr. The henchman then invited Matthias and murdered him in a similar manner. Immediately after, Thomas's two sons Iacobus and Iustus were summoned by the authorities and executed together with their grandmother Martha (1551/2–1613), though Thomas's wife Iusta as well as his unnamed daughter were spared.[56]

The martyrdom of Thomas and Matthias in Arima was first reported to Western readers by Pedro Morejon (1562–1639), a Spanish Jesuit who had been stationed during the above-mentioned series of events in Nagasaki, in a book published in Mexico in 1616. But the immediate source for our play must have been the later Latin account by the Flemish Jesuit Nicolas Trigault (1577–1628) which appeared in Munich in 1623, since only this version recounts the bloody banquet (Morejon simply says that the two martyrs were killed by trickery).[57] Trigault himself was somewhat of a celebrity among European Jesuits around 1620 as he had gone on a personal tour from 1614 to 1618 through Catholic circles, including those in the Holy Roman Empire, with the aim of drumming up financial and personal support for the Eastern missions. His main expertise was actually on China, to which he had been assigned from 1610 until his death (reputedly by suicide) in 1628.[58] But during his lifetime he also published two books on Japan in response to popular demand and the 1623 volume, which served as the source of at least seventeen Jesuit plays other than *JM*,[59] covered events that transpired from 1612 to 1620.

The martyrdom of Thomas and his family was to become a popular theme in Jesuit dramaturgy, and more than a dozen versions other than *JM* are known, from the one in Eichstätt in 1626 to Kortrijk in 1745.[60] The story indeed contains a number of themes that cry out for dramatic treatment (especially of the early modern Jesuit kind), from the tearful farewell between

Thomas and his children (which may have resonated with boys in boarding school and their parents), treacherous murder committed during a party, and the unshaken piety of the hero's sons and other family members in following his shining example to the bitter end.

JM takes major liberties with history by replacing the local dynast Naozumi/Michael with the country's ruling hegemon Ieyasu/Daifu. None of the other Jesuit plays on the martyrdom of the Honda family is known to have made such a change, instead opting to keep Michael who does have a dramatic appeal (of sorts) as the apostate son unworthy of his pious parent.[61] But the insertion of Daifu as the dynast in charge, while being a bold departure from Japanese history, does allow *JM* to explore issues of secular political motives and conflict between personal feelings and public responsibility lurking behind religious persecution, themes which may have especially engaged a German audience in the middle of the Thirty Years' War (1618–48) as will be discussed below. In contrast to the thoroughly villainous Fujihiro/Safioye, Daifu in *JM* is depicted as a surprisingly moderate, albeit pagan, persecutor who is reluctant to put Thomas and his family to death and is forced into doing so only by the perceived need to uphold national security and regal authority. While the dramatic representation of Daifu owes much to existing Jesuit dramas which *JM* mined extensively as will be pointed out in 2.3, it does accord uncannily well with the popular Japanese perception of Ieyasu as an Augustus (23 BCE–19 CE)-like founder of a political system that was to usher in more than two centuries of peace and prosperity to the war-torn nation.[62]

The martyrdom of the Honda family is reported only in Western sources and no contemporary Japanese accounts are known to survive. The *kirishitan* community of Arima was eradicated in the aftermath of the Shimabara Rebellion (see 1.1), a condition which likely explains why local memories of the event did not survive. The bodily remains of Thomas and his family were however recovered in the immediate aftermath of their martyrdom and eventually made their way via Nagasaki to Macau and are preserved to this day in the latter city in its Museum of Sacred Art and Crypt.[63] Together with associated manuscript notes of Morejon which also survive,[64] these relics are an invaluable material witness to the martyr account that was transmitted and later disseminated widely in print and on stage.

Context of reception: The Koblenz Jesuit College in 1625 and Philipp Christoph von Sötern (1567–1652)

The Jesuit college of Koblenz was established in 1581 in the order's Lower Rhine Province. From its beginning, the college, like the city itself, was closely connected to and dependent on the powerful Prince Electorate of Trier. The prince elector of Trier, who was also its archbishop, resided since the Middle Ages on the fortified Ehrenbreitstein hill which looms over the city across the river Rhine. The Jesuits already had a school in Trier by 1561, but since the local population in and around Koblenz was also said to be in need of their spiritual direction and education, arrangements began to be made in the 1560s to invite them to this city below the Ehrenbreitstein.

By 1580, a suitable place with stipend had been made available to the Jesuits in the city centre by the then archbishop and prince elector, Jakob von Eltz-Rübenach (1510–81), and instruction began in 1581/2. The college building was renovated and expanded in the subsequent decades and is still in use today as the *Rathaus* or town hall in the centre of the old town. From its foundation up to the early seventeenth century, the Koblenz Jesuit college grew to house about 300 students every year and provided the kind of humanistic education sketched in 1.2 above. It did not, however, reach the stature of such major Jesuit colleges as those of Munich or Vienna, which had upwards of 1,000 students each and counted internationally renowned humanists among their teachers.[65] Unlike these better-endowed peers, the Koblenz college also lacked a dedicated theatre, meaning that its dramatic performances, including *JM*, had to be staged either in a large hall (in the college itself or in some other building belonging to the city or to the archbishop/prince elector) or some large open space outdoors.[66] Still, within the city and its surroundings the college remained the foremost place of learning, and although its location, administrative structure and name have all changed, the school officially continues to this day as the Görres-Gymnasium of Koblenz.[67]

JM was produced in this academy in 1625, at a time of great crisis not only for the city and the Prince Electorate but for all of Europe. For the continent then was in the middle of the Thirty Years' War when major powers from Spain to Sweden clashed in Central Europe in what is remembered to this day as one of the greatest human catastrophes to befall the early modern West.[68] Koblenz and the Jesuit college did escape the immediate impact of the war until 1632, when French and Swedish forces clashed over the city. Battles nonetheless were taking place in neighbouring territories, as for example in 1621 when the Italian-Spanish general Ambrogio Spinola (1569–1630) (whose cousin Carlo Spinola (1564–1622), incidentally, was a Jesuit missionary in Japan and was martyred there)[69] used Koblenz as a base from which to overrun the Protestant Rhenish Palatinate to the south.[70]

Koblenz indeed occupies a strategic chokepoint, the confluence (the city's name derives from the Latin term *ad confluentes* ('at the confluence')) of the major natural waterways of the Rhine and the Mosel, and the locale surfaces repeatedly in military history. Julius Caesar (100–44 BCE) is thought to have built his famous bridge somewhere nearby, and already in the reign of emperor Tiberius (42 BCE–37 CE, r. 14–37 CE) a permanent Roman military camp stood in what is today the centre of Koblenz.[71] In the modern period the city went back and forth between French and German hands, and the Ehrenbreitstein Fortress housed an American garrison in the aftermath of the First World War (1914–18).[72]

As mentioned above, in 1625 Koblenz had not yet come under direct fire, but it did become the stage of a political conflict of historic significance precisely in that year. The then prince elector and archbishop of Trier, Philipp Christoph von Sötern (Figure 2), was an ambitious and controversial figure who had a penchant for grand building projects and renaming areas under his control after himself.[73] He was born of a Protestant father and a Catholic mother and was baptised Lutheran but converted to Catholicism after which he received a Jesuit education. In 1623, after rising through the ranks of Catholic church hierarchy, Sötern reached the pinnacle of his career and was crowned archbishop and prince elector of Trier. As a holder of this coveted office in the Holy Roman Empire, he was expected to support the Habsburgs and specifically the Spanish Netherlands in their military operations, yet the location of his territory as well as (as some claim) his insatiable need to finance his grand building projects made him a prime target for French overtures.[74]

As prince elector, Sötern presided over the *Landtag* or regional diet, and as the entry in the annals of Koblenz college, the sole external testimony of the work, makes clear, it was during its extraordinary session in the summer of 1625 that *JM* was performed in front of him and the assembled estate representatives. The relevant entry[75] is as follows:

> *reverendissimus et illustrissimus archiepiscopus noster, praebito de Iaponensibus martyribus dramate Latino, quod sibi cum statibus, id temporis hoc loco maiore numero convenientibus, pergratum fuisse prolixe monstravit, in pristina erga nos benevolentia retentus est* ('Our most reverend and illustrious archbishop, after a Latin drama concerning the Japanese martyrs was performed, which he effusively declared was extremely enjoyable for himself as well as for the estates (i.e. diet representatives), who were gathered at this time here in large number, retained his pristine goodwill toward us').

What the annals do not report is that the diet of 1625 was a political disaster which eventually contributed (together with his many other missteps) to Sötern being rejected by his subjects and imprisoned by the Holy Roman

Figure 2 Philipp Christoph von Sötern, Austrian National Library/Vienna, 1627 (PORT_00058793_1).

Emperor. A complaint later made by members of the diet to the imperial court reports that among other outrages, Sötern in 1625 demanded that they vote for a twenty-five per cent sales tax on wine to finance Spinola's army, and that he rammed through the bill by making his soldiers quarter with the ecclesiastical dignitaries (who were most vocal in their opposition) until they capitulated.[76] His blatant abuse of arms to bend the will of diet representatives has been regarded as a highly unusual and remarkable event in early modern political history.[77] When one takes into account this tense background, the macabre humour and extravagant theatrics in some scenes of *JM* may be appreciated all the more as desperate attempts at entertainment in a desperate situation. One may be reminded of the burlesques of Aristophanes (*c*. 446–*c*. 386 BCE) produced against the background of the Peloponnesian War and dysfunctional Athenian politics, even though the latter's plays are obviously of a different literary calibre.

Finally, Sötern's equally disastrous ventures into international politics deserves consideration in relation to *JM*. Even though, as mentioned before, he was expected to be a dependable ally of the Habsburgs in the Thirty Years' War, he eventually turned out to be a weak link in a chain that broke. From the early stage of his office, he felt himself repeatedly let down by his supposed Catholic allies as they failed to provide promised stipends and refused to support his attempts to reclaim control of the wealthy St. Maximin's Abbey in Trier. By the summer of 1625, the relationship between Sötern and the Spanish Habsburgs had become frosty, and the archbishop was becoming proportionately more open to overtures from the famous French statesman Cardinal Richelieu (1585–1642) who was intent on gaining any allies he could (including Protestants) in order to weaken Spain and the Holy Roman Empire and was ready to offer financial incentives.[78] Thus, the mention in *JM* I.3 of Spanish expansionism as a contributing factor in provoking anti-Christian persecution in Japan, while perhaps surprising in a Catholic context (even when spoken by an antagonist and agent of the devil), may have found a receptive ear in Sötern, the play's guest of honour. Whether *JM* increased his hostility towards Spain or not, his intrigues were eventually destined to bury him in infamy as his later invitation of, or at least lack of opposition to, French and Swedish forces to occupy parts of his own territory was to bring about his political downfall and darken his reputation in German Catholic history.[79]

Manuscripts and editorial principle

The text of *JM* is preserved in two manuscript groups in the Koblenz Landeshauptarchiv (LHA), namely Abt.117 nr. 706 (henceforth *A*: Figure 3) and nr. 716 (henceforth *B*). The manuscripts come from two large stashes of booklets and loose leaves which were discovered in the Koblenz gymnasium archive in the late nineteenth century and transferred to the then Staatsarchiv Koblenz. Originally labelled Abt. 117 nr. 593, the stashes turned out to be schoolwork papers, mostly dramatic texts. Local historians Paul Bahlmann (1857–1937) and Wilhelm Josef Becker (1890–1974) attempted to separate the individual pieces and correlate them with dramatic productions mentioned in annals associated with the Koblenz Jesuit gymnasium, and based on their efforts nr. 593 was further subdivided into nrs. 700–37.[80]

As was recognized early on,[81] however, their attempt to create order out of chaos sometimes led to even greater confusion as many of the texts did not match the dramatic performances in the annals. While Becker's early-twentieth-century study[82] is still the most comprehensive overview of the Koblenz Jesuit plays available, there certainly remains much room for further archival and codicological work. Of the nearly forty plays identified by Becker,[83] *JM* is only the second piece to be published after the drama on Saint Judoc (*c.* 600–668) which was edited as a local gymnasium class project in the 1970s.[84]

A recent re-examination of this Koblenz Jesuit schoolwork archive[85] has further revealed the existence of a few other pieces that are related to *JM* in content. Nrs. 722 and 723 both record a drama on the two Jesuit saints Loyola and Xavier (henceforth *I&X*) which was staged in 1622 to celebrate their canonization[86] and contain passages that overlap with *JM* I.5, I.6 and II.1. Similarly, nr. 727, internally identified as a *tragicomoedia Constantinus Baptizatus appellata* ('tragicomedy entitled *Constantine Baptised*', henceforth *CB*) is a drama of unknown date[87] which has textual overlaps with *JM* I.6 and III.1. These overlaps occur in exclusively in the chaotic and fragmentary *A* and not *B*, a fact which, combined with the relatively polished, coherent state of *I&X* and *CB*, suggests that not only with *I&X* (which definitely precedes *JM*) but also with *CB*, *JM* was the borrower, not vice versa. Lastly, in nr. 711, a file consisting of a collection of rough drafts, there exists a German translation in rhyming verses of *JM* I.2 which may very provisionally be dated to after 1661.[88] These are all traces that suggest an active process of *contaminatio* ('contamination'), to use Roman comic terminology,[89] taking place in the Koblenz Jesuit theatre and merit further investigation.

To come back to *JM* proper, the manuscript groups *A* and *B* display substantial overlap indicating that they stem from an identical piece centred on the martyrdom of Honda Heibyōe/Thomas and his family. *B* is a continuous manuscript of thirty pages containing an integral text of a play, except that it lacks the usual prefatory material such as title, list of characters and prose summary. It is folded neatly into a booklet and its modern, stamped page-numbering follows the original sequence. *A* on the other hand is a collection of drafts and notes totaling sixty-six pages written in different hands on several different sizes of paper, with some internal overlap in addition to substantial overlap with *B*. While the sheets of *A* have been grouped correctly in the sense that they stem from the same play, its modern stamped page numbers are often incorrectly sequenced and do not follow the original manuscript order which can be reconstructed based on content as well as external features such as paper size and quality. Based on my own on-site examination of *A*, I identified the following sub-groups (by stamped folio numbers arranged in actual manuscript sequence): 3→4→29→30→31→32 →33→34 (henceforth A^1); 1→2→35→36 (A^2); 37→38 (A^3); 39→40→41→42 (A^4); 43→44→45→46→47→48 (A^5); 5→6→7→8→9→10→11→12→13→ 14→15→16→17→18→19→20→21→22→23→24→25→26→27→28 (A^6); 51 →52→49→50[90] (A^7); 53→54→65→66→55 (A^8); 57→58→59→60→61 →62→63→64 (A^9). These nine sub-groups are independent of each other in the sense that they each show no internal overlap and are drafts of discrete portions of the play (none is complete) that presumably emerged during the production process which must have involved numerous checks and revisions. While *A* as a whole is in an obviously unfinished state, its text is more expansive; where it overlaps with *B*, *A* as a rule is longer and more elaborate, and it also contains entire scenes that are missing from *B*.

Since neither *A* nor *B* has a title, the one given in this volume is a provisional reconstruction based on the annal entry cited above (see 2.2). The modern archival folders in LHA are entitled *Idolomania* ('Idolomany') (*A*) and *Martyres Iaponiae sive Daifu rex Iaponiae* ('Martyrs of Japan or Daifu, king of Japan') (*B*), and Valentin, following Becker, calls the play *Martyres Iaponenses sive Idolomania* ('Japanese Martyrs or Idolomany').[91] These appellations are all conjectures based on the annal entry, manuscript content, or both. The actual title used at the performance may well have been different from all of these; for example, the playbill of the 1626 Eichstätt version of the same martyrdom (though with demonstrably different plot details) bears the title *Iustus et Iacobus pueri Iapones martyres* ('Iustus and Iacobus, the Japanese boy-martyrs').[92]

The state of manuscripts sketched above creates a major editorial challenge. While one possibility was to give a shorter version substantially following *B*, in the end the editor decided to combine both *A* and *B* to give the longest possible version, incorporating all of the former including marginal additions and even crossed-out lines (which are so indicated in the commentary). This is because lines and scenes present in *A* (including portions crossed out) but missing in *B* add much to the *JM*'s comic potential and performative scale and reflect the considerable ambition, though not necessarily the actual staging capability, of its production team. This means among other things that

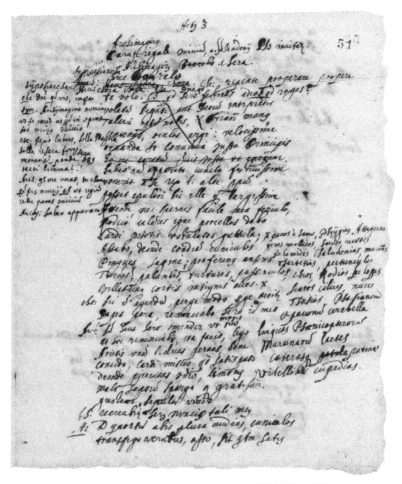

Figure 3 Manuscript: *A*.51, containing 1061–105 of *JM*, LHA/Koblenz,
seventeenth century (Best. 117 Nr. 706: 51).

the placement of some of the scenes found only in *A* is conjectural as will be
explained in the notes. Whether the actual performance was closer to the
cleaned-up text of *B* or the eclectic and maximally expansive version given in
this volume must remain a matter of speculation.

Due to the current imperfect state of knowledge regarding the production
process of Jesuit plays as well as the chaotic nature of the surviving

manuscripts the editor also decided not to adopt the classical philological norm of establishing a stemma and trying to arrive at a definitive text, however this is defined,[93] under the assumption that what one can recover in a case like *JM* is, at best, a textual ground plan (or series of ground plans in successive stages of revision) of the actual performance which can never be reconstructed in full short of the invention of the time machine. Emendations are kept to the minimum; even when the syntax or metre can be 'fixed' with a little tinkering, these passages are as a rule left as they are, with metrically problematic lines listed in scene summaries of the commentary. The edition in this volume is one that attempts to do the fullest possible justice, based on available evidence, to the imagination, humour and creativity (despite an often wobbly command of Latin) of those who staged near-contemporary Japan in Koblenz for a moment of pious relaxation during the charged summer of 1625.

Stylistics and literary heritage

Linguistically and stylistically, *JM* belongs squarely to the tradition of humanistic Neo-Latin which is rooted in the Graeco-Roman literary milieu but incorporates certain post-classical elements (see 1.2). So, while its metre and formal dramatic structure are derived from classical Athenian and Roman theatre, it also contains a mix of mediaeval and early modern elements as will be sketched out in this section. As a performative text preserved in drafts, many of which may have been made by the student actors themselves,[94] it also displays numerous rough edges that would have been smoothed out in printed texts. In this sense, *JM* must be more typical of the approximately 100,000 Jesuit plays that are estimated to have been staged in the order's schools, rather than the few hundred polished samples that made it to the press.[95]

JM's four-act structure is somewhat unusual for a Neo-Latin play (five acts being the preferred classical norm) but by no means unique. Each act is followed by a sung or chanted chorus, and some scenes also have sung parts, all features not unusual in plays of this kind.[96] At 1,600 lines, *JM*'s reconstructed length is comparable to that of many classical tragedies but is on the short side if one considers other Jesuit plays which often exceeded 2,000 lines, with one exceptional case forging on for as many as 12,127 lines.[97]

Most of the Latin vocabulary of *JM* is what one may term classical, but a small number of words of obviously non-Graeco-Roman origin such as Buddhist terms (e.g. *Xacas, Amidas*) and Japanese proper names (e.g. Arima, Daifu), presumably taken from printed missionary reports such as Trigault's, are used freely. A few less obviously post-classical words such as *encomiasta* ('eulogizer': 10) and *depraedico* ('advertise': 662) are also found, which however are attested in printed Neo-Latin texts and simply indicate that the early modern understanding of correct Latin was slightly different from the modern philological one.[98] In terms of vocabulary, the only really black sheep (so to speak) are the nonce-words *servito* ('to keep, preserve') used twice in our text (134. 440) and *debustuatum* ('burned down': 487) which appears once, whose meaning however could be easily guessed by those familiar with the language.

Most of the script is delivered in iambic trimetre, which is the regular metre for dialogues of Greek drama and Senecan tragedy, or in senarius, its looser Roman comic variety.[99] For simplicity's sake, in the commentary both schemes will be often subsumed under the term senarius even though some passages, especially (but not only) those cribbed from printed Jesuit dramatists, are in the more astringent iambic trimetre. Comic iambic octonarius also makes a brief appearance in I.6. Anapaestic dimeter, iambic dimetre (alternating with trimetre), dactylic hexameter, elegiac couplet, Sapphic stanza, and hendecasyllable are classical lyric schemes which *JM* uses more or less correctly and would not be out of place in Senecan tragedy,[100] even though there are occasional problems with scansion. Hypermetry, hypometry or other metrical shortcomings are especially common in iambic trimetre/senarius, a characteristic shared by other late-sixteenth- and early-seventeenth-century manuscript Jesuit plays from German speaking areas which tend to fall noticeably below the polished metrical standard of printed texts.[101] There are also three passages (1087–93, 1531–4, 1539–44) that are demonstrably cribbed from prose sources even though they are arranged in the manuscript to look like senarius.

Furthermore, two extended passages (774–893, 1566–99), are written in loosely accentual rhymed verse. Of these, 774–893 was definitely sung to music as the manuscript assigns voice types such as bass and baritone to individual characters.[102] There are also two cases (897–900, 1527) of traditional Catholic prayers of mediaeval origin inserted verbatim, as well as one passage (326–45) where an edict is delivered in prose. All of these non-classical metrical features find parallels in other Jesuit Neo-Latin plays.[103]

The mixture of classical and later elements is also in evidence when one looks at literary echoes and borrowings. Echoes of Seneca (146–8, 208–9, 580–4, 765–71, 1336, 1337, 1344, 1449–50, 1498) are the most numerous, and there are those elsewhere of Virgil (773, 1010, 1030, 1031, 1041, 1380), Horace (65–8 BCE) (1059, 1165, 1212, 1414, cf. also 693, 1009), Ovid (43 BCE–18 CE) (152, 156–7), Cicero (276), possibly Persius (34–62) (1184–6) and Juvenal (?–after 127) (651–2). But the targeted cribbing of six humanist authors, four of them Jesuits, is of greater importance for our understanding of the production of *JM*.

For scenes of feasting and food preparation, we can see that *JM* owes much to the French humanist Jean Tixier de Ravisi (*c.* 1470–1542) and the Portuguese Jesuit dramatist Luis da Cruz (1543–1604). Among the works of Tixier, who at one time taught at the Parisian college of Navarre,[104] is a Latin conversation manual with the simple title *Dialogi*,[105] from which a list of obscure food terms (many of them connected to Mediterranean locales far removed from the Far East) totalling seven lines (1087–93) is lifted. Tixier's prose text is copied in the right margin of *A.*51 (Figure 3) and was perhaps meant to be reworked into iambic trimetre/senarius later (in our text they are distributed into a rough equivalent thereof). Cruz is one of the justly celebrated luminaries among the Jesuit dramatists and taught for many years at the university of Coimbra[106] which also was the *alma mater* for many of the missionaries in Japan. More than half of the ostensibly Buddhist hendecasyllabic hymn in *JM* I.6 and much of the kitchen banter in III.1 come from his two biblical allegorical dramas *Prodigus*[107] (*P*) and *Vita Humana.*[108] (*VH*), which were first performed in the mid- to late-sixteenth century in Coimbra and were printed in Lyon in 1605.[109] There is also an echo of his *Sedecias*[110] in 1170 and 1175.

There is another intertextual connection between Coimbra and *JM* involving the Scottish humanist George Buchanan (1506–82). Like some of his peers, during much of his active career Buchanan held an ambiguous attitude toward the Catholic church, though he moved decisively to the Scottish and English Protestant side toward the end of his life. At one point of his multifaceted career he joined the teaching staff at Coimbra but fell under suspicion of heresy and was subsequently transferred to a monastery in Lisbon (1551–2), where he famously whiled away his confinement by translating the Psalms, possibly from the original Hebrew, into Latin lyric metres.[111] *JM*'s Sapphic chorus for I is mostly made up of lines lifted from Buchanan's translation (*BP*), while the one for II in the same metre may have been penned anew.

Finally, some of the most dramatic and politically charged scenes in *JM* turn out to be heavily indebted to works of three Jesuit dramatists, Jakob Pontanus (1542–1626), Bernardino Stefonio (1560–1620) and Nicolas Caussin (1583–1651). From Pontanus's *Eleazarus Macchabaeus*,[112] (*E*) a biblical martyr drama set in the mid-second-century BCE Palestine/Israel, are lifted a few lines expressing threat (1467–9) and defiance (1440–1) in persecution. From Stefonio's *Crispus*[113] (*C*), a political tragedy dramatising Constantine the Great (272–337)'s execution of his son and title character (*c.* 295–326) due to slander, and his *Flavia*,[114] which revolves around the confrontation between the pagan cult leader Apollonius of Tyana (*c.* 3 BCE–*c.* 97) and the impeccably Christian Flavian clan, come numerous lines containing reflections of political and religious nature which are incorporated in I.3, II.3, III.2, III.3, and IV.3, 4, 5, 6 as pointed out in the commentary. Finally, from Caussin's three martyr plays *Theodoricus* (*T*) which features Boethius (480–524/5) and his family, *Felicitas*[115] (*F*) which showcases the title character (*c.*101–*c.*165) and her sons executed under Marcus Aurelius (121–80), and *Hermenigildus*[116] (*H*) which is set in the Visigothic court of the sixth century, are lifted dozens of lines spoken both by persecutors and the persecuted in II.3, III.3, and IV.3, 5 and 6.

These borrowings not only improve *JM*'s Latinity but also add much to its dramatic force and philosophical depth. Of the three, Caussin and Stefonio lived particularly close to centres of political power and their real-life court experiences seem to have suffused their historical plays with political verve. Stefonio spent decades as a professor in the Collegio Romano, the very hub of global Jesuit educational network,[117] while Caussin rose in the ranks to become confessor to King Louis XIII of France (1601–43) in 1637 before clashing with Richelieu and being sent away to exile in Rennes.[118] A modern scholar sees in their works dramatic illustrations of baroque philosophical and religious thinking concerning the slippery slope of power and the proper Christian response to tyranny and political oppression.[119] If so, the composer(s) of *JM* may be commended for their acute perception and dextrous application of borrowed material though a less kindly reader may see plagiarism at work.[120] Through these intertexts we can see a bold literary alignment, a palimpsest as it were of mid- to late-imperial Rome with early modern Japan, of rulers like Marcus Aurelius and Constantine with Ieyasu/Daifu, and of victims of political violence such as Saint Felicitas and her sons, Boethius and his wife and children, and Crispus Caesar with the martyrs of Japan. These early modern intertexts in *JM* show that fellow European Jesuit playwrights not only supplied samples of good Latinity to German schoolchildren but also dramatic and cognitive idioms with which to understand and recreate events taking place in the contemporary Far East.

Victor the Japanese (Munich 1665)

Origin and transmission: From Osaka in 1597 to Europe in the 1660s

The second play in our collection, *Error Fortitudinis Profanae a Sacra Correctus in Victore Iapone* ('Error of Profane Fortitude Corrected by Sacred Fortitude in Victor the Japanese', henceforth *VJ*)[121] performed in Munich in June 1665, is also based on a specific event which took place, according to

Jesuit accounts, in early 1597 in the city of Osaka, a mercantile hub near the ancient capital of Kyoto in Japan's Kansai region. The historical namesake of *VJ*'s title character, Victor Noda Gensuke (active 1590s), was a Japanese Catholic convert and a member of the Osaka magistrate (*bugyō*)'s office which was in charge of maintaining public order under the command of the central government. Andreas Ogasawara (active 1590s), who appears as Victor's son in *VJ*, was likewise a Catholic convert and resident of Osaka. Andreas was also a member of the famed Ogasawara clan which since the thirteenth century had been in charge of safeguarding and teaching archery, horsemanship, and general etiquette appropriate for the hereditary warrior class.[122] Andreas is first mentioned in missionary reports as a landlord who sheltered several Jesuit priests early in the wave of persecution that culminated in the so-called Martyrdom of Twenty-Six Saints[123] (see also 1.1).

According to missionary accounts Victor and Andreas were mutual acquaintances though not family members, and both kept company with Paulo Miki (1562–97), a Japanese Jesuit brother who became one of the twenty-six martyrs, while the latter were kept imprisoned in the neighbouring city of Kyoto before being marched south to their execution ground in Nagasaki. Quite likely it is through Miki's pre-execution oral report to the Portuguese Jesuits stationed in Nagasaki that we have the following anecdote about Andreas and his father around which *VJ*'s plot revolves.

Living with Andreas during the turmoil in the Kyoto-Osaka area was his octogenarian father by the name of Ginsei (active 1590s), a fresh convert who had been baptised only half a year previously. When Ginsei heard about the persecution, he angrily began to gird himself for battle against the enemies of his newfound faith. Andreas discreetly admonished his aged father that the proper Catholic way of martyrdom, taught by their Jesuit mentors, was to submit patiently to the sword, but the son's words only added fuel to Ginsei's anger. In a paroxysm of rage, he began to swing his sword as if to practice fighting off enemies of the faith, much to the mirth of some Christian bystanders. Andreas then tried another tack, suggesting that Ginsei take refuge with his newly born grandson in order to continue the ancient and honoured lineage while the rest of the family joined the martyrs, a counsel that predictably only stoked his anger further. But when Ginsei worked off some of the heat with his martial exercise and went indoors, he was astonished to find members of the household, including women and children, preparing their best clothes and putting their rosaries and other devotional articles in order. When he learned that they were doing so in preparation for martyrdom, their quiet example succeeded where Andreas's words failed. The old man became ready to join the martyrs and threw down his arms, providing a happy denouement to the little drama.[124]

The earliest known sources that mention this tale are two Jesuit letters, both sent from Nagasaki in the middle of March 1597. These letters by Luís Fróis (1532–97) and Pedro Gómez (1535–1600), both Iberian Jesuits, are mainly concerned with the twenty-six saints, and Andreas, his father Ginsei and Victor are just some of the innumerable minor side characters that populate the saga. Fróis and Gómez, who incidentally were both competent Latinists, wrote these accounts in vernacular languages (Portuguese and Spanish, respectively) as was usual at that time (cf. 1.2 above). Fróis' report, in a version edited on its way to Europe by Valignano, was subsequently translated into several languages including Latin and disseminated widely in Europe.[125]

VJ however may not be directly indebted to any of the late sixteenth- to early seventeenth-century editions of Fróis' letter; instead, the most likely source is an Italian book by the Jesuit archivist and historian Daniello Bartoli (1608–85). Bartoli, at the command of Jesuit Superior General Vincenzo Carafa (1585–1649), spent thirty-five years of his life crafting a monumental history of the Jesuit order, and the part describing missionary activity in Japan, comprising five books, appeared in 1660.[126] There is evidence that Bartoli's account was read and used for dramatic production even before *VJ* in Munich. In September 1663, two years before *VJ*'s composition, the Munich Jesuit college staged a spectacle featuring the famous *kirishitan daimyō* Ukon (see 1.1) as the main character. The Munich Ukon production, being the major theatrical show of the year, was performed no fewer than three times in front of distinguished audiences including the prince elector of Bavaria.[127] The script of this Ukon play has not survived, but its bilingual Latin-German playbill has, and Bartoli is cited as the source.[128] One detail in *VJ* also points to Bartoli as the likely source, namely the appearance of Leo and Quirinus who watch and mock Victor's martial exercise in I.5. The presence of unnamed Japanese converts who stood by and laughed at Andreas's father brandishing his weapon is a detail that Valignano edited out of Fróis' manuscript and thus did not appear in the earlier printed reports of the martyrdom, but Bartoli's account restores these merry bystanders.[129] Presumably Bartoli, the indefatigable archive hunter, saw and took note of Fróis' unabridged manuscript account in Rome.

There are a couple of possible reasons why Andreas's father comes to be called Victor in *VJ*. In the original story, as mentioned above, Victor and Andreas were fellow converts in the same city and not family members. It is not difficult however to see how Victor could be erroneously conflated with Andreas's father. In Bartoli as well as in other published accounts, the story of Andreas's quarrel with his father was preceded by two episodes featuring Victor Noda.[130] In the first of these, Victor is said to have tried to join the martyrs together with his entire family and gotten upset when a Jesuit father dissuaded him from forcing his dependants to face certain death. In the second episode, Victor and Andreas, together with a few others, are reported to have engaged in a debate as to who would be the worthiest to be executed together with their imprisoned fellow believers. Victor is thus represented as an enthusiastic would-be martyr and Andreas's rival in religious ardour. A modern German retelling of the episode even mistakenly turns Victor into Andreas's son,[131] showing how prone to confused interpretation these personal connections are. But in the case of *VJ*, the conflation may also have been intentional. Victor's name, which has the same meaning in Latin as in English, fortuitously matches the main theme of the play which is the triumph of the truly Catholic way of martyrdom over the *error profanus* ('profane error') of military resistance against persecution. The name furthermore is connected in a roundabout fashion with the local dignitary whose death *VJ* was meant to commemorate, as will be explained in the next section.

In the denouement of *VJ*, Victor and Andreas merrily march off to martyrdom together with their family and friends, but there is no historical evidence that any of them were executed for their faith during or immediately after the persecution of 1596/7. There is a record of a *kirishitan* Ogasawara family whose members were put to death for their faith in 1636,[132] but their relation to Andreas's branch cannot at present be determined. The Ogasawara clan itself has survived and actively professes martial arts and traditional feudal etiquette to this day.[133]

The context of reception: The Munich Jesuit College and the dramatic wake of Franz Fugger (1612–64)

The Munich Jesuit college was founded in 1559 under the chief initiative of Albert V (1528–79), duke of Bavaria and champion of the Counter-Reformation. Compared to Koblenz, Munich is a city that emerged late in regional history; but by the beginning of the sixteenth century it had become the capital of a united Bavaria and soon commenced a meteoric rise as a major Catholic base in the confessional battleground of the southern German-speaking area. By the early seventeenth century, student numbers in the Munich college had risen to around 1000~1400, a level maintained well into the subsequent century. Munich also became host to internationally renowned Jesuit dramatists such as Jakob Bidermann (1578–1639), Jakob Gretser (1562–1625) and Jakob Balde (1604–68), whose works, both printed and in manuscript, continue to be studied to this day.[134] The school, today known as Wilhelmsgymnasium, has since undergone major transformations but remains a leading humanistic academy in Southern Germany.[135]

In 1623 the secular duke of Bavaria also became, like the archbishop of Trier, a prince elector of the Holy Roman Empire and it was with this august office in attendance that the near-annual gala plays of the academy were regularly performed.[136] The prince elector and duke of Bavaria was in turn a generous patron and provided material and financial support to the school's theatrical productions which worked hand-in-hand with his Counter-Reformation agenda.[137] Within this rich and well-maintained tradition of Munich Jesuit theatre, Japanese elements appeared with some regularity. Already in 1597, in a play commemorating the consecration of St. Michael's Church adjoining the college, Japanese characters appeared among a train of visitors paying homage to the archangel, a dim reflection of the Tenshō embassy which had visited southern Europe less than a decade ago.[138] In 1631 a *comico-tragoedia* ('comico-tragedy') featuring Hideyoshi/Taicosama was performed, and several other Japan plays followed suit in the seventeenth to eighteenth century.[139] The 1663 Ukon play mentioned above was performed three times on three consecutive days with each show lasting five hours.[140]

The 1665 performance of *VJ* in contrast was a small-scale, internal classroom exercise presumably not open to the public. Based on the manuscript's titular information it can be dated to June that year, though neither the college's diary nor its annals mention it.[141] Still, the explicit association made in its colophon with the piece that follows (see Figure 4) helps pinpoint the historical occasion that engendered it. This was the death of Franz Graf von Fugger-Weißenhorn-Nordendorf (Figure 5), a local patron of the Jesuit order and a member of the powerful and wealthy Fugger family, at the battle of Mogersdorf/Saint Gotthard. This battle was fought on 1 August 1664 between the Ottoman army and a coalition commanded by the Holy Roman Empire around the named locale, in what is now the Austro-Hungarian border.

The colophon of *VJ* records the name of the author and the scribe, who is said to have copied the subsequent *epinicion* ('victory ode') as well. In the manuscript volume, *VJ* is indeed followed by a poetic work consisting of a little more than 660 lines.[142] The latter work may be styled an epyllion or short epic, and its author as well as copyist, recorded in its colophon, are the same as those of *VJ*, namely Jakob Wiestner (1640–1705) and Franz Max Luz (1648–?)[143] respectively. The titular information further informs us that it is a victory ode for Franz Fugger sung by the students of the poetic class, that is to say the same as those who acted in *VJ*, on 2 April 1665, i.e. two months before the play.

This appended epyllion (henceforth *FE*) is an embellished retelling of the deeds of Franz Fugger during the Austro-Turkish war of 1663 to 1664, culminating in his death on the battlefield. The narrative opens with the

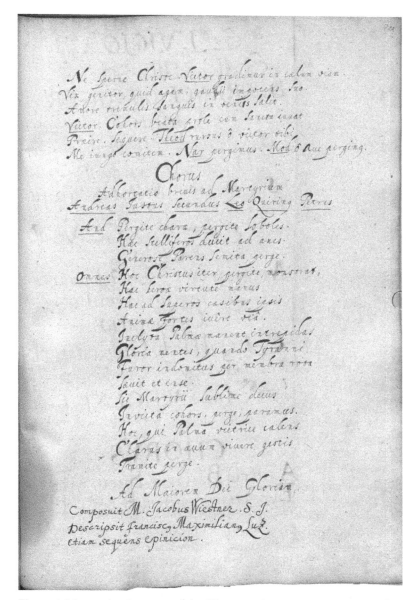

Figure 4 Manuscript: Last page of the *VJ* manuscript, containing 819–40 and the colophon, BSB/Munich, 1665 (CLM 1554: 211r).

Figure 5 Franz Graf von Fugger-Weißenhorn-Nordendorf, Austrian National Library/Vienna, 1664 (PORT_00062804_01).

description of Mars and Enyo lamenting the lack of warlike spirit among Europeans and summoning Fugger from southern Germany to join the battle against the Ottomans; it proceeds to relate how Fugger and his soldiers sail down the Danube to join the grand coalition being assembled by the Holy Roman Emperor; how news of the Ottoman capture of Novi Zrin in present-day Croatia shakes the Western forces; the circumstances on the battlefield, starting with the ferocious cannon attack followed by equestrian battle on the banks of the river Rába; the retreat of the German contingent when faced with numerically superior Ottoman forces, and Fugger's heroic attempt to stem the tide; his death at the hand of a cowardly Ottoman sniper (modelled on Melanippus in Statius *Thebaid* 8.716–21), and his dying wish for Habsburg victory addressed to Mars; and Mars' answer in the form of the arrival of a French contingent, just in time to reverse the scale of battle against the Ottomans. The concluding polymetric section drives home the message that Fugger brought a truly Christian victory over infidel forces with his heroic death and exemplary piety despite overwhelming odds. Fugger is presented as a classical hero, the centrepiece of an epic battle between European Christians and Eastern invaders in a language echoing Virgil and Statius and recalling among other precedents the Persian invasion of ancient Greece (at one point, the Ottomans are called Achaemenids). There is also a comparison made in the end between Fugger and a storm-battered trade ship that arrives safely at port laden with treasure from Peru, a simile that may possibly be seen as a thematic bridge between the *FE* and the prologue with the Dutch sailor in *VJ*.

First-hand historical accounts however paint a far less glamorous picture of the battle and the part played by Fugger. As the Ottomans prepared their westward march yet again in the beginning of 1663, the Holy Roman Emperor Leopold I (1640–1705) had to hastily gather a contingent of multi-ethnic, multilingual forces including those from western German-speaking areas and France. The hodgepodge coalition suffered severely from a lack of adequate provisions far from home in the hot summer of central Europe; many soldiers were incapacitated and had to be left behind, and Fugger himself became gravely ill and almost dropped out during the long march.[144] Early on the day of the battle, Ottoman forces crossed the river Rába and attacked their opponents stationed on the other bank, routing the poorly supplied and already exhausted defenders and spreading panic and rumours of unstoppable Turkish advance deep into Austrian territory. Fugger died of a single gunshot wound in the head sustained during the initial stampede, and the confusion was so great that a rumour circulated soon afterwards that he was killed by friendly fire.[145] Fortunately for the Habsburg side however, later on the same day its commanding general Raimundo Montecuccoli (1609–80) succeeded in regrouping the coalition and counterattacked the Ottomans who had occupied the town of Mogersdorf, driving them back into the Rába (where many of them did drown) and literally snatching victory from the jaws of defeat.[146] This near-miraculous victory nonetheless was soon tarnished by what many considered to be the outrageously unfair peace treaty of Vasvar, which was signed barely ten days later and under which the Ottomans were not only allowed to keep Transylvania but even promised monetary tribute from the Holy Roman Empire.[147] Leopold I may have correctly foreseen that he did not have the resources needed to push back the Ottomans any further and that the latent French threat in the opposite flank demanded his more urgent attention.[148]

In the meanwhile, Fugger's body was ceremoniously conveyed to Ingolstadt and interred in the city's Moritzkirche on 24 August 1664. A Latin epitaph, which once existed in the church but is now reportedly lost, told, among other things, that Fugger fell as a 'victor against the Turks' (*victor contra Turcas*) 'to become a triumphant general in heaven' (*ut caelo triumphator exstaret*).[149] It is not difficult to see how the twin works composed less than a year later by the then young teacher of poetry Wiestner and performed by the students of the Munich Jesuit academy celebrated or, to phrase it in another way, put a brave face on the ambiguous death of their noble patron by stressing the theme of sacred Christian victory. Fugger's death in a controversial military campaign was painted in the finest heroic colours using epic themes in *FE* in April. Then in June, a Japanese character by the name of Victor was brought on stage to drive home the notion that apparent earthly defeat at the hands of non-Christians can really be a splendid Christian victory in disguise. Wiestner pulled off this literary commemoration of Fugger's demise in true Jesuit Neo-Latin style, combining Catholic theology with classical tropes and a dash of exotic elements. Theatrical performance to mark a funeral of an illustrious figure is itself a classical Roman custom;[150] thus the choice of genre (albeit as a classroom exercise instead of the annual spectacle) itself would have been a nod to the humanistic tradition for which the Munich academy was famous.

Wiestner's literary efforts may have come with earthly rewards as well. Fugger and his wealthy family were generous supporters of the Jesuits, including their university in Ingolstadt,[151] where Wiestner was to hold a professorship and become an internationally celebrated scholar of canon law.[152]

Manuscript and editorial principle

The text of *VJ* is preserved in CLM 1554, a bound manuscript volume currently housed in the Bavarian State Library (BSB) which consists of declamations (i.e. classroom exercises) of the Munich Jesuit academy from 1582 to 1665. The manuscript anthology includes dialogues, epigrams, plays, and sermons which were copied out year after year to make up a literary scrapbook. *VJ* followed by *FE* stands at the end of the volume.

Like the other pieces in the volume, both *VJ* and *FE* are written in a neat, clear hand and are almost entirely free of scribal errors, in marked contrast to the unfinished state of *JM*. *VJ* is also furnished with a carefully lettered title and colophon as well as summary and character list at the beginning of every scene. The edition in this volume reproduces the single text in CLM 1554: 195r. –211r. including the scene summaries and character lists. The few emendations made by the editor are explained in the commentary. Again in contrast to *JM*, as the manuscript text of *VJ* was penned down as a literary monument to be preserved and admired alongside other Neo-Latin productions of this famed academy, this edition tries to do justice to the provenance by giving a clean and standardised version of this belletristic piece.

Stylistics

VJ with its 840 lines is about as long as the shortest classical Greek and Roman plays.[153] It consists of three parts plus prologue and the tripartite structure is by no means unique among Jesuit plays.[154] Each part is structured like an act and is divided into scenes with dialogues delivered in iambic trimetre, while its end is demarcated by a choral passage in different metrical schemes, on which more will be said below.

VJ's vocabulary and syntax adhere closely to classical standards. A few Japanese loanwords and proper names are admitted (such as the usual *Xacas*, *Amidas* and *bonzius* as well as Taicosama) but are used sparingly outside of the prologue which needs them to sketch the setting. While throughout *JM* one sees real as well as made-up Japanese place and personal names scattered liberally, *VJ* is much more classical and even the Japanese characters are identified exclusively by their Western baptismal names (except for the regent Taicosama, who never appears on stage). Some early modern Neo-Latin authors explicitly state that Japanese words and proper names that they use are unfortunate though necessary barbarisms[155] and it is presumably in keeping with such a sentiment that *VJ* restricts these foreign lexical elements to the absolute minimum.

Unlike *JM*, *VJ* betrays virtually no trace of cribbing, even though in this regard some caution is in order since a large amount of Jesuit Neo-Latin literature which Wiestner could have consulted remains in manuscript form and could not be examined in preparation for this edition. There are just two Senecan tags that can be securely identified (1, 232, cf. 245), which is somewhat surprising as *VJ*'s style is otherwise highly reminiscent of Roman tragedy. One line which expresses the commonplace sentiment, that no one with the right religious conviction is too young to die a martyr (701), is quite similar to a line in *JM* (1463), which in turn is lifted from *F*;[156] as young martyrs, Japanese or otherwise, are such a staple in Jesuit plays, a line like this could have been common currency in the genre.

The metre displays close adherence to basic classical quantitative rules. Most of the play is delivered in iambic trimetre of the kind seen in printed Jesuit plays. Some of the few anomalies may be due to miscopying, and rare cases of hiatus and synizesis can be paralleled in Senecan tragedy or at least early modern editions thereof.[157] The choral passages at the end of I and III are in anapestic dimeter, the most common lyric metre in Senecan tragedy. The chorus at the end of II on the other hand is a somewhat unusual combination of iambic trimetre with iambic dimeter/iambic dimeter catalectic. The former metre, the same as in the dialogues, is used by Victor and Theodorus whereas Andreas and his friends chant in the latter which, while used elsewhere in Jesuit plays,[158] is reminiscent also of the scheme combining quantity with accent that is associated with Ambrose of Milan (*c.* 340–397) and was frequently employed in medieval church hymns.[159] Here we see a neat correlation of content with form, as the pagan sentiment of armed resistance to persecution is expressed in classical metre while the eminently Catholic ideal of a willing embrace of martyrdom is expounded in a rhythm often heard in church services.

Wiestner, a young teacher in his twenties when he composed *VJ* as well as *FE*, seems to have been a skilled versifier and a role model within the Jesuit Latin educational system which, as sketched above, was geared toward imitative production rather than philological research. In the seventeenth century, the Bavarian Jesuits were in the midst of its golden age of Neo-Latin literature[160] and Wiestner, who spent most of his life as student and professional in their midst, must have been steeped to the core in this humanistic ambience. Also worth mentioning is the fact that at the very time that he was writing *VJ*, the Munich academy was editing one of the jewels of Bavarian Neo-Latin, Bidermann's posthumous dramatic collection, which came out the following year.[161] *VJ* may thus be reasonably regarded not only as a case of reception of Japanese elements in European Neo-Latin but also as a minor star in the brilliant constellation of Bavarian Baroque humanism.

Notes

1 The Nestorians came first to China, followed by Catholic Franciscans in the thirteenth century. See e.g. Ding 2006.
2 For the Jesuit order and early modern academic culture see e.g. O'Malley 1993: 253–64.
3 A term popularized by Boxer 1951.
4 Yoshishige appears in several Jesuit plays, including one performed in Koblenz in 1622; see note in 2.3 below and Immoos 2005A: 366–7.
5 *kirishitan*, from the Portuguese *cristão* ('Christian'), is the historical term for early modern Japanese followers of Catholicism.
6 See e.g. Hesselink 2016: 4–6 for a historical overview of Jesuit political activity in mid- to late-sixteenth-century Japan.
7 On the Japanese Jesuit seminary in the early modern period see e.g. Moran 1993: 165–9.
8 See Cooper 2005.
9 See Schwemmer 2022: 51–2.
10 See e.g. Moran 1993: 155.
11 See e.g. Moran 1993: 15–19
12 See Boxer 1951: 56–72

13 In a twist of fate, the assassin's daughter, Tama (1563–1600), later known as Gratia Hosokawa, became a famous Catholic convert and heroine of several Jesuit plays. See e.g. Dietrich 2000: xviii–xix and Takao 2019: 98–101.

14 Taico or Taikō is a court title which Hideyoshi obtained in 1591 and by which he was widely known in Japan. -sama is a Japanese honorific. See e.g. Hesselink 2016: 284–5.

15 Compare e.g. Trigault 1623: 14 with Moran 1993: 94

16 The possibility of Catholic missionaries having been agents of the Iberian imperial agenda is an understandably sensitive topic to this day. For an episode involving the Philippines-based Jesuit Alonso Sánchez (1547–93) allegedly suggesting the Spanish crown to invade Japan and China see e.g. Giraldez 2015: 67–8.

17 See Shimizu 2012.

18 See e.g. Moran 1993: 80–1 and 182–3.

19 Daifu is a court title which Ieyasu obtained in 1596 and by which he became widely known. -sama is an honorific as in Taicosama. See e.g. Hesselink 2016: 285.

20 The image of the peaceful, united and prosperous Europe in marked contrast to the war-torn and indigent Japan was inculcated e.g. to the Japanese Jesuit students in the Latin text prepared for them in 1590. See Sande (1590) 7.

21 For the interactions between Adams, the Dutch, the Jesuits and Ieyasu see e.g. Clulow 2013: 57–8.

22 For Jesuit plays on Ukon see e.g. Wimmer 2005: 34–7.

23 On the Shimabara rebellion see e.g. Clements 2016.

24 Cieslik 2004: 419–32.

25 For an overview on these different kinds of early modern Jesuit accounts on the Far East see further Collani 2005: 267–82.

26 For popular anti-*kirishitan* literature in early modern Japan see Leuchtenberger 2013. On other Japan-themed Jesuit plays see Immoos 1981, Jontes 1984, Takenaka and Burnett 1994, Weber 1997, Pass and Kalicki 2000, Wimmer 2005, Oba 2016, and Keener 2021.

27 For Jesuit accounts as sources for early modern Japanese linguistics and tea ceremony see Kishimoto 2006 and Smutny 2016, respectively.

28 For a comprehensive catalogue of archaeological and historical records concerning early modern Catholic evangelization and subsequent persecution see Gonoi 2021.

29 See Watanabe 2018: 104–7.

30 For evidence on these earliest Jesuit plays on Japan see e.g. Oba 2016: 45.

31 For a rough estimate of the quantity of Japan-themed early modern Jesuit plays (up to 650) see Immoos 2005B: 373.

32 Cf. e.g. Griffin 2017: 231–4.

33 Just to give one example, the performance of a play (probably produced by the Franciscans, language unknown) on Japanese martyrs is recorded to have taken place in Manila, Philippines on 9 December 1619. See Retana 1910: 29.

34 For a preliminary overview of early modern Neo-Latin genres on Japan see Watanabe 2018.

35 See Korenjak 2016: 254.

36 See e.g. O'Malley 1993: 254–7.

37 For an exploration of the manifold traditions that coalesce in early modern European Neo-Latin religious drama see Parente 1987.

38 For the curriculum of Jesuit schools in the early modern period see e.g. O'Malley 1993: 215–25 and McCabe 1983: 3–10.

39 For Latin conversation and composition in contemporary Western academia see Minkova 2014: 86. For the production of Neo-Latin classical quantitative verse today see Money 2015: 877–8

40 Tunberg 2014: 76.

41 See e.g. Sidwell 2015.

42 See e.g. Haskell 2014: 785

43 For typical later careers early modern Jesuit students see e.g. McCabe 1983: 11–18.

44 For languages used by early modern Jesuits in and around Japan see Moran 1993: 37–8.

45 See e.g. Watanabe 2020: 203–8 on Jesuit Latin education in early modern Japan.

46 See 1 *Cor.* 9.19–23.

47 See further Rosenstatter 2010: esp. 29–30 on Jesuit academic culture behind these plays.

48 Play listed in Jontes 1984: 46 and Valentin 1983–4: 109.

49 For Thomas Honda Heibyōe's career as reconstructed from historical records see Kataoka 2010: 131–3.

50 As reported in Morejon 1616: 11 and Trigault 1623: 45–6.

51 See e.g. Trigault 1623: 119.

52 For Japanese views concerning Fujihiro's social standing see Miyake 1956: 76–7.

53 For an overview of Fujihiro's early career and his appointment as governor of Nagasaki see Hesselink 2016: 133–7.

54 For modern Japanese historians' assessment on Fujihiro's governorship see Miyake 1956 and Shimizu 1975.

55 For an overview of Fujihiro's activities around Arima in 1612–13 see Miyake 1956: 82–5.

56 So Morejon 1616: 19–21 and Trigault 1623: 122–30.

57 Cf. Morejon 1616: 19–20 with Trigault 1623: 126. For a description of Trigault's 1623 Munich publication see Kapitza 1990: 450–5.

58 For Trigault's mysterious demise see Logan and Brockey 2003.

59 For a list of known Jesuit plays based on Trigault 1623 see Collani 2005: 270–1.

60 For known plays on Thomas Honda Heibyōe and his family other than *JM* see Jontes 1984: 49, Proot 2002: 36–7, Staud 1994: 115–16, 128, 195, Valentin 1983–4: 112, 143, 262, 272, 302, 441, 589, 618, 641 and Wimmer 2005: 27–8.

61 For examples of Michael/Naozumi on the Jesuit stage see Szarota 1980–7: III.1.198 and Bahlmann 1896: 276–7.

62 See Haga 2021 for a comparison between Tokugawa Japan and imperial Rome.

63 See Oda 1985: 113–18.

64 See Cieslik and Sakuma 1974: 19.

65 For an overview of the early history of the Jesuit college in Koblenz see e.g. Becker 1982: 10–12.

66 For a list of locations in Koblenz where Jesuit plays may have been performed see Bellinghausen 1973: 160.

67 See e.g. the school website in https://www.goerres-koblenz.de/unsere-schule/tradition-und-moderne/geschichte/ (accessed 18 February 2022).

68 See Wilson 2009.

69 For Carlo and Ambrogio Spinola see Omata 2020: 7–8, 27–31.

70 See e.g. Wilson 2009: 300.

71 For the history of Roman Koblenz see Belllinghausen 1973: 36–69.

72 See Zuber 2016: 70–4.

73 For Sötern's megalomaniac and short-lived geographic and architectural achievements see e.g. Bellinghausen 1973: 172–3.

74 For an overview of Sötern's life and political intrigues see Weber 1969.

75 KS Best. 222 A.685: 68v.

76 The complaint is reproduced in Hontheim 1750: 300.

77 For a modern assessment of Sötern's handling of the 1625 *Landtag* see Dillinger 2008: 68–9.

78 For an analysis of Sötern's shift of allegiance from the Habsburgs to the French see Abmeier 1986: 4–9 and Weber 1969: 32.

79 For a German Catholic historian's condemnation of Sötern see Duhr 1907–28: 2.1.25.

80 For an account of the discovery of these manuscripts and early attempts to catalogue them, see Bahlmann 1896: 80, Becker 1919: 7–8 and Michel 1919: 93–4.

81 See Becker 1919: 7.

82 Becker 1919.

83 See Becker 1919: 8–15.

84 See Haas 1977 and 1982. Based on its hand this piece is likely from the seventeenth century, but its production date is unknown.

85 Most of the information given in this paragraph was uncovered by Dr Antonia Kariasl in her research in the LHA in September 2021. I am most grateful to Dr Karaisl for sharing her unpublished findings, including images of manuscripts and transcripts pointing out overlaps with *JM*.

86 Becker 1919: 12 says 1623, but KS Best. 223 A684 (the annals of the Marian sodality of Koblenz): 63r.-v. clearly states that the performance took place on 15 August 1622. *I&X* V.4 is of special interest as it is set in Bungo and features Xavier debating with and winning against local Buddhist priests in front of the *kirishitan daimyō* Yoshishige (see 1.1 above), showing that Japan was represented, albeit briefly, in the Koblenz Jesuit theatre at least once prior to *JM*.

87 Cf. Becker 1919: 8 and Bahlmann 1896: 80. As *CB* incorporates lines from Cruz's *Prodigus* which was published in 1605 (see below 2.4) and was likely cribbed for *JM* in 1625, its date may be presumed to lie between these two ends (i.e. 1605–25).

88 LHA Best. 117 nr. 711: 9–11 and 85–7. 86 contains a draft of a letter dated 1661 or 1667.

89 See e.g. Barsby 1999: 16–17.

90 50 however does not include any script but is a draft outline of scenes.

91 Cf. Valentin 1983–4: 109 with Becker 1919:13.

92 For a description of this *perioche* see Boge 2001: 361.

93 For an overview of traditional methods in editing Neo-Latin texts see e.g. Sidwell 2017: 400–3.

94 For the possibility that students sometimes took part in the creation of scripts in early modern Jesuit plays see Duhr 1907–28: 2.1.686.

95 For an estimate of the quantity of staged vs. printed Jesuit plays see Grund 2015: 113–14.

96 For typical numbers of acts and other structural characteristics of Jesuit plays see Barea 2013: 553–5.

97 See M. Riley's edition of Carolus Kolczawa S. J., *Tyrannis triumphans et triumphata, seu Anglia* http://www.philological.bham.ac.uk/tyrannis/ (accessed 6 September 2021).

98 For differences between Neo-Latin and (the usual modern understanding of) classical Latin see e.g. Sidwell 2015: 19–23.

99 On the senarius and other Roman comic metres see e.g. Barsby 1999: 290–304.

100 For an overview of metrical schemes in Senecan tragedy, the number-one metrical model for Jesuit dramatists, see e.g. Fantham 1982 104–15.

101 For examples of and discussions on loose metrical standards in Jesuit plays from German-speaking areas see Bauer and Leonhardt 2000: 101–4, Tilg 2005: 44–5 and Abele 2019: 160–6.

102 I thank Harris Makoto for secure identification of these voice types in the manuscript (email dated 11 June 2020).

103 See Bauer and Leonhardt 2000: 104–6, Torino 2007: 687 and Abele 2019: 160–6.

104 See Ferrand 2014: 1069.

105 Citation in commentary by folio number in Tixier 1615.

106 On Cruz' educational and literary career see Büttner 2004: 26–31 and Barea 2013: 624–5.

107 Citation in commentary by line number in Fernandes and Castro 1989. The passages from *P* also occur in *CB*, so the borrowing in *JM* may very well have happened with *CB* as an intermediary (see 2.3 above).

108 Citation in commentary by line number in Barbosa and Pinho 2011.

109 For an overview of these two plays see Frèches 1964: 139.

110 Citation in commentary by line number in Büttner 2004.

111 For Buchanan's career and his verse translation of the Psalms see Green 2014: 466–8. Citation in commentary is by psalm and line number in the online Philological Museum http://www.philological.bham.ac.uk/ buchpsalms/contents.html (accessed 6 September 2021).

112 Citation in commentary is by page number in Pontanus 1600. On his career as a dramatist see Rädle 2013: 266–8.

113 Citation in commentary is by act/line number in Torino 2007. On Stefonio's major dramatic works see Chevalier 2013C: 75–80, 97.

114 Citation in commentary by line number in Jesuits 1634.

115 See Garrod 2019 on Caussin's *Felicitas*.

116 Citation of all of Caussin's plays in commentary is by page number in Caussin 1621. For Caussin's major dramatic works see Chevalier 2013B: 431–4, 437–40, 448–50.

117 For Stefonio's career see Chevalier 2013C: 97.

118 For Caussin's life and career see Hocking 1943: 14–17.

119 See Chevalier 2013A: 258.

120 For views on plagiarism in the early modern Jesuit dramatic context see Abele 2018: 167–78. *JM* as a performative text not intended for publication would have had great license as per contemporary mindset.

121 Play listed in Jontes 1984: 47 and Valentin 1983–4: 261.

122 See Yamada 2003: 74.

123 For a summary of historical accounts on Victor and Andreas Ogasawara see Yūki 1994: 31, 37, 74, 79.

124 This summary is based on the Japanese translation of Fróis' manuscript letter in Yūki 1994: 88–90.

125 See Yūki 1994.

126 For an overview of Bartoli's work on Japan see Collani 2005: 280–2. Scioli 2013 has a modern critical edition.

127 See AZPJ Signatur 41-6.4; 511–12.

128 For a reproduction of the playbill see Szarota 1980–7: II.1.535–46 and Kapitza 1990: 629–33.

129 The passage is question is in Scioli 2013: 304–6.

130 Cf. Yūki 1599: 47–51 with Scioli 2013: 304–5.

131 Huber 1954: 102–4.

132 On this martyrdom see Mizobe 1990.

133 See e.g. Ogasawara 2020.

134 On student numbers and major literary figures among the faculty of Munich Jesuit academy in the early modern period see Selbmann 1996: 9–21 and Schmid 2001: 136–40.

135 See e.g. the school website in https://www.wilhelmsgymnasium.de/ (accessed 9 September 2021).

136 See e.g. Bauer and Leonhardt 2000: 12 and Rädle 2013: 269.

137 On Jesuit theatre and Counter-Reformation see Rädle 1979.

138 See Bauer and Leonhardt 2000: 268–75. On the Tenshō embassy see 1.1 above.

139 See Valentin 1983–4: 131, 243, 486, 527, 775, 794, 804.

140 BSB CLM 1551: 101r.

141 Cf. BSB CLM 1551: 111v.–112r. and AZPJ Signatur 41–6 Abt.4: 527.

142 BSB CLM 1554: 211v.–221v.

143 Franz Max Luz came from a well-connected local political family, graduated from the Munich academy in 1666 and became a courtier later in life. I thank Mr. Peter Kefes biographical information on Luz (email to Antonia Karaisl, 13 July 2021).

144 See Kunnert 1963: 306.

145 See Kunnert 1963: 307–8.

146 For a general overview of how the battle proceeded on that day see Toifl 2016.

147 On the controversial aftermath of the battle see e.g. Yilmaz 2016: 26–8.

148 See e.g. Rohrschneider 2016: 117–18.

149 For a full transcription and description of the epitaph see Kunnert 1963: 310.

150 For the connection between funerals and Roman theatre see e.g. Manuwald 2011: 245.

151 For the Fugger family's (especially Franz's) support of the Jesuit university in Ingolstadt see Kunnert 1963: 310–11.

152 For Wiestner's later illustrious career as a legal scholar see Duhr 1907–28: 3.544–6.

153 As a comparison, Euripides *Cyclops* is 709 and Plautus *Curculio* is 729 lines long.

154 For another Jesuit play (performed in Munich in 1598) with three parts (*partes*) see Rädle 2013: 241.

155 For examples of early modern Neo-Latin authors' apologies for using Japanese terms see Watanabe 2018: 109–11. For the uneasy mix of Japanese and classical Graeco-Roman elements in Jesuit plays in general see Weber 1997: 5, 9. For the restrictive lexical stock of belletristic Neo-Latin see Helander 2014: 39.

156 See note to *JM* 1463.

157 See e.g. notes to *VJ* 206 and 248.

158 See Bauer and Leonhardt 2000: 130–2 and Tilg 2005: 318–20.

159 See e.g. Pöhlmann 2020: 112.

160 See e.g. Schmid 2001: 137–8.

161 Bidermann 1666; I thank Fidel Rädle for pointing this detail out to me.

Japanese Martyrs: Latin Text

Prologus

2 angeli.
Angelus 1: Salve, *Angelus 2*: fave, *Ambo*: spectator integerrime;
    superi iubent, medioximi volunt;
Angelus 2: En, nos tenellae praesides pueritiae,
    curae iuventus est quibus.
Angelus 1: Nunc Christianorum tenera succendere   5
    pubis paramus pectora.
Angelus 2: Fratrum par Arimensium, par nobile,
    rei gerundae sunt caput.
Angelus 1: Quorum fuimus olim duces certaminum,
    encomiastae nunc sumus.   10
Angelus 2: In Christianos aestuat dux Arimae
    iussu Daifu Caesaris.
Angelus 1: Vanos deos et numina imperat coli;
    sed Christiani respuunt.

1–32 The prologue is spoken by the guardian angels of Iustus and Iacobus, the boy-martyrs. The angels inform the audience that the play centres on this pair who were beheaded, following the brave example set by their father and uncle, after spurning the threats of the tyrant of Arima who was acting at the behest of Daifu. This summary differs from the actual play in two points: 1) While it identifies Iustus and Iacobus as the main characters, the *JM*'s main heroes (at least for up to two-thirds of it, until they are martyred) rather are their father Thomas and uncle Matthias; 2) The tyrant or ruler of Arima proper, historical Arima Naozumi/Michael, never appears in the play and is represented by the national hegemon Tokugawa Ieyasu/Daifu instead (see Introduction 1.1 and 2.1). The differences may simply be due to hasty planning, but another possibility is that our piece recycles the prologue of a still earlier play which featured Iustus and Iacobus prominently and in which Naozumi/Michael did appear. There is however no record of such a piece having existed (which does not mean that there never was one).

The text of the prologue is found only in *B*. The metre is iambic trimetre alternating with iambic dimetre, a scheme familiar e.g. from Horace *Epodes* 1–10.

Japanese Martyrs: Translation

Prologue

2 angels.

Angel 1: Greetings, *Angel 2*: please be silent, *Both*: most honourable spectator;
thus heavenly deities command, and middling ones wish.

Angel 2: Behold, we are the guardians of tender children,
who watch over youth.

Angel 1: We are now preparing to set on fire   5
the hearts of Christian adolescents.

Angel 2: A pair of brothers from Arima, a pair of nobles,
is our main subject.

Angel 1: We once led them in their struggle,
and now we eulogise them.   10

Angel 2: The leader of Arima boils with anger against the Christians
at king Daifu's command.

Angel 1: He orders the worship of vain deities and spirits,
but the Christians refuse.

---

1 *spectator integerrime*: The primary referent may be archbishop and prince
elector Sötern, the spectacle's guest of honour (see Introduction 2.2).

2 *superi iubent, medioximi volunt*: In Plautus *Cistellaria* 512, deities are divided
into the *superi*='heavenly', *medioximi*='middling/earthly', and *inferi*='infernal
(i.e. of the underworld)' ones. In Christian, including Jesuit, Latin on the other
hand, the *superi* commonly refers to the holy trinity as well as the saints and
archangels. It may be that *medioximi* here is a playful self-reference made by
the guardian angels as entities that rank lower than the *superi*.

9–10 *quorum … sumus*: What the guardian angels mean is that they once led
their charges (Iustus and Iacobus) in their struggle for successful martyrdom
and that they are now praising them on stage.

10 *encomiastae*: encomiasta, from the Greek ἐγκωμιαστής, is not found in
L&S, Forcellini or NLW but is attested in printed Neo-Latin texts (see e.g.
Locre 1608: 49).

11–12 *dux … Caesaris*: What is said here is closer to documented history
than to what actually follows on stage (see note to 1–32 above).

Angelus 2: Tandem tyrannus illustri binos loco   15
    sisti iubet puellulos.
Angelus 1: Tentat dolis, addit minas et verbera;
    stat uterque flecti nescius.
Angelus 2: Et fortiter cum patre patruo et suo
    pro lege Christi concidunt.   20
Angelus 1: Dant colla fatali ferro puelluli,
    legem dei ne polluant.
Angelus 2: Puerile sanguen et animos tam nobiles
    probant boni, stupent mali.
Angelus 1: Pars magna scelus hoc exsecratur principis   25
    caelumque plausu personat.
Angelus 2: Tantum est; cothurnus forte maior est pede
    parantque magna parvuli.
Aetatulae veniam date; superis placent
    vobisque placeant parvuli.   30
Adeste faciles arbitri spectaculi!
    Tentasse satis est parvulis.

I.1

Belial, Astaroth, Idolomania, Crudelitas, Impietas.
Belial: Quis umquam, amabo, parricidam carnifex
tam verberavit aspere ac enormiter,

---

16 *puellulos*: *puellula* is classical but not the masculine *puellulus*. The latter however is attested elsewhere in Neo-Latin (see e.g. Tixier 1616: 58).

28 *magna parvuli*: *et* or *at* is crossed out between these two words in the manuscript.

33–140 I.1. This is a kind of second prologue in which demonic figures (Idolomany, Cruelty and Impiety in *A¹*, Belial and Astaroth in *B*) discuss their plan to retake Japan, a land that Xavier and his followers had claimed for Catholicism, by using Safioye as their chief earthly agent.

The text presents a major editorial challenge as the two extant versions, in *A¹* and *B*, have substantial textual overlap yet feature different characters and end up with noticeably different tones. The longer *A¹*, which alone has Idolomany's extended monologue (51–86), gives a more diabolical image of the infernal forces. The somewhat shorter version *B* has a lighter note, kicking

Angel 2: Finally the tyrant orders two little boys of illustrious birth   15
   to be brought in front of him.
Angel 1: He tempts them with tricks, and adds threats of beatings;
   both boys persist, incapable of being shaken.
Angel 2: And bravely they die together with their father and uncle
   for the law of Christ.   20
Angel 1: The little boys stretch out their necks to the fatal sword,
   lest they dishonour the law of God.
Angel 2: The boys' blood and spirits so noble
   rouse the praise of good people, and the surprise of bad ones.
Angel 1: The majority detest this crime of the prince   25
   and heaven resounds with applause.
Angel 2: That is all; perhaps the buskin is too large for the foot
   and small children are preparing big things.
Be kind to the children; the small ones are pleasing to heavenly beings,
   may they also be pleasing to you.   30
Be favourable judges of this spectacle!
   For the little ones, it is enough to have tried.

I.1

Belial, Astaroth, Idolomany, Cruelty, Impiety.
Belial: What executioner, I beg you, ever thrashed
a parricide so harshly and monstrously

---

off with a comic exchange (33–50, found only in *B*) between Belial who
complains about the thrashing he has received from Lucifer for losing Japan
and the tongue-in-cheek consolation offered by Astaroth. As for the rest,
87–9 are found only in *A¹*, and from 90 on the two versions overlap except
that 93–7, 115–21, and 126–34 appear only in *A¹* and 105–6 (*divum …
lignario*), 114, 122, and 140 only in *B*. In this edition, all lines after 51 are
assigned to speakers as in *A¹*. In *B*, 90–2, 110–14, 121, and 135–40 are spoken
by Belial and 99–109 by Astaroth.

The metre up to 134 is senarius, with many problematic lines (38, 43
(*versus mancus*), 51, 57, 58, 95, 109, 112, 114, 119, 122, 132, 134 (*versus
mancus*). 135–40 is in dactylic hexametre.

33 *Belial*: Belial the demon appears frequently in the Old and New Testament
(e.g. *Deut.* 13.13, *2 Cor.* 6.15) as well as in early modern European demonology
(see e.g. Weyer 1577: 919–20).

quam Lucifer profanus ille me modo   35
nihil merentem? O ut meum tergum, caput,
O crura fracta! Quis mihi auxiliabitur?
Frater Astaroth, venito, curre, advola!
Astaroth, quibus cavernis delitescis, Astaroth!
Astaroth: Quid lacrimaris, Belial? Quid me vocas?   40
An quid tibi, mi frater, evenit mali?
Quid, Belial, tantum gemis? *Belial*: Me perditum,
O me afflictum!
Astaroth: Dic! *Belial*: Imperator ipse noster Lucifer
horribiliter, immaniter, crudeliter   45
me verberavit! *Astaroth*: Quo reum crimine? Suae
laesaene maiestatis? *Belial*: Ah, ah, Astharoth,
Iaponiam turbandam mihi dederat, ah, ah,
adversa sors artes omnes lusit meas.

   –   –   –

Astaroth: Cavebo, ne, ut tu, pessimis tracter modis.   50

   –   –   –

Idolomania: Idolum ego dea, domina Iaponiae
orbisque novi; ego matre sata Superbia
Erebique hiantis Dite, diabolorum omnium
fetura pessima, fera crudelissima,
inimica caelo furia, quae hoc efflictim ago,   55
ut, pace turbata, orbis in Tartara ruat.
Sed quid morarum necto moras tam diu?
Ego non furorem insaniam, ut Maenas, meum?
Hoc ense mille, mille sternam millia,
ita populabo capita, sic pedes metam,   60
ita penetrabo viscera, ita praecordia.
Mene otiosa, sedem ut occupet Iaponum

---

38 *Frater Astaroth*: Astaroth is also well known from the Old Testament (e.g. *Judg.* 2.13) as well as early modern demonology (see Weyer 1577: 921). *frater* is used here in the sense of friend or colleague.

50 *cavebo … modis*: This line appears in *B* near the end of the scene immediately before the pronouncement in dactylic hexametre by Belial (135–40). In the manuscript the line begins with *parebo*, and above it is

as that profane fellow Lucifer did to me just now,   35
me, who had done nothing wrong? O, look at my back, my head,
O my broken legs! Who will help me?
Astaroth, brother, come, run and fly!
Astaroth, in which caves are you hiding, Astaroth?
Astaroth: Why are you weeping, Belial? Why are you calling me?   40
My brother, did anything bad happen to you?
Why do you groan so much, Belial? *Belial*: I am done for,
O I am hurt!
Astaroth: Speak! *Belial*: Our commander, Lucifer himself
horribly, monstrously, cruelly   45
thrashed me! *Astaroth*: What crime were you guilty of? Of
lèse-majesté? *Belial*: Ah, Ah, Astaroth,
he had given me Japan to shake it up. Ah, Ah,
adverse fortune disappointed all of my tricks.

–   –   –

Astaroth: I will take care so that I won't be treated horribly, like you.   50

–   –   –

Idolomany: I am the goddess of idols, mistress of Japan
and of the New World; I was born of mother Pride
and of Hades, king of gaping hell. Of all the devils
I am the worst brood, the most cruel beast,
a fury hostile to heaven, and I work assiduously for this aim,   55
that peace be broken and the world crash down into hell.
But why do I keep on tarrying so long?
Shall I not, as a Maenad, rage with my accustomed furor?
[*Swinging a sword held in her hand*] With this sword, I will strike
    down one thousand, one million,
thus [*Sweeping above*] will I gather heads as booty, thus [*Sweeping
    below*] will I shear off legs,   60
thus [*Making stabbing motions*] will I pierce entrails, and thus, hearts.
Am I to be idle, while I let a Roman priest,

---

written *vel, cavebo*. The latter reading is adopted here (the choice does not
affect the overall meaning or metre). The line is assigned in Belial in the
manuscript but context dictates that it must be attributed to Astaroth. In this
edition the line is placed here in order to make its connection with the
Astaroth-Belial exchange clearer.

55 *furia*: Cf. note to 502.

nostram Latinus praesul, Ausonius popa,
hoc patiar? Hoc impune dextera perferet?
Regina quid Iaponiae possit potens,   65
patebit omni in orbe; quid necto moras?
Patrare quidquid triste, detestabile,
difficile, grave, terribile, sceleratum queo,
aggrediar, audebo, magis ausura in dies.
Me continenter duce, triginta tres popas   70
a primo eorum capite Petro, dextera
cruenta regum (vah, recensens gestio)
adusque Melchiadem neci crudae dedit.
Et nunc patiar, ut gens Iaponensis, fide
quae tota perstat, stringat in caput meum   75
perfida machaeram? Omnisque plebs colat sacra
lingua nefanda, quae scelestus Xavier
praecepta docuit, templa consurgant polo?
Per Amidae pudenda sacra, per et Xacae
manes nefandos, fulmen ignitum Iovis,   80
per Styga iuro, per et cuncta deum numina,
non patiar! Ita me iuvet Acheron bonzius,
ita me Amidas propitius et Phlegethon beet!
Ubi, ubi tyrannis impia, ubi inferae Stygis
horrenda monstra? Adeste, adeste, vos dea   85
Orientis evocat, moras quid nectitis?

70–3 *Me continenter . . . dedit*: The reference here is to early Roman Catholic popes from Peter (?–64/68) to Melchiades (?–314), also known as Miltiades, who according to church tradition occupied the office from the beginning of Christianity to the end of official Roman imperial persecution in 313. The Catholic church today numbers Melchiades/Miltiades as the thirty-second pope, but different succession lists existed in the past (see e.g. O'Malley 2010: 16–17).

75 *tota*: Idolomany speaks here of all the Japanese nation going over to Catholicism, a statement that is to be taken proleptically or as a rhetorical exaggeration. Cf. also 90.

79 *Amidae . . . Xacae*: *Amidas* and *Xacas* are the most frequently mentioned Buddhist terms in early modern Jesuit accounts. They correspond respectively to *Amitābha* or *Amida*, the principal deity in Pure Land Sect Buddhism, and Gautama Buddha (fifth or sixth century BCE?) of the Shakya (hence Japanese

a Western pontiff, occupy our seat in Japan?
Shall I let this be? Shall I quietly put up with this?
What the powerful queen of Japan is capable of, 65
all the world shall see; why do I tarry?
Whatever depressing, detestable,
difficult, onerous, terrible, criminal thing I can do,
I shall try and dare, and day by day I am going to dare even more.
Under my continuous leadership, thirty-three pontiffs. 70
beginning with their founder, Peter, were given over
by the blood-stained kings (Oh, I am so happy to recall this!),
to horrendous murder, all the way to Melchiades.
And now, shall I let the Japanese nation, who all
persist in their faith, disloyally draw their sword 75
against my head? Should all the people cultivate with their voice
the abominable sacred precepts, which Xavier, the criminal,
taught them, and should their churches rise up to the sky?
By Amida's shameful rites, by the abominable spirit
of Shaka, by Jupiter's fiery thunderbolt 80
I swear, and by all the divine powers of the gods,
I shall not allow this! May Acheron the bonze thus help me,
may Amida and Phlegethon propitiously bless me!
Where, where is the impious tyranness, where are the horrendous monsters
of infernal Styx? Come here, come here, the goddess of the Orient 85
summons you, why do you tarry? [*Cruelty and Impiety arrive on stage*]

Shaka, Latin *Xacas*) clan (see e.g. Washizuka and Goepper 1997: 13–16), the very founder of Buddhism. Here and elsewhere they seem to be generic and undifferentiated Japanese pagan deities.

80–1 *Iovis … Styga*: Graeco-Roman paganism and Buddhism are often mentioned in the same breath in *JM*, as in other Jesuit plays set in Japan. In the early modern Catholic view, Eastern pagan religions like Buddhism were another form of demon-worship once practised by the ancient Greeks and Romans (see e.g. Urbano 2005: 84). Thus it should come as no surprise that in *JM* Graeco-Roman deities are shown worshipped alongside Buddhist ones by the Japanese and that these gods sometimes appear on stage to join forces against the Catholic Church (see also Introduction 1.2).

82 *Acheron bonzius*: No such bonze appears in any of the subsequent scenes, but the proper name, used for the underworld in classical Latin (see *L&S* s.v.), is an appropriate one for a friend of Idolomany.

Crudelitas: Augusta, multum salve, dic, quid imperas?
Impietas: Quae causa nos huc accivit tanti mali?
Idolomania: Audite facinus dirum et illaetabile:
Gens Iaponensis tota perstat in fide   90
colitque sacra plebs omnis, quae Xavier
docuit scelestus; crux, templa insurgunt polo.
Impietas: O facinus exsecrandum et inexpiabile!
Hoc Christianorum Iaponensium scelus
feram? Mariae natum sic plebs colet?   95
Tantum patiar Impietas scelus? Testor deos
divasque omnes, per sceptra iuro Tartari,
hac Christiadum gentem dextra perdam, opprimam!
Crudelitas: Ille ego Britannos orbe seclusos dolis
gyrare qui tot annis novi, forcipes,   100
rotas, palos, cruces, sicas, ignes, faces
cultoribus Romanae sedis intuli;
Iaponia quoque sentiet ultrices manus.
Optatus est in aula nobis regia
Saphioia, divum contemptor, nobilis   105
qui factus ex fabro quondam lignario
et artifex modo principem locum tenens;
Iovem tuetur et Amidam, colit deos.
Hic faber et princeps omnis fiet mali.
Idolomania: Rem acu. In me nulla tentandi residet mora.   110
Saphioia regem incautum versabit dolis.
Hunc aggredere, tyrannis, inflammes praecordia.

---

98 *Christiadum gentem*: B has *Iaponenses*. The reading of *A¹* adopted here is metrically superior.

99–100 *Ille ego Britannos ... novi*: The idea that demonic forces were attacking the Catholic church both in Europe (mainly through Protestants) and elsewhere in the world (mainly through pagans, like the unconverted Japanese) is one that is repeated elsewhere in early modern Jesuit literature (see e.g. Döpfert 2017: 52, 66. For a similar view expressed in Spain in 1617 see Roldán-Figueroa 2021: 209–11). Just in such a vein, Trigault 1623: 21 reports the aural appearance of a demon in Japan who announced (through

Cruelty: Many greetings, empress; speak, what is your command?
Impiety: What occasion for such great evil summoned us here?
Idolomany: Hear this horrid and unhappy deed;
all of the Japanese nation persists in its faith,   90
and all the people cultivate the rites, which Xavier,
the criminal, taught them; their cross and their churches rise up to the sky.
Impiety: O execrable and inexpiable deed!
Shall I endure this crime at the hands of
Japanese Christians? Shall the people thus worship Mary's offspring?   95
Shall I, Impiety, put up with such a great crime? I swear by all
the gods and goddesses, I swear by the sceptre of hell,
that I shall destroy, I shall crush the Christian nation with this, my right
     hand! [*Gestures with her right arm*]
Cruelty: I am that one, who for so many years have been able to
spin around the Britons, cut off from the world, with my trickery; I have   100
with tongs, wheels, stakes, crosses, daggers, fire, and torches
tortured the followers of the Roman See;
Japan, too, will feel my vengeful power.
There is a man chosen by us in the royal palace,
Safioye, who despises heavenly beings, who became   105
a noble out of a woodworking carpenter,
our master artisan, who has just now come to a princely station;
he honours Jupiter and Amida, and worships the gods.
He will be our prince and craftsman for all our evil deeds.
Idolomany: You hit the nail on its head. I will try this out without delay.   110
Safioye will work on the clueless king with his trickery.
Take him on, tyranness, inflame his heart!

---

a local individual whom it had possessed) that true Christians in the East
would be subjected to the same assaults as in Britain.

103 *ultrices*: B has *has meas*. The reading of *A¹* adopted here is slightly more
expressive.

105–6 *Saphioia … lignario*: *A¹*, having only *Saphioia lignarius quondam
faber*, is more concise. On Safioye's model Hasegawa Fujihiro and his social
background see Introduction 2.1.

110 *Rem acu*: *rem acu tango* is a common proverb used by Plaut. (*Rudens*
1306) and many others. See also 179.

Ego interim turbabo regna Bungica
et arte, quicquid potero, efficiam mea;
statuas ab alto, idola pontificantium,   115
demoliar, et praesulum flammis dabo
aras sacratas, funditus aequabo solo
aedes divorum, templa, fana, rebellium
capita, gregemque Christi Acherontici absument rogi.
Impietas: Ego furorem insaniam meum in Indiis   120
nec patiar illuc nomen inferri dei.
Iungendae sunt vires, ac arma duplicanda;
noctes diesque pervigil totos agam
leonis instar rugientis obambulans,
ut capta praeda destinetur Tartaro.   125
Idolomania: Nunc ergo coniurata pugnemus manu,
arma duplicemus, pereat impium genus.
Ferenda templis dona constructis focis;
si respuat, succumbat atro funere
aut exulet suis fugatus sedibus.   130
Crudelitas: Iuro tibi omnem fida, quam potero, operam
praestare, magnus ita me iuvet Diespiter.
Impietas: Ita me Amidas propitius et Xacas beet,
fidem irrefractam servitabo.
Idolomania: Iam gaudere potest Stygiae regina cavernae, 135
in nigris gestire queunt cacodaemones antris;

---

113 *regna Bungica*: Referring to Bungo (southern Ōita prefecture today), the feudal realm of Ōtomo clan, whose member Sōrin was one of the early *kirishitan daimyō*. By the early seventeenth century, the successors of Sōrin had abandoned Catholicism and persecution was flaring up in Bungo as well (see Introduction 1.1).

115 *statuas … pontificantium*: Referring to sacred images (of saints etc.) used in the Catholic church. *pontificans* in the sense of 'holder of the pontificate, pope' is attested from late antiquity (see Forcellini s.v.).

118 *divorum*: Emended from *deorum* in *A¹*, which does not suit the context since gods in the plural denote pagan polytheism in Jesuit literature. The *divi* on the other hand can mean heavenly beings such as saints.

123 *leonis instar rugientis*: The image of the devil going around like a roaring lion waiting to devour its victim is also found in 1 *Pet.* 5.8.

Meanwhile, I shall shake up the kingdom of Bungo
and will accomplish whatever I can with my artifice;
I will demolish the statues and idols of popes   115
from their foundations, I will hand over to flames
the sacred altars of the priests, I will raze to the ground
the houses of the saints, and hellish pyres shall consume
the churches, chapels, the rebels themselves, and the flock of Christ.
Impiety: I shall rage with my furor in the Indies,   120
and will not let the name of God be brought in there.
We must join forces and redouble our arms;
I will spend all my nights and days awake,
roaming round like a roaring lion,
so that my captured booty may be destined to hell.   125
Idolomany: Now therefore, let us fight with joined hands,
let us redouble our arms, let the impious crowd face doom.
Pyres should be made, and offerings should be brought to temples;
if they refuse, let them die an atrocious death
or go to exile, away from their own homes.   130
Cruelty: I faithfully promise to devote all of my effort that I am
capable of, may Jupiter so help me.
Impiety: May Amida and Shaka so bless me,
I shall keep my loyalty unbroken.
Idolomany: Now, the queen of the Stygian cavern may rejoice,   135
the cacodaemons can exult in their black caves;

---

134 *servitabo*: *servito* is a nonce-word, an invented frequentative of *servio* or
servo; unless it is a scribal error for *servabo*. But *servitat* also occurs in 420
and 440, where the form is required by metre (see also Introduction 2.4).

135–40 These lines are in dactylic hexametre, which adds an air of gravity
and portent as the demonic figures look with approval upon their human
protégé Safioye entering the stage.

136 *cacodaemones*: From the Greek κακοδαίμων ('ill-omened'). Applied to
Socrates (*c.* 469–399 BCE) (Aristophanes *Clouds* 104) among others, this
word is frequently used in Neo-Latin in the sense of devil or demon (see
NLW s.v.)

Iaponidae Xacam, Daibundum et numina falsa
supplicibus rursum votis ad sidera tollent;
Virginis et Christi laudes nomenque peribunt.
Sed prodit princeps, socius iam retia pandet.   140

I.2

Saphioia, 2 bonzii.
Saphioia: Quos colligavit cultus una sacratior,
sacri deorum praepotentum servuli,
quid agimus? Impia Christiadum gens
almae per urbis compita meat libera.
Nescio quis intimas voret nostras furor   145
penitus medullas atque per artus volat
visceribus ignis mersus et venis latens.
Ut agilis altas flamma percurrit trabes,
totas populatur sic nocuus venas furor.
Bonzius 1: Quae causa tanti latitat interius citi   150
furoris? Ecquid flamma principium nocens?
Dic, fare, principiis eundum est obviam,

---

137 *Daibundum*: The term comes from the Japanese *daibutsu* ('great Buddha'). Transcribed as *daibutu*, the term appears in the reports of Trigault (1622: 3, 372–3, 508) to mean the colossal statue of Buddha whose construction in Kyoto was inaugurated by the national hegemon Hideyoshi in 1586. Completed in 1612, this particular *daibutsu* was subsequently lost to natural disasters, but similar earlier colossi survive in Nara and Kamakura and are major tourist attractions today (see e.g. Matsuo 2007: 81–4)

141–207 I.2. Safioye airs his complaints about persistent stress and insomnia to two Buddhist priests and wonders what is causing them. The latter suggest that he is in fact suffering from pious anxiety arising from the neglect of traditional Japanese religion and the invasion of Christianity. Safioye embraces this answer and the three agree to launch an anti-Christian persecution using the authority of Daifu, who is to be persuaded that the scheming Catholics are bringing natural as well as human-made calamities upon Japan.

the Japanese will raise up to the stars Shaka, Daibutsu,
and their false divinities with supplicant prayers again,
and respect for the names of the Virgin and Christ will perish.
[*Sees Safioye approaching stage*] But our leader comes forth; our ally
   will now lay his snares.   140

I.2

Safioye, 2 bonzes.
Safioye: You whom our truly sacred religion bound together,
you, holy servants of the most potent gods,
what are we doing? The impious Christian tribe
comes and goes freely through the streets of our mother city.
Some kind of rage is devouring my innermost   145
marrows deep inside and a fire courses through my limbs
submerged within my entrails and hidden in my veins.
Just as a flame might run nimbly through high beams,
so a harmful rage is wrecking all my veins.
Bonze 1: What reason for such a great rabidness could be hidden   150
inside? Is fire a harmful first principle in any way?
Speak out, evils must be met at their start, head-on,

The scene is found only in *A¹*. Since the text is placed immediately after
the previous scene in *A¹* and is entitled *scena 2da*, it was clearly planned to be
staged at this point. The manuscript character list contains, in addition to
Safioye and the two bonzes, *2 ephebi* who do not appear in the scene as
preserved. The metre is senarius, with many problematic lines (143, 146, 162,
166, 167, 176, 180, 181, 204, 205).

146–8 *penitus ... trabes*: The words are taken from Seneca *Phaedra* 642–4,
except for the non-metrical *per artus volat* which in the original is *per venas
meat* (642). In Seneca the title character is describing an illicit passion for her
stepson; here it refers to a soon-to-be articulated sense of anxiety over paganism
under attack. What is being described in both cases is a sentiment that is
justified from the viewpoint of the speaker but unjust from that of the audience.

152 *principiis eundum obviam*: The phrase recalls Ovid *Remedia Amoris* 91,
where the poet speaks of the need to resist erotic impulse at its start (*principiis
obsta*).

ne posita semel longinquitas vix temporis
ulla erui inde videat, aut si fors videt,
sat difficulter inveteratum tollier   155
malum inde cernat. Sera medicina est, mala
dum longiores invaluere per moras.
Saphioia: Incognita Podalirii nobis sacra
est hactenus ars, nec corpora nostra Machaones
herbis male valentia nedum salubribus   160
fovere. Utrimque me incognitum vexat malum:
Populatur ingens flamma animum intus meum,
et licet amoeno fulgeat Hesperus polo,
nox atra furvis flammeos umbris tegat
caelos, suetis Phoebe decurrat bigis   165
revecta, vel ad ortum revisat Thaumantias
lucem, expers quietis dego, fugit inscius
somnus oculos nec ulla quies fessum invenit.
Bonzius 2: Fors insuetae quibo causam pandere,
flammae medullas devorantis intimas.   170
Saphioia: Pandito. *Bonzius 2*: Cultorem te deorum sedulum
novi, pietatis integrum rarae virum;
tuam deorum cultus exagitat sacer
mentem neglectus, quem gens barbara, impia,
effera, cruenta, Christiadum gens horrida   175
deridet ore et prosequitur dicax votis
indigna Phoebeae nitore lampadis
ast digna cavo carcere tenebrosi specus.

156–7 *sera medicina est … moras*: Again the language is close to Ov. *Rem. am.* 91–2 (*sero medicina paratur/cum mala per longas convaluere moras*), where the topic is the danger of delay in resisting erotic impulse. The lines also recall *P* (see Introduction 2.4) 389–90 (*at longa mora/inualuit: omnis sera medicina est modo*), where the kind father Androphilus (who stands for God the father) expounds in a long monologue on the need to keep debauchery away from youth.

158–9 *Podalarii … Machaonis*: Podalirius and Machaon are two mythical doctors and sons of Asclepius, the god of medicine. They are both said

lest lengthy delay, if it interposes itself, should with difficulty
allow for a cure, or, if it should allow for a cure,
it would prove difficult to remove the already rooted   155
evil by that time. Care comes too late, when illness
has become strong through too lengthy a delay.
Safioye: The sacred art of Podalirius has been unknown
to me so far, nor have the likes of Machaon cured
with any of their salubrious herbs my sick   160
body. The unknown disease attacks me on two fronts:
A monstrous fire is devouring my spirit inside;
and whether dawn shines from beautiful heaven,
black night covers the flaming sky with its dark
shadows, returning sister moon runs the course on her accustomed   165
chariot, or goddess rainbow revisits the rising
sun, I am left without repose; sleep, the stranger, flees
from my eyes, and no rest comes to my exhausted self.
Bonze 2: Maybe I can explain the reason for the unusual
fire that is devouring your innermost marrows.   170
Safioye: Explain! *Bonze 2*: I know you to be an assiduous worshipper
of the gods, a good man of rare piety;
neglect of the sacred religion of the gods
disturbs your mind, our religion which the barbarous, impious, wild,
bloody, and horrid tribe of Christians   175
are deriding with their tongues, and are attacking loudly with prayers,
a tribe unworthy of the rays of Phoebean lamp
but worthy of a gloomy prison in a shadowy cave.

---

to have put their skills to use in the Trojan War (see e.g. Homer *Iliad* 2.731–2; *Ilias Latina* 218).

161 *utrimque*: corrected from *utrique* in manuscript.

166 *Thaumantias*: An alternate name for Iris, the goddess of rainbow (see e.g. Virgil *Aeneid* 9.5).

178 *ast ... specus*: The manuscript has *ast digna cavo carcere, et saxo horrida/at digna nocte tenebrosi specus*. The line has been rearranged slightly to combine these words in a way that suits both sense and metre.

Saphioia: Rem acu tetigisti; causa flammae sat meae
liquet. At quis maleficam Christiadas urbis luem   180
pestemque cunctis arcere licet modis?
Bonzius 2: Cum nos cruore Christiadum fuso manus
rigare sacras non deceat, pandam tamen
modum, media, viamque quis premi queat.
Toti pavendus gestat orbi fulgida   185
sceptra Daifusamus hostis gentis impiae,
deorum amicior. Sacro utendum est dolo.
Saphioia: Quis ille dolus, quae fraus faciet nobis fidem?
Bonzius 2: Quodcumque terrens regna divexat malum,
quaecumque fruges perdit aerugo satas   190
et quisquis artus rodit atrox pectoris
morbus, malorumque omnium clamabimus
reos, et avito exterminandos limite,
ni grande brevi solo aequari imperium velit.
Bonzius 1: Necto alia retia, novos apparo dolos,   195
quis involutus piscis hamo noxius
superis graviores pro meritis poenas luat.
Saphioia: Eloquere! *Bonzius 1*: Primos fulgido conquirere
in imperio honores et altos stringere
laudum titulos, nec opibus nec Tyrio satis   200
fulgere murice, sed diadema per nefas
prensare clarum Christiadas tumidos loquar.
Saphioia: Datis quiesco consiliis. Probo data.
Temptare non nocet, ut mens mea autumat.
Bonzii ambo: Dii ergo superi, medii, vos supplices   205
precamur, adeste supplicibus, vestros pio
thure cumulabimus tholos nos servuli.

---

179 *Rem acu tetigisti*: See note to 110 for the proverb. Safioye here repeats the
expression of Idolomany, whose earthly instrument he is.

186 *Daifusamus*: This refers to Daifu, modelled on the historical figure
Tokugawa Ieyasu (see Introduction 1.1). *Daifu* (indeclinable), *Daifusamus*
(second declension), and *Daifusama* (first declension) are all used for this
same character in *JM*.

Safioye: You hit the nail on its head; the reason for my burning sickness
is clear enough. But in what ways can we completely keep away   180
the harmful Christian pest and disease afflicting our city?
Bonze 2: Although it is not fit that we should stain our sacred hands
with the blood of the Christians, nonetheless I shall explain
the mode, medium, and way in which they can be crushed.
Daifusama, the awe of the entire world, holds the shining   185
sceptre; he is an enemy of the impious tribe
and more friendly to the gods. We must use holy deception.
Safioye: What deception, what trick will make us believable?
Bonze 2: Whenever some terrifying evil disturbs the realm,
whenever some disease destroys planted crops,   190
whenever some atrocious sickness gnaws at the muscle
of the heart, in short, of every evil we will proclaim them guilty
and worthy of being banished from their ancestral lands,
unless our ruler wishes to see his great empire reduced to the ground
     in no time.
Bonze 1: I am coming up with another trap and am preparing new
     tricks   195
so that the bad fish, caught with the hook,
may pay a heavier penalty to the gods, as it deserves.
Safioye: Explain! *Bonze 1*: 'They are aiming for the foremost
honours in our august empire, and are plucking off high titles
that earn praise, are not content with wealth, or the glitter of   200
Tyrian purple, but are out to snatch the glorious crown
through their crime, these haughty Christians' – so will I say.
Safioye: I am relieved by your plans. I approve of what you have to
     offer.
There is no harm in trying, as my opinion goes.
Both bonzes: O gods above, gods in the middle, we humbly   205
pray to you, come to us, your supplicants, we will load
your temples with incense, as we are your humble servants.

---

187 *Sacro . . . dolo*: The Jesuits themselves were often accused in the sixteenth
and seventeenth century by both Catholics and non-Catholics of using 'pious
fraud' to promote their own supposedly devious agenda (see e.g. Pavone
2005). Here the kind of conspiracy theory under which the Jesuits laboured
is foisted upon Japanese Buddhists.

I.3

Daifu, Saphoia, 4 consiliarii, satelles.
Daifu: Aequalis astris gradior et cunctos super
altum superbo vertice attingo polum.
Tandem potenti sceptro rebelles premo,   210
bellace dextra tutus adversam ferox
terram dux factus; ora reprimit et trucis
quisquis tyranni fuerat impius comes
tacet et merito gloriae tulit partes meae.
Nunc summa teneo decora, nunc solio fruor.   215
Terrae Facatae, regna mihi Bungae, Figen
Tensae, Chicu dant supplices bello manus.

208–317 I.3. Daifu is introduced exulting over his recent victories and
conquests, but his counsellors suggest the need for continued vigilance.
Safioye enters on cue to inform him of the new and imminent danger arising
from the Christians who are said to be not only trampling on traditional
Japanese religion but also acting as scouts for the Spanish, who have already
conquered the Philippines and are supposedly intent on invading Japan.
Safioye adds that the brothers Thomas and Matthias are foremost among
these internal fifth column. Daifu, shaken by the warning, orders the
proclamation of an anti-Christian edict and sends out a minion to summon
Thomas and Matthias for trial.

This scene is preserved in A^1 and *B*. Lines 225–30 and 290–301 are only in
A^1, while 211–15, 218–21, and 233 are only in *B*. The character list in *B*
includes Thomas and Matthias who do not in fact appear in this scene. The
scene is placed immediately after I.2 in A^1 and I.1 in *B*. The placement in this
edition follows A^1 and the general flow of the plot.

The metre is senarius, with a number of problematic lines as usual (210,
214, 220, 223, 224, 233, 257, 281, 292, 293, 296, 299, 307, 312, 313, 315).

208–9 *Aequalis ... polum*: These lines are taken from Sen. *Thyestes* 885–6,
where Atreus exults over the revenge he is exacting on his brother, having
murdered his children and about to serve them to their father as food. The lines
may be understood as a generic statement of impious hybris for which however
neither Atreus in *Thyestes* nor Daifu in *JM* suffers any earthly retribution.

211–15 *Bellace ... fruor*: These lines are written in small letters on the right
margin of *B*, and later crossed out. Thus, they may not have made it to the final

I.3

Daifu, Safioye, 4 counsellors, minion.
Daifu: I walk as tall as the stars, and towering above everyone else,
I touch high heaven with my proud head.
At last, I crush the rebels with my weighty sceptre,   210
strong in my warlike hand, I press upon hostile
land, having become its leader; and whoever
had been an impious companion of the dire tyrant now keeps his mouth
    shut
and is silent and has rightly become part of my glory.
Now I am on my beautiful summit, now I enjoy my throne.   215
The lands of Hakata, the realms of Bungo, Hizen,
Tenka, and Chiku extend their suppliant hands toward my might.

---

performance but do explain the ground for Daifu's exultation. The tyrant (212) whose impious companions Daifu says he has silenced may refer loosely and ahistorically to Hideyoshi/Taicosama, the previous hegemon who passed away in 1598, or to his son Hideyori (1593–1615), known as Cubosama in Jesuit accounts, whom the historical Ieyasu drove to suicide after the historic date of this play (see Trigault 1623: 375–8 and Henshall 2013: 433).

215 *nunc ... fruor*: This line again echoes Sen. *Thyestes* 887 (*Nunc decora regni teneo, nunc solium patris*). See note to 208–9.

216 *terrae*: The manuscripts have *terras* functioning as the object of *premo* in 210, which it immediately precedes in the main text without the marginal addition. The case is here changed to fit the syntax necessitated by the marginal insertion of 211–15.

216-17 *Facatae ... Chicu*: Some of these Japanese place names are real and others fanciful. *Facata* is today Hakata in Kyushu, historically one of the oldest urban centres in Japan and now a ward within Fukuoka city. *Bunga* stands for the domain of Bungo (see Introduction 1.1) while *Figen* is the domain of Hizen which roughly corresponds to the eastern parts of Saga prefecture today. *Tensa* is derived from the Japanese word *tenka*, spelled *tenca* in Jesuit Latin (see Trigault 1623: 387, where there is a printed marginal note: *An Tensa? ut alii*), which literally translates as 'under heaven' (i.e. the known world, but frequently used in the sense of Japan). *Chicu* is a fanciful place name presumably derived from Chikuzen or Chikugo, both historical Japanese domain names that are spelled *Chicugen* and *Chicugo* respectively

Quis me per orbem mortalis beatior?
Nihil esse certum constat et constat nihil,
hoc praeter ipsum, instabilis fortuna licet,   220
virtute nixa servat in rebus fidem.
Fortuna nobis prospero vultu favet,
arridet, et instabiles aliis rotas dea
uni Daifu immobiles stabilivit ovans.
Non iam rigentes aere turmas, nec ducem   225
depressa tellus pondere armorum gemit.
Non bella clangunt horrida truces bucinae,
enses cecidere flammei, dirae minae,
ardor strepentis iam litui horridus silet.
Hac pace fruar et Caesaris sceptro nego   230
posthac ferendos mobiles regni exitus.
Consiliarius 1: Utinam quod optas, Caesar, eventus probet!
Hac pace dummodo placidus aspiret Zephyrus!
Daifu: Nil metuat ille, cuius invictas opes
trabeata virtus laude numerosa extulit.   235
Xacae sum amicus, militum numero potens,
fortis sagatus, ira si bello tumet,
felix togatus, arma si condit quies.
Quidquam hic vereri provide, timidi est nimis.
Consiliarius 2: Nihil noceri posse tu tibi putas?   240
At ego inveniri posse non paucos reor,
qui si nocere non queant, tentent tamen.

---

in Jesuit Latin. Overall, this list of geographical names would have meant little to the audience in Koblenz other than giving a sense that Daifu has been expanding his realm in a series of victories, making him appear (against documented history; see Introduction 1.1 and note to 211–15) to be a triumphant national hegemon already by the dramatic setting of 1613.

220 *instabilis fortuna licet*: In *B* these words are written above *nempe sed si quam*.

221 *servat in rebus fidem*: In *B* likewise these words are written above *spondet incertis fidem*.

What mortal is there more blessed than I throughout the entire
    world?
That nothing is certain, is certain; nothing is settled,
except for this one thing, that although Fortune is fickle,   220
when she is supported by virtue, she keeps her promise in human affairs.
Fortune favours us with a happy visage,
the goddess smiles and her wheels, which are wobbly for others,
she has made firm and stable for me, Daifu, alone, and applauds.
Now, neither bronze-clad troops nor any military commander   225
makes mother earth, weighed down with heavy arms, groan.
Fierce battle-trumpets do not blare out war,
flaming swords and dire threats have ceased,
the resounding clarion with its terrible gleam is now silent.
I shall enjoy this peace, and shall henceforth refuse to let my kingly sceptre   230
put up with an uncertain future when it concerns my kingdom.
Counsellor 1: May the future prove your wishes correct, O king!
May Zephyr blow calmly on this peace!
Daifu: He, whose invincible resources are supported by stately power
with its abundant honour, should have nothing to fear.   235
I am a friend of Shaka, I am a powerful leader with a large army,
a courageous commander, when wrath calls to war,
a happy civilian, when peace puts away arms.
It is a sign of cowardice to foresee any danger now.
Counsellor 2: Do you think that no harm can be done to you?   240
I on the other hand think that not a few people can be found,
who, even though they cannot harm you, may nonetheless try.

---

233 *Hac . . . Zephyrus!*: This non-metrical line is added in the right margin
of *B*.

238 *felix togatus*: *A¹* has *fortis togatus*, repeating *fortis* from the previous line.
The reading of *B* adopted here is slightly more elegant.

239 *Quidquam . . . nimis*: This line echoes *C* (see Introduction 2.4) II.258:
Omnia vereri provide, timidi est nimis. The same line as in *C* also appears in
Drexel *Iulianus Apostata* (henceforth *IA*) 635. In both contexts, they are used
by members of the Roman imperial court to warn ruling emperors not to
become complacent in their rule.

Consiliarius 3: Nihil hic vereri provide stupidi est nimis.
Ne fide, Caesar; saepe nautas inscios
ad saxa torquet aura quae belle vehit.   245
Daifu: Non hunc beatum rere, qui solio manum
subnixus alto despicit vanos metus?
Consiliarius 4: Illum beatum iudico, si quis pedem
utrimque referens, sede se media tenet
nec cuncta semper anxius misere timet   250
nec dissolutus mente nil umquam timet.
Daifu: Ergo nocere Caesari quisquam volet?
Consiliarius 1: En, imperator, hunc roga quantum tibi
a Christianis hinc et inde impendeat
malum. *Daifu*: Quid est? Saphioia, cur fers huc gradum?   255
Saphioia: O magne Daifu rex, aeternum tibi
regnoque vivas; nos Christiadum furor tuo
stitit coactos hic tribunali sacro.
Daifu: Itan', Saphioia? Fare, quid portas mali?
Quis debitum diis honorem sustulit?   260
Saphioia: Periere regis funditus anathemata,
religio concidit; exulat nomen procul,
afflicta foede iura pietatis iacent.
Daifu: Quis tam nefandi conscius monstri locus?
Quod quereris, edic; gravius incertos tenes.   265
Saphioia: Verbo docebo; dii occiderunt patrii,
simulacra templis, imperator, hinc et hinc
quassata squalent. Quis queat digne eloqui?
Non Iuppiter, non Aesculapius ullibi,
nemo deorum sartus aut tectus manet.   270
Et insulas quas nostro conspectu mare
tenet (Philippinas dicit gens barbara)
armis nefandis Iberus iam possidet

243–5 *Nihil . . . vehit*: These lines combine *C* II.259 (with the addition of *hic nihil*) and II.267–8 (with the addition of *Ne fide, Caesar* before *saepe*). Again this is a generic piece of courtly political advice.

248–51 *Illum . . . timet*: These lines are again lifted from *C* II.260–3. *IA* 637–8 uses the first two of these four lines. Again the statement is a piece of generic political advice from a courtier to a hegemon.

Counsellor 3: It is a sign of stupidity not to foresee any danger now.
Do not be confident, O king; sailors are often unknowingly
dashed against rocks by the wind that seems to be carrying them well.   245
Daifu: Do you have doubts, if someone rests his hands on a throne
and looks down with contempt on empty fears, whether he is happy?
Counsellor 4: I regard that one to be happy who, having his feet
planted apart, keeps himself in the centre of his seat.
He does not anxiously and miserably fear everything,   250
nor is he without any fear at all, with his mind relaxed.
Daifu: So, you think that anyone wishes to harm me, the king?
Counsellor 1: Look, supreme commander, ask this man about the great
evil that comes from the Christians and threatens you
from all sides. *Daifu*: [*Seeing Safioye entering*] What is it? Safioye,
    why do you come here?   255
Safioye: O great Daifu, king, may you live forever
for yourself and for your realm; the madness of the Christians
has forced me to stand here before your sacred tribunal.
Daifu: Is it so, Safioye? Speak, what evil tidings do you bring?
Who destroys the honour that is due to the gods?   260
Safioye: The king's offerings have altogether perished,
religion is dead; its name has gone far off to exile,
the laws of piety are prostrate, having been shamefully abused.
Daifu: What place is privy to such unspeakable monstrosity?
Speak out what you are complaining of; you torture me with uncertainty.   265
Safioye: I shall say in a word; our paternal gods have fallen,
their images are strewn everywhere in temples, supreme commander,
desecrated. Who can explain this in a worthy manner?
Neither Jupiter nor Asclepius nor any of the gods
remain properly maintained or housed anywhere.   270
And those islands, which the ocean holds within
our view (barbarians call them the Philippines),
are occupied now by the Iberians with their nefarious arms,

---

267 *hinc et hinc*: A¹ has *hinc et inde* whose meaning is almost identical, but
the reading of B adopted here is metrically superior.

271–5 *Et insulas … feret?*: The idea that the Iberians, especially Spaniards,
were using Catholic evangelisation as a front for their imperialist ambitions is
one that found traction in the early seventeenth century both in the Far East
and in Europe (see Introduction 1.1 and 2.2). Indeed, at this time the spectre

tuum, Daifu, sitiens nostrumque sanguinem;
et Iaponum tellus sinu tales feret?   275
Daifu: Quousque tandem patiar illudi mihi?
Profecto inanes Caesaris gessero notas
vacuumque nomen regis et partes ducis,
si, me rectore, divorum cultus ruat
vertatque regnum Iaponum gens impia.   280
Saphioia: Iendonia de gente Matthias eius quoque
germanus Thomas et nescio quae non cohors
adglomerat, inopum Christiano coetui
datura nomen. Coepta ni, Caesar, tuo
prohibentur ausu, funditus quassa occident   285
brevi deorum templa, religio, fides.
Defende, Caesar, occasum regni tui;
nomenque divum regis obiectu preme!
In te suprema, Caesar, incumbit salus.
Daifu: Vera retulisti? Sceptra quaerit imperii,   290
quod mage ferox gens Christiadum ridet deos?
Eoa litare pertinax thura Iovi
denegat? Tremendo non supplex Marti cadit?
Amidaene suetis orbat aras hostiis
cunctisque sacris victimas negat diis?   295

---

of Spanish incursion was arguably much closer to home for the residents of Koblenz than for those of Japan, as the prince electorate of Trier was serving as a base for forces from the Spanish Netherlands fighting in the Thirty Years' War. The city of Bacharach, for example, which was taken from the Protestants by Spinola's army in 1620 (see e.g. Mortimer 2015: 222 and Introduction 2.2), is only forty kilometres south of Koblenz. In contrast Manila is about 2000 kilometres south of Nagasaki, and it is a gross exaggeration to say that the Philippines is within visible distance from Japan (cf. 271).

275 *feret?*: So A^1. B has *fovet* which also suits the context and metre but *feret* with its future rather than present tense is slightly more preferable in this rhetorical question.

276 *quousque tandem*: This phrase from Cicero's *Catiline* I.1.1 has been parodied endlessly in Latin literature (cf. e.g. Apuleius *Metamorphoses* 3.27 and Dyck 2008: 63).

the Iberians, who are thirsting for your blood, Daifu, and ours;
should the land of Japan, too, enclose such people in its bosom?   275
Daifu: How long shall I let them make fun of me?
Surely, I would be carrying the kingly insignia in vain,
my regal title as well as my position as leader would be meaningless,
if the religion of the gods should collapse under my watch
and the impious tribe should overturn the realm of Japan.   280
Safioye: Matthias from the family of Yendono as well as his
brother Thomas and some other rabble
congregate, ready to become members of the
destitute Christian crowd. Unless their plans are stopped,
king, by your initiative, soon the temples   285
of the gods, religion, and our faith will be shaken and completely
    destroyed.
Take guard, king, against the destruction of your realm;
and shield the name of the gods with your regal protection.
Our utmost safety, king, depends on you.
Daifu: Is what you report true? That they seek the sceptre of command,   290
that these excessively barbaric Christians deride the gods?
They refuse to offer oriental incense
to Jupiter? They do not fall suppliant in front of fearsome Mars?
Do they deprive Amida's altars of their usual sacrifice
and refuse to offer victims to all of the sacred gods?   295

---

278 *vacuumque*: So *A¹*. *B* has *vanumque*, which also fits the sense and metre.

279 *me rectore*: *A¹* switches the order of these words, but the reading of *B* adopted here is metrically preferable.

281 *Iendonia*: The invented family name *Iendonus* is used for the Honda family for most of this play, although Feibioye, from the Jesuit transcription of Thomas's Japanese (actually first or personal) name Heibyōe, also appears later (1299–1300, 1488). Iendonus is presumably made up of *Iendo*, so spelled e.g. in Trigault 1623: 388, the new Tokugawa capital at that time (former Edo, known today as Tokyo), with the Japanese honorific *-dono* (Latinized as *-donus*) (or rather a part thereof) tacked on to the end.

283 *adglomerat*: An irregular transitive use of an intransitive verb.

Haec audis et vides summo, Iuppiter, polo?
Nondum trisulco in Styga gentem demergere
paras? Adhuc tibi mihique vivit noxia?
O summe praepotens Iuppiter, caelo tona,
intende dextram, vindices flammas para,   300
omnemque ruptis nubibus gentem quate!
Quis hoc iniquum facinus aequi fecerit?
Quis Amidam, quis Daibut spretos feret?
Iendonii fratres ferro cadent meo
cruciarii, ni tempserint legem impiam.   305
Consiliarius 1: Invicte, vive, Caesar, et terror ducum;
gentem rebellem terris proscribe tuis.
Edicta valvis stent publica regni tui
munita signis, exsulet dirum genus.
Consiliarius 2: Consilia velox praeripe et primas moras; 310
Iendonios tribunal ad tuum voca.
Daifu: Vos agite, fidi proceres, quam citissime
regni probra monstraque nostri exquirite,
et crastino sistite tribunali reos.
Satelles: Rex, imperare tuum est, at nostrum iussa facere. 315
Daifu: Aulam petamus. Pendeat signis tribus
edictum –.

308–9 *edicta . . . genus*: The edict mentioned here is loosely based on the one promulgated in 1612, which applied officially to the few domains directly administered by the Tokugawa clan, as well as the later one of 1614 which applied to all of Japan and led to the great 1615 expulsion of the *kirishitan* (see Introduction 1.1). For specific local anti-Christian edicts promulgated in Arima in 1613 (different in substance and more locally conditioned than in *JM*) see e.g. Trigault 1623: 44.

316 *signis tribus*: These 'signs' may be the regal seals mentioned above (308–9), but the mention of number three may also recall the accusation against Christ placed on the cross in three languages (cf. *Lk.* 23.38).

Do you hear and see this, Jupiter, from the summit of heaven?
Are you not yet preparing to hurl them down into Styx with your
three-pronged bolt? Do they keep on living and doing harm to you and
    me?
O Jupiter highest and most powerful, thunder from your sky,
stretch out your hand, prepare your vengeful flames,   300
split your clouds and shatter all these rabble!
Who would think that this criminal deed is permissible?
Who would put up with abuse against Amida, against Daibutsu?
The Yendono brothers will fall by my sword,
those gallows-birds, unless they cast away their impious ways.   305
Counsellor 1: May you live, invincible king, fear of the leaders;
proscribe the rebellious crowd in your lands.
Let your published edict be fixed to doors, armed with the seal
of your kingship, and let the evil tribe go to exile.
Counsellor 2: Grab hold of the counsel quickly, and do not tarry;   310
summon the Yendonos to your tribunal.
Daifu: Get to work, my faithful leaders, as quickly as you can,
seek out the guilty monstrosities of our realm
and bring the accused to my tribunal tomorrow.
Minion: King, it is your job to command, ours to follow your order.
    [*Leaves stage*]   315
Daifu: Let us go into our court. Let the edict be displayed
with three signs. [*Leaves stage with his followers*].

317–54 I.4. Anarchus, a public herald, announces a decree which commands
all citizens and residents of Japan to offer sacrifice to traditional Buddhist
deities and threatens those who disobey with exile or capital punishment.
The populace on stage applauds the proclamation. Archias, Anarchus's
assistant, expresses his forebodings that the edict will bring about bloodshed,
but the latter assures him that they have nothing to fear. Both Anarchus and
Archias are characters invented for the occasion. In *P* there is a dissolute
youth named Anarchus ('unruly' in Greek). The name Archias would be
familiar to any early modern Jesuit student as that of the Greek poet Aulus
Licinius Archias (fl. *c*. 120–61 BCE)) whom Cicero defended in a speech
which became a perennial school favourite (see e.g. Jesuits 1600: 144).

I.4

Anarchus praeco, populus, Archias satelles.
   Anarchus: Adeste, summi, imi, medioximi,
audite regis magni Iaponiae edictum;
adeste omnes Christicolae, sacrificuli,
coriarii, carbonarii, mensarii,   320
dites et inopes, nobiles, ignobiles,
magni et parvi, et mandata Daifu accipite:
Quisquis Xacae, Daibut, divisque ceteris
Sabaea thura non tulerit, luet nece.
Os premite, aures arrigite, verba advertite: 325
'Imperator Daifusama, invictus, augustus, maximus,
potentissimus, pater patriae etc.
Beneficiis immortalibus a diis hactenus affecti,
utpote quibus imperia nostra quanta, quanta
sunt, quantaque umquam futura erunt, accepta   330
penitus ferimus ferreque semper debemus, ingrati
profecto et impii prorsus fuerimus, nisi (de hac quando
parem iis referri gratiam numquam posse minime

The text given here is a combination of what is preserved in *A³* and *B*. *A³* has 325-54, i.e. the edict in prose (after a one-line introduction) and the exchange between Anarchus and Archias. *B* has 317–24, i.e. the gist of the edict delivered in senarius. In *B*, this announcement of the edict is followed immediately by the heated exchange among Thomas, Matthias and other *kirishitan* about how to act in response to it (I.8).

The composition and placement of this scene is provisional. *A³* is codicologically a free-floating unit, written on both sides of a single sheet of paper which originally could have lain anywhere in the stash of drafts. In *B* on the other hand this scene is preceded by the monologue of the church and the consolation of the angel or Christ (I.7). The announcement of the edict seems to follow naturally the court scene with Daifu and others, and the current placement does allow the first line (317) to form one metrical line in senarius with the last words of I.3.

The scene uses senarius for 317–25 and 346–54 (problematic metre: 318, 319, 349) and prose for the edict in 326–45. The line break in the prose text follows that in the manuscript.

I.4

Anarchus the herald, people, Archias the minion.

    Anarchus: Come, you most noble, you most abject, and you in the middle!
Listen to the edict of the great king of Japan;
come, all Christians, serving priests,
tanners, colliers, bankers,   320
rich and poor, nobles, ignobles,
great and small, and listen to the command of Daifu:
Whoever does not carry Sabaean incense to Shaka,
Daibutsu, and the other gods, shall pay for this with their lives.
Keep silent, pluck up your ears, and pay attention to these words: 325
'The supreme commander Daifusama, invincible, august, greatest,
most powerful, father of the fatherland etc.;
whereas we have so far been touched by the kind deeds of the
    immortal gods,
inasmuch as to them we consider our empire, however much
it is, and however much it will be, to be entirely   330
due, and ought to consider to be due always, we surely
would be ungrateful and impious altogether, unless (since concerning
    this favour
we are not at all ignorant that we can never return equal gratitude

---

317 *summi ... medioximi*: A common classical tripartite division, applied here to social classes; see also note to line 2.

320–2 These three lines are written as two in the manuscript, with the sole line break after *nobiles*. The lines have been rearranged here to fit the metre.

324 *Sabaea thura*: The Sabaeans, a South Arabian ethnic group, were famous in Graeco-Roman antiquity for producing fine incense. Sabaean incense (*Sabaeo thure*) appears as an offering in the Paphian temple to Venus in Virgil *Aen.* 1.416–7.

326–45 The language of the edict is a parody of dense legalese. After a huge preamble that takes up more than two-thirds of the text, the substance of Daifu's order is given succinctly in 340–5. This generic edict does not demonstrably correspond to any single historical Japanese anti-Christian proclamation (see further Introduction 1.1 and note to 308–9).

326–7 *invictus, Augustus ... pater patriae*: These pompous titles all have their origins in late republican to early imperial Rome. For *pater patriae* see e.g. Cic. *In Pisonem* 3.

ignoramus) de hac saltem qualicumque animi significatione
testificanda non aliquando cogitemus. Quocirca Amidae   335
optimo maximo, magnisque Iaponum diis, Xacae et Daibut,
pro singulari eorum merito publicas sollemnesque sup-
plicationes et sacrificia pie decernimus, statuimus,
imperamus. Et vobis quotquot Iaponiam habitatis cives
inquilini, convenae, imperiali hoc edicto notum   340
testatumque facimus. Deorum igitur delubra omnes
adeant, deos religiose colant, thure victimisque
placent, proque pio imperatore, reipublicae florenti statu, vota
faciant atque supplicent. Secus qui fecerint impii
habentor exiliique aut capitis poena mulctantor.'   345
Populus: Dii servent, dii fortunent et beent Caesarem!
Anarchus: Nunc quoque sublimi hoc ad legendum propalam
Caesareum suffigamus edictum loco;
fixum haeret. *Archias*: Haereat fixum ferale (ita enim animus
praesagit mihi) diploma. O quantum cladium   350
metuo quantumque sanguinis brevi dabit!
Anarchus: Hoc nos curamus scilicet, illi viderint.
Nos, Archia, extra telorum iactum sumus.
Archias: Putas. Sed regiam nunc tempus repetere est.

I.5

Idolomania, Antibarzanes, Barzanes.
Idolomania: Applaude coeptis, Auster, applaudat polus;   355
faustis eunt alitibus isthaec consilia.
Nunc legibus victricibus manus meae

---

353 *extra ... sumus*: A common proverbial expression since antiquity (see
e.g. Erasmus 1703: 147–8).

to them) we should not rarely think about testifying this state of the mind,
of whatever kind. Wherefore, to Amida   335
the best and greatest, and to the great gods of Japan, Shaka and Daibutsu,
for their singular merit we piously decree, constitute,
and command public and solemn supplications
and sacrifice. And to you, however many of you inhabit Japan as
native citizens or visitors, we make this known and attest this   340
by this imperial decree. Therefore let all come to
the temples of the gods, worship the gods correctly, placate them with
incense and victims, and on behalf of the supreme commander and the
     flourishing
state of the republic, let them make vows and supplicate. If any people
     act otherwise, let
them be considered impious and let the punishment of exile or death
     be meted out to them'.   345
People: May the gods protect, may the gods give good fortune and their
     blessings to our king!
Anarchus: Now, let us also affix this royal edict on a high
place to be read, out in the open; [*With Archias' help, affixes the text of
     the edict above*]
it is affixed. *Archias*: Let this fatal (for so my own mind
presages) document be affixed. O how much disaster   350
do I fear, and how much bloodshed will this soon result in!
Anarchus: We take care of our own business to be sure, and let them
     take care of theirs.
We, Archias, are beyond the range of fire.
Archias: So you think. But now it is time to return to the palace. [*Archias
     and Anarchus leave stage*]

I.5

Idolomany, Antibarzanes, Barzanes.
Idolomany: Applaud our attempt, south wind, and let heaven also applaud; 355
our plans are proceeding on a sure footing.
The king is now a pawn in my victorious hands

355–84 I.5. Idolomany summons two bonzes by the name of Antibarzanes
and Barzanes to hasten to Arima and fan the flames of persecution. The
bonzes are lazy and reluctant to keep up their paces with Idolomany,

subiectus est Caesar, iugo domitus meo.
Patente sorpsit ore dira toxica,
furoris alti virus exhausit nocens,   360
votis cruentam aggressus est necem malis.
Christiadum avet sanguine sitim compescere
effuso, Diocles alter in regno suo.
Fortuna, perge prospera et inceptis fave.
Surunga, Bungo, Figen, totaque regia   365
rursus Daibundo supplices tendunt manus.
Arima sola restat, ubi Ausonius popa
hostis Daibut sceptra contorquet manu.
Huc tela vertam, nec prius cedam loco;
bellace dextra mordeat subiectus humum.   370
Agite igitur, pigra pecora, cito, cito per aera.
Antibarzanes: Ego prae malitia tibiae hercule haud queo.
Barzanes: Via longa desperare me fessum facit.
Idolomania: Age, quisque scopis insideat eques; Xacas

---

whereupon the goddess orders them to fly on broomsticks. Following this sage advice, they all arrive safely and quickly in Arima.

The placement and composition of this and the following scenes are somewhat uncertain. The sole surviving text is in *A²* and its heading simply states *scena*, with no number given. *A²* as a whole is one piece of paper folded to form four sides, one of which contains I.5 and the rest parts of I.6.

The manuscript has the sub-heading *Idolomania cum bonziis*, hence the two characters other than Idolomany are presumably Buddhist priests who play a prominent part in the following scene as well. The bonzes' names are written out only as *Antibarz* and *Barz*, but these can securely be expanded to Antibarzanes and Barzanes respectively based on a similar scene in *I&X* (see Introduction 2.3) in which these names are clearly legible. Barzanes appears in Diodorus Siculus (*c.* 90 BCE–*c.* 30 BCE) 2.1 as the name of an Armenian King. Antibarzanes is presumably formed simply out of Barzanes.

This scene is delivered entirely in senarius. Metrically problematic lines: 370, 371, 376, 377, 378, 379, 381 (*versus mancus*), 382.

359 *sorpsit*: The common perfect form of *sorbeo*='I swallow' is *sorbui*, but the collateral form *sorpsi* is found in late antique grammarians as well as in compounds. See L&S s.v.

and subject to my control.
He has swallowed my dire poison with an open mouth
and has imbibed the noxious venom of profound madness.   360
He has started on his evil way towards bloody murder.
He longs to quench his thirst by spilling Christian
blood, imitating Diocles in his own realm.
Goddess Fortune, go on merrily and favour our plot.
Suruga, Bungo, Hizen, and all of the court   365
again stretch forth their suppliant hands toward Daibutsu.
Arima remains the only place where the Ausonian priestling,
the enemy of Daibutsu, wields his sceptre.
I shall turn my arms in that direction, nor will I be the first to give way;
let my adversary, struck down by my warlike arm, bite the dust.   370
[*Calling on Antibarzanes and Barzanes*] So come now, you lazy cattle,
     quickly, quickly through the open!
Antibarzanes: I really cannot, because my leg is useless, by heavens!
Barzanes: I am tired and the long way makes me lose hope.
Idolomany: Come, each of you should ride astride on a broom [*All of
     them ride astride broomsticks*]; Shaka

---

362 *Diocles*: Alternate name for Diocletian (244–311), the Roman emperor who initiated the last major anti-Christian persecution; see e.g. Lactantius *De mortibus persecutorum* 9.

364 *Surunga*: Suruga was the ancient domain and home territory of Ieyasu, roughly corresponding to Shizuoka prefecture today. It seems to be listed here simply as a generic place name along with Bungo and Figen/Hizen (see also note to 216–7).

366 *Ausonius popa*: A contemptuous reference to the Roman pontiff and by extension to his priests. Ausonia is the ancient name for Italy, and *popa* is a derogatory term for priest (cf. Persius 6.74) as well as perversion of *papa*, the popular appellation of the pope.

374 *scopis insideat eques*: Idolomany suggests that they all ride on broomsticks and fly through the air. Popular belief that human followers of the devil (i.e. witches) fly on broomsticks is well attested in early modern trial records from German-speaking regions (see e.g. Lindauer 2012: 371).

Amidasque divi nos citos super aera   375
pernice cursu vectitabunt. Sed ne noceat
Circaeus aer, Cerberi hanc spumam sumite.
Ne laedat hostis, hoc schedium pectus firmet.
Adversus Euri flabra his occurrite plumis.
Antibarzanes: Itane tuti super aethera volitabimus?   380
Idolomania: Ita, ita volemus.
Videtis, ut belli iam peregimus viam?
Tenemus Arimam. Gratias tibi, Xaca,
Antibarzanes: tibi, maxime Amida, *Barzanes*: diis, deabus omnibus!

I.6

2 bonzii, populus, Christiani, Geta.
Bonzius 1: En tibi libamen, magne rerum conditor,   385
Amida; fruere, O deus ter optime maxime.
Dicite carmina, dicite, pueri,
Amidae magno, Xacae magno,
date festivis orgia saltibus,
festivo plausu placate deos!   390
Bonzius 2: Amidas Indum servitat orbem,
Amidas horrea replet oryza,
Amidas dolia replet Baccho.
Amida maxime, serva mundum,
serva cunctos, Amida, Iapones.   395
Dicite carmina, canite, pueri,

381-2 A crane or some such device may have been used here to simulate Idolomany and the two bonzes flying over great distance. A nearly identical scene of flying bonzes was previously staged in Koblenz in 1622 (cf. *I&X* I.6 and Introduction 2.3).

385-496 I.6. Two Buddhist priests, likely identical to Antibarzanes and Barzanes in I.5, celebrate a pagan sacrificial feast with the locals. Some Christians in the crowd refuse to join and the priests order them to be arrested and imprisoned. The remaining celebrants keep up their music and

and Amida, the heavenly beings, will carry us quickly through the air   375
in a swift journey. So that Circe's wind would not harm you,
however, take this froth of Cerberus. [*Gives them the froth*]
Lest our enemy do us damage, let your breast be armed with this amulet.
     [*Gives them amulets*]
Resist the blasts of the west wind with these feathers. [*Gives them feathers*]
Antibarzanes: Thus protected, will we fly above air?   380
Idolomany: Yes, yes; let us fly. [*They fly up, then descend onto a different
     scenery*]
Do you see how finely we have finished our journey?
Now we are in Arima. Thanks be to you, Shaka,
Antibarzanes: to you, greatest Amida, *Barzanes*: to all the gods and goddesses!

I.6

2 bonzes, people, Christians, Geta.
Bonze 1: Look, here is an offering to you, great creator of things,   385
Amida; enjoy it, O thrice good, greatest god!
[*Begins to sing*] Sing the song, sing, boys
to great Amida, to great Shaka,
celebrate the revelry with festive dance,
please the gods with festive applause.   390
Bonze 2: Amida preserves the Indian world,
Amida fills the granary with rice,
Amida fills up jars with wine.
Amida greatest, save the world,
save, Amida, all the Japanese people.   395
Sing the song, sing, boys,

---

festivities. But the party begins its downward spiral as the two priests proceed
to verbally abuse the statue of Amida for refusing to drink from their hands.
Then, while they are happily consuming the wine that had been offered to
Amida, a servant comes with the unhappy news that their house has been
struck by a thunderbolt and burnt down (presumably as punishment for
their impious incontinence). The incensed priests thrash the statue of Amida
before scurrying off stage.

The text combines contents of A^2 and A^9. What is in A^2 forms the bulk of
the scene (385–98, 419–96), while from A^9 comes the festive chant or song of

date festivis orgia saltibus,
festivo plausu placate deos!
Bonzii et populus: Amida, salve, salve, Daibut,
patriae parens, Iaponum caput.   400
Annue votis pie precantum,
suscipe laetus dona clientum.
Date festivis orgia saltibus,
fundite laetis carmina vocibus,
dicite Io, dicite paean,   405
Amidam magnum colite Xacam.
Resonent montes, resonent fontes,
concinant valles, resonent calles,
date iucundam nymphis umbram.
Laeta sereni festa triumphi.   410
Amidas Indum servitat orbem,
Amidas ornat Cerere corbem,
Amidas implet dolia Baccho,
Amidas omnes replet Iaccho.
Prodeat ergo florida Chloris,   415
iubilet ergo regia solis.
Io triumphet, Io triumphet,
resonet Bacchus, festa coronet.
Bonzius 1: Nunc adeste, cives, cura magnorum deum;

---

the bonzes and the people (399–418). The latter is in the same metre as those
sung by the two bonzes taking turns in 387–98 and repeats some of the lines
or phrases therein (cf. 389 and 397 with 403; 391 with 411; 392–3 with 412–
3); these details make it likely that it is the text of the song that is referred to
in the stage direction *cantus et saltus* in A^2 (after 399 in our text). A^9 as a
whole forms an independent booklet of six sides on which sung texts (399–
418, 774–891) are written. The first song (399–418) is entitled *Bonzii et
populus deo Amidae divinos honores decernunt* in A^9.

The placement of the scene is conjectural. Our text in A^2 starts with a
simple *scena* (without any number) followed by the character list *Duo bonzii,
4 pueri, populus*. The *pueri* or boys may have been silent characters or some
or all of the singers. The scene contains substantial overlaps with *I&X* I.8 and
CB 1.4 (see Introduction 2.3), meaning that it was recycled from earlier local
theatrical material with some slight changes to fit the new context.

celebrate the revelry with festive dance,
please the gods with festive applause.
Bonzes and people: Hail, Amida, hail, Daibutsu,
father of our fatherland, chief of Japan.   400
Give your nod to the prayers of pious worshippers,
take up with joy the gifts of your followers.
Celebrate the revelry with festive dance,
pour out songs with happy voices,
say 'hurrah', sing the paean,   405
worship great Amida, worship Shaka.
Let the mountains resound, let the fountains resound,
let the valleys sing in unison, let the footpaths resound,
give the nymphs a pleasant shadow.
This is a happy festival of serene triumph.   410
Amida safeguards the Indian world,
Amida gives bread to our basket,
Amida fills jars with wine,
Amida fills everyone up with Bacchus.
Let flower-bedecked Chloris therefore come forth,   415
let the court of the sun therefore shout with joy.
Hurrah, triumph, hurrah, triumph,
let Bacchus resound, let him crown the festival.
Bonze 1: [*Resumes normal speech*] Now come, citizens, you care of the
    great gods;

The majority of the scene is delivered in senarius, with the following
exceptions: Anapestic dimetre in 387–418; dactylic hexametre (Greek) in
423–4; hendecasyllables in 444–72; octonarius in 477–9, 490–1. There are a
number of metrically problematic lines as usual: 390, 392, 396, 398, 400, 401,
408, 412, 419, 420, 422 (Greek), 425 (*versus mancus*), 431, 432, 437, 451, 461,
474, 476, 480, 481, 482, 483, 484, 485, 488, 491, 492, 496 (*versus mancus*).

386 *optime maxime*: optimus maximus is a classical epithet traditionally
reserved for Jupiter; see e.g. Cic. *Natura Deorum* 3.87.

391 *servitat*: See note to 134. Cf. also 411.

400 *patriae parens*: See note to 326–7.

415 *florida Chloris*: A learned reference; Chloris is said to be the original
Greek name of Flora, the Roman goddess for flowers; see Ov. *Fasti* 5.195–6.

genua recurvi et prona bracchia mecum   420
passi, litate victimas bonis diis.
τίς τῇδε; *Populus*: πολλοὶ κἀγαθοί.
Bonzius 1: Ζεῦ βασιλεῦ, τὰ μὲν ἐσθλὰ καὶ εὐχομένοις καὶ ἀνεύκτοις
ἄμμι δίδου, τὰ δὲ λυγρὰ καὶ εὐχομένοις ἀπαλέξειν.
Libate omnes!   425
Populus: Hanc vos, dii, pultem probate, maximi.
Bonzius 1: Hoc thure, dii deaeque, placati date,
quod voce maesta et corde amaro poscimus.
Populus: Hoc thure, dii deaeque, placati date,
quod voce maesta et corde amaro poscimus.   430
Bonziius 2: Et vos negatis Amidae litare munera?
Christiani: Diis thura vestris numquam litabimus
nec Christianos nos, o praeses, hoc decet.
Bonzius 2: Ergone Christum colitis? *Christiani*: Ita colimus eum.
Bonzius 2: Ergone falsum nomen est magni Amidae   435
et nos scelesti, qui Amidam facimus deum?
Christiani: Si libere loqui licet, ea est opinio.
Bonzius 1: Vah, impudens os! Labra dira comprime!
Ite ocius satellites, ite ocius,
ligate sacrilegos catenis ferreis   440
et in profundos carceres detrudite!
Vos interim virili estote pectore,
festisque lucem hanc gaudiis traducite.
    Antistrophe
Salve, Xaca sagax, Daibut, salve!

422–4 Prior to 422 in the manuscript is the stage direction: *in genua procumbunt*. The Greek in these lines is written clumsily with numerous spelling errors which are corrected in this edition. κἀγαθοί (422) is restored from *CB* (24) (see Introduction 2.3) as what is in *A²* is hopelessly jumbled. 423–4 in *A²* are also riddled with errors in but the lines clearly come from the prayer to Zeus in Ps.-Plato *Alcibiades* 2.143a and *Anthologia Palatina* 10.108. To reflect the arcane air of the original, the English translation of these lines is sourced from Benjamin Jowett (1817–93)'s nineteenth-century rendition of *Alc*. (Jowett 1892: 544).

with bent knees, with me, and with outspread 420
arms, offer your victims to the good gods.
[*Sees a group approaching*] Who cometh hither? *People*: Many a goodly one.
   [*Everyone genuflects*]
Bonze 1: [*Chants to a statue of a god*] King Zeus, grant us good, whether
   prayed for or unsought
by us; but that which we ask amiss, do thou avert.
[*To the people*] Now, all, give offerings. 425
People: [*Bringing bowls of porridge to religious statues*] Gods and
   goddesses greatest, try this porridge.
Bonze 1: [*Bringing or lighting incense in front of the statues*] Gods and
   goddesses, be satisfied with this incense and grant
what we ask for with our sad voice and bitter hearts.
People: Gods and goddesses, be satisfied with this incense and grant
what we ask for with our sad voice and bitter hearts. 430
Bonze 2: [*To a crowd of people standing apart*] And you refuse to give
   offerings to Amida?
Christians: We will never offer incense to your gods,
nor is this fitting to us Christians, O presiding one.
Bonze 2: So, you worship Christ? *Christians*: Yes, we worship him.
Bonze 2: So, is the name of great Amida a lie 435
and are we criminals, we who style Amida a god?
Christians: If we may speak freely, that is our opinion.
Bonze 1: O what impudent attitude! Shut close your inauspicious lips!
[*Calling to some guards nearby*] Come quickly, minions, come quickly,
bind the sacrilegious crowd in iron chains 440
and throw them into the bottom of the prison!
[*To the remaining crowd*] You however in the meanwhile, be of manly spirit
and go through this day with festive joy.
               Antistrophe
[*Begins to sing*] Hail, sage Shaka, hail, Daibutsu!

443-4 *Antistrophe*: This word appears before the hendecasyllabic chant of 444-72, which is found in A^2 immediately after I.5 but is transposed here where the manuscript has the notation *cantus iterator et saltus*. This position of the hymn is supported by the structure of the similar scene in *CB* I.4. This hymn is presumably labelled *Antistrophe* in relation to the prior chant in anapestic dimeter (386-418).

Xacae nectite metra mixta nervis!   445
Mystae, plaudite; laus superba Xacae,
clarisque undique floreat triumphis.
Crines implicet alma Baccha Xacae,
myrtus vinciat aureos capillos.
Quis non ornet eum cui Chinense   450
regnum ac Indicus orbis thura libat?
Dives est Amidas freti lapillis,
Lydi pondera luculenta iactat.
Salve, Xaca sagax, Amida, salve!
Amidae nectite metra mixta nervis,   455
mystae, plaudite; laus superba Xacae.
Dum membris valido sumus vigore,
laeti gaudia gaudeamus omnes.
Bacchus laetitiae minister adsit,
nutantem rosa verticem coronet,   460
priusquam approperet tremens senectus.
Nati de nihilo in nihilum rotamur
et tamquam levis aura dissipamur;
ergo dum fuga detinetur, ante
quam pennis volet, unde non redibit,   465
paucis hic hilares fruamur horis.
Omnes: Ergo dum melior virescit aetas,
saltantes grave taedium levemus,
plaudamus pedibus leves choreas.
Ars dicat numeros canora vocum,   470
hinc addat fidicen lyram iocosam,
inflabit calamos choraulus inde.
Bonzius 1: Amida, fames te vexat et ventris furor;
dies abiit quartus ex quo nihil cibi
gustasse te puto; nunc inediam hanc dissipa!   475
Hem, renuis? Aperi labra, ni velis insigniter
comedere fustuarium; hem, in diabolorum omnium nomine,

457–72 These lines are lifted from a scene of dissolute Epicurean feast in
VH, with slight modifications. 457–61 copy *VH* 3405–9. *Dum . . . vigore* (457)
is modified from *Dum florem redolet suum iuventa* (*VH* 3405) and *priusquam
. . . senectus* (461) comes from *priusquam fugiat decor iuventae* (*VH* 3409).
These are minor changes that do not alter the meaning or metre of the
passage and suit the current context better. 462–66 are cribbed from *VH*

Strum with your chords mixed rhythms for Shaka! 445
Mystic priests, applaud; let there be superb praise for Shaka
and let him be honoured everywhere with brilliant triumph.
Let the kindly Bacchant arrange her hair for Shaka,
let myrtle bind her golden hair.
Who would not honour the one to whom the realm of 450
China and the Indian world offer incense?
Amida is rich in pearls of the sea,
And he boasts of his glittering Lydian hoard.
Hail, sage Shaka, hail, Amida!
Strum mixed rhythms for Shaka with your chords, 455
mystic priests, and applaud; let there be supreme praise for Shaka.
While solid strength is still in our limbs,
let us all be happy and rejoice.
Let Bacchus come to serve us joy
and let roses crown our drooping heads, 460
before tremulous old age approaches.
Born of nothing, we roll away to nothingness
and melt away, just like a light breeze;
so, while the end is still away, before
we go our winged ways from where there is no return, 465
let us be happy and enjoy here our brief moment.
All: So, while the better part of our age is still flourishing,
let us dance and lighten our heavy tedium,
let us beat the earth with our feet in nimble dance.
Let musical and artful voices modulate the rhythm, 470
let the string-player add light-hearted tune with his lyre here,
there, the flute-player will blow into his reeds.
Bonze 1: [*Speaking to a religious statue*] Amida, raging hunger in the
    stomach is troubling you;
this is the fourth day that you have eaten
nothing, I think; now break your fast! 475
Hey, do you refuse? Open your mouth, unless you want to eat
blows; hey, in the name of all the devils

3400–4 and are especially notable for expressing a typically Epicurean nihilist sentiment. 467–72 again crib *VH* 3410–15. In early modern Western thought Epicureanism and Buddhism were often linked as two manifestations of basically identical hedonistic and atheistic libertinism; see e.g. Rubiés 2020.

477 *fustuarium*: *fustuarius* is a recherché word attested in Cassiodorus (*c.* 485–*c.* 585) *Variarum* 4.10.3.

vora; nisi ederis ego tibi cerebrum excerebravero!
Sceleste, non vorabis? Aegerne es, sanusne? Vis potum?
Etiam recusas vinum tam nobile?   480
Bonzius 2: Fors de tua non captat scyphum manu?
Experiar ego; videtis, annuit mihi ut bibam.
Bonzius 1: Quid? Tu quod paratum numini? Bibas, bibo.
Bonzius 2: Sed en, quis properat tam concito cursor gradu?
Geta, quid portas? *Geta*: Malum hercle, malum ingens;   485
domicilium vestrum ictu subito fulminis
debustuatum; auditis hoc? *Bonzius 1*: Perii hercule!
Bonzius 2: Et ego profecto funditus perii!
Bonzius 1: Amida, Amida, haeccine est fides data? O nefas!
Nunc ego te pro merito tuo genialiter tractabo!   490
Exite, virgae; virgidemiam hodie tibi lautam concinnabo,
Amida, tax, tax, tuo insonabit tergo!
Iterate, virgae; plusculum morosus est
Amidas; deinceps simile si tentaverit
Amidas, peribit inter occisissimos!   495
Bonzius 2: Fugiamus hinc.

I.7

Ecclesia, Christus.
Ecclesia: Rector deus, quousque sanguinario
tuum sub urso fremere spectabis gregem
et fulminantem differes manum? Trahit,

---

485 *Geta*: The Getae were an ancient Thracian tribe, and its singular form Geta appears as the name of a slave in Terence *Phormio* and *Adelphoe*.

487 *debustuatum*: A nonce-word formed from *bustum*; cf. also forms like *bustuarius*.

491 *virgidemia*: A word used memorably in Plaut. *Rud.* 636.

gobble up; unless you eat, I will beat your brains out!
You criminal, you don't swallow? Are you sick or healthy? Do you
    want a drink?
[*Holding a cup to the statue*] Do you even refuse such noble wine?   480
Bonze 2: Maybe he doesn't want to take the goblet from your hand?
[*Taking the cup from the hand of Bonze 1*] I will try; see, he nods, telling
    me to drink.
Bonze 1: What? You are drinking what was prepared for divinity?
    You drink, I drink. [*The two proceed to drink copiously*]
Bonze 2: [*Seeing Geta running onto stage*] But look, who is running
    in here with such a quick pace?
Geta, what news do you bring? *Geta*: Bad news, by Hercules, hugely
    bad news;   485
your house was burned down completely by a sudden
thunderbolt; are you listening? *Bonze 1*: I am done for, by Hercules!
Bonze 2: And I am surely done for completely!
Bonze 1: Amida, Amida, is this your good office to us? O, unspeakable!
Now I will treat you merrily, as you deserve!   490
Come out, rods; Amida, you will get a goodly harvest of blows today,
Amida, your back will resound 'whack, whack'!
[*Starts beating the statue with a stick*] Repeat the blows, rods; Amida
    is a bit too
naughty; if Amida tries a similar trick
again, he will be a goner right away!   495
Bonze 2: Let us get away from here. [*The bonzes leave stage*]

I.7

Church, Christ.
Church: God our ruler, for how long will you watch
your flock groaning under the bloody bear
and delay the use of your thunderous arm? Everywhere

---

492 *tax, tax*: The onomatopoeia appears in the context of beating a slave in
Plaut. *Persa* 264.

497–561 I.7. The Church personified delivers a monologue complaining of
savage persecution instigated by Safioye and calls on God for help. Christ (or
an angel, see below) appears in response to comfort her. At the end of the

raptat, trucidat Christianos undique   500
ferox tyrannus, mucro longinqua nece
hebetatus obrigescit, effuso natant
cruore vici; cladibus tantis darent
lacrimas vel hostes. Unus infandi artifex
auctorque Saphioia exitii stupet   505
duratque mentem; Bungum stagnat sanguine
arsit Facata, nunc Arimenses agros
cruore foedare appetit, scelerum omnium
faber vaferrimus. Deo neophytus
si quis dicavit nomen, en capiti minax   510
impendet ensis, vix sacri e baptismatis
redit lavacro Christianus, et sibi
cruces, catastas, ignes, globos, necem
ipsam parari cernit, in veterem iterum
ni iuret errorem et deum eiuret suum.   515
Tu cui nil est difficile, nihil impervium,
regnator orbis deus, multam hanc ne sine
in te tuumque filium rabiem! O deus,
ostende fraudes, subdolorum numinum
contunde vires, te boni tantum colant,   520
mali extimescant, caelitum et hominum patrem!
Christus: Gens cara Christo, cara gemmeo polo
cara aligeris et caelitibus carissima,
dilecta mea, unica ab aevo sponsa electa mihi,

---

exchange, the Church expresses her resolve to endure all manners of violence and to sacrifice her very life for Christ.

The scene survives in three versions, namely in A^4, A^6, and B. Of these, B has only 497–521 and 550–3; A^4 has all lines except 560–1, while A^6 lacks 522–3, 529–35, and 544. The second character, who most plausibly is to be identified as Christ based on his spoken lines (see esp. 524, cf. also 536 and 560), is however labelled *angelus* in A^4 and B.

I.7 is placed between I.3 and I.4 in B., II.1 and I.8 in A^4, and I.3 and II.4 in A^6. Our placement of the scene, based on the overall plot movement and A^4, is provisional and conjectural.

The metre is senarius except for 550–1 in dactylic hexametre and 552–3 in elegiac couplet. Lines with problematic metre are 509, 513, 517, 524, 536, 537, 548, 549, 554, 558.

Christians are dragged off and slaughtered   500
by the ferocious tyrant, the sword is blunted, encrusted
with long bloodshed, the streets
are flowing with blood; faced with such great calamities,
even an enemy would weep. The planner and originator
of the unspeakable carnage, Safioye, alone looks on in wonder   505
and keeps his mind obstinate; Bungo has become a pool of blood,
Hakata has been burned down, now he seeks to pollute
the fields of Arima with bloodshed, that most cunning artificer
of every crime. Whenever any novice
dedicates himself to God, behold, a threatening sword   510
hangs over his head, hardly has he come back as a Christian
from the fountain of sacred baptism, and he sees
crosses, gallows, fires, bullets, and murder itself
being prepared for him, unless he swears to uphold
his former error and abjures his own God.   515
You, to whom nothing is difficult, nothing impervious,
God, ruler of the world, do not allow this great
madness against you and your son! O God,
expose the deception, crush the strength of
deceitful spirits, let only the good worship you,   520
let the evil fear you, father of heavenly beings and of humans!
Christ: Flock dear to Christ, dear to the starry heavens,
dear to angels, and dearest to heavenly beings,
my beloved, chosen ages ago as my only bride,

---

499 *differes*: B has *differs*, but *differes* in *A⁴* and *A⁶* is metrically superior.

513 *globos*: *globus*, meaning any round or spherical body in classical Latin, can among other things refer to a firearm projectile in Neo-Latin. See e.g. Besold 1620: 4. Cf also 642.

518 *tuumque filium*: *A⁶* has *tuorumque*, which is metrically inferior.

524 *ab aevo*: So *A⁶*, *A⁴* has *in orbe*, which changes the sense from a temporal to a geographic one.

mentem quis innocuam, maeror, luctus, dolor   525
subiit, tenet, premit? Intrepida et immobilis
constans, ut hactenus, mane; constantibus
laurea coronae praemia debentur viris.
Tellure ut innatas recondit altius
annosa quercus flante radices Noto   530
strindenteque Euro, Borea, Aquilone, fortior
deridet impetus; fortiores proelio
sic vos redite, malaque sufficiant novas
vires animo; caduca, fluxa, levia
passos meliora, firma, certa vos manent.   535
Ecclesia: O pie Iesu, suavitas mentis meae!
Silere nequeo, nec lacrimis temperare queo,
dum te tyrannum cerno transfossum plagis.
Commota veluti vexat undas aequoris
procella, amoeni vanescit lumen poli,   540
nec una nox est, densa tenebras obruit
caligo et, omni luce subducta, fretum
caelumque miscent, undique incumbunt simul
rapiuntque pelagus Eurus et Boreas, Notus,
aequalis orbe Christiadum nostro venit   545
genti procella, minantur spumea aequora,
bacchatur, ardet, frendet, insanit, furit
in nos tyrannus, in unicam Christi sponsam
sponsique caput machaeram vibrat insanus furor.
Christus: Pelle metus, nec funde graves, Ecclesia, questus; 550
opprimere haud poterit, premat, esto, Marte tyrannus;
sanguine fundata est ecclesia, sanguine crevit,
 sanguine florebit, sanguine finis erit.
Ecclesia: Revixit animus, cessit omnis e corde dolor,
nil iam pavesco, tela vibrentur manu,   555
fremat tyrannus, saeviat Ditis specus,

536–8 In A^4 these lines are placed toward the end of the scene between our 553 and 554, but their position in A^6 which we follow here fits the flow better.

543–4 These lines are combined into one in A^6 as *caelumque miscent Eurus et Boreas furens*. Here we give the more expansive version of A^4.

what sadness, mourning, grief has come, holds and presses upon   525
your innocent mind? Intrepid and unshaken,
you must remain steadfast as before; laurels, crowns,
and prizes are earned by steadfast men.
Just as an old oak tree drives deep down its
own roots into the earth, while the south wind blows,   530
and stronger than the raging western and northern winds,
it laughs at their threats, so you, too, return
to battle stronger, and let adversity supply your mind
with fresh strength; having endured passing, fickle, and easy trials,
you may look forward to better, firm, and certain rewards.   535
Church: O pious Jesus, you sweetness to my mind!
I cannot keep silent, nor can I hold back my tears,
while I see you being pierced with wounds inflicted by tyrants.
Just as a raging storm whips up waves
on the sea, when the light of happy heaven vanishes,   540
nor is it simply night, but dense darkness rolls up
the shadows, and with all brightness gone,
the west wind, north wind and south wind mix the sea with the sky,
and from all directions they veer in at once and take hold of the ocean,
just so, a whirlwind is coming in our world to the Christian   545
flock, the frothing waves threaten
and the tyrant raves, is aflame, gnashes his teeth, rages
and roars against us, and crazed furor shakes its sword
against the sole bride of Christ and the very bridegroom.
Christ: [*Chants*] Let go of your fears, Church, nor pour out heavy
    complaints;   550
the tyrant cannot crush you at all, though he may oppress you with war;
the church has been founded with blood, it grew with blood,
 it shall flourish with blood, the end will come in blood.
Church: My mind has been resuscitated, every pain has left my heart,
I now fear nothing, let arms be brandished by the hand,   555
let the tyrant roar, let Hades' cave rave,

552–3 This elegiac couplet on the bloody beginnings of Christianity is
found, with minor variations such as *coepit* for *crevit* (552), or *succrevit* or
proficiet for *florebit* (553), in numerous early modern European texts. See e.g.
Reusner 1600: 21 and Strasser 2015: 558–9.

556 *Ditis specus*: A⁴ has *Tartarea cohors*, which is metrically inferior.

flammis adurat, sulphura emittat Styge;
non ego cruces diras, faces pavesco et minas.
Nostra venerando fixa sit uni spes deo.
Tibi, Christe, vitam, tibi roseo stat sanguine   560
litare niveam cordis et amoris hostiam.

I.8

Petrus, Paulus, Iohannes, neophyti, Thomas, Matthias.
Petrus: Auresne falsus verberat rumor meas,
in Christianum edicto iam totum gregem
saeviri? *Paulus*: Verus, ah, nimium rumor volat!
Omnes: Occidimus, occidimus, occidimus!   565
Petrus: Nescio quis artus occupet tremor meos
et gelidus ossa paene disrumpat pavor
animumque dirus involvat terror meum.
Ast quid ego loquor? Gravis data sat causa est metus;
quis non pavescat, sibi sciens insidias,   570
mortem, cruces, rotas, flammas, pararier?
Ego dum meditor paratus aerumnas, graves
voluto casus, quos blanda, innocua et sacra,
pacifica, clara Christiadum gens perferat,
in pectora gelidus coit, fateor, cruor.   575
Sed cur fata, sortem, tempora arguo tristia?
Non illa fortuito veniunt casu; suo

562–649 I.8. Japanese Christians Petrus, Paulus, Iohannes and several novices exchange news concerning Daifu's anger as well as the oncoming persecution and lament the fall of their church which Xavier established with such great dedication. Thomas and Matthias however console and embolden their fellows with a barrage of biblical exemplars. Their counsel is effective and the characters express a common resolve to offer themselves up to God in their upcoming trial. I.8 has many parallels with I.7; there are several lines that repeat or echo those in the previous scene (cf. 513 with 571, 560–1 with 648–9, 623 with 559) and the overall development from lament to consolation culminating in renewed resolve is also common to both. I.8 is thus an earthly reflection of the heavenly allegorical action in the previous scene, with Thomas and Matthias taking the place of Christ (or the angel) and the other

let them singe with flames, let them emit sulphur from Styx;
I do not fear dire crosses, torches or threats.
Let our hope be affixed to venerable God alone.
I have decided, Christ, to offer to you, to you, with my rose-coloured blood,   560
my life, as the snow-white sacrifice of my heart-felt love.

I.8

Petrus, Paulus, Iohannes, novices, Thomas, Matthias.
Petrus: Is it a false rumour that reaches my ears,
that the entire Christian flock is now under savage attack
through an edict? *Paulus*: Ah, the rumour is all too true!
All: We are done for, done for, done for!   565
Petrus: An uncertain fear grips my limbs
and a cold tremor shakes my bones
and dire terror fills up my mind.
But what am I saying? There is a grave cause for fear;
who would not be afraid, knowing that trickery,   570
death, torture, wheels, flames are being prepared for oneself?
When I, ready for these trials, think of our worries, and revolve in my mind
the harsh calamities which the graceful, innocent, sacred,
peaceful and distinguished flock of Christians must endure,
my blood, I admit, grows cold and congeals in my breast.   575
But why should I blame the fates, or chance, or these harsh times?
They do not happen because of fickle fortune; God

Christians reflecting the stance taken by Church. Cf. also I.1 and I.2 (esp. 110
and 179), in which Safioye is pictured as the earthly agent of Idolomany.

Our text for I.8 combines what is in *B*, *A⁴* and *A⁵*. *B* has 562–5, 599–613,
and 617–20. *A⁴* has only 595–613 and 617–20, while *A⁵* has all lines except
562–5, 613, and 617–20. The placement of the scene is again conjectural, as
the lines in *B* are actually part of I.4, while in *A⁴* this scene is followed by II.1
and in *A⁵* by our 1.9. The placement in this edition follows the general
arrangement of *A⁵*.

The metre is loose senarius throughout, with many problematic lines (565,
570, 576, 579, 587, 589, 599, 608, 621, 628, 632, 643, 645, 647) as usual.

562 *falsus*: corrected from *falsas* in *B*; cf. 564 *verus*.

praevisa tempore numen emittit polo.
Paulus: Nostra Daifusamam lumina videre flammeum,
qualis per arva Libycus invasit leo,   580
fulvam minaci fronte concutiens iubam,
vultus furore torvus atque oculis, truces
gemitus, et altum murmur, et gelidus fluit
sudor per artus, spumat, ac volvit minas.
Sic ipse contra Christiadas probos atrox   585
certamen animo commovet. Nuper ego sic
in Christiadas fulminantem flammeis
oculis, vultu, gestu, manibus et vertice
vidi, et proceres una affremuerunt diu.
Iohannes: Altus licet usque membra maeror comprimat,   590
exedat ingens luctus et tristis dolor,
dum Christianos Daifusami furor
perdere laborat noxius, iraque flammea
bis mille parat neces quibus sacrum eruat,
decorumque nomen Christiani sopiat,   595
maerore pulso, remeat in cor gaudium
novoque gaudio salit, ut in gemmeos
se nostra caelos lucifica mens erigit.
Aeterne rerum omnium moderator deus!
Viden' ut tuo opus numine exstructum cadat?   600
Arimensium non sublevabis amplius
miserum genus? Capiti tyrannus imminet
Iaponidum et patriae communis plurimum
angit clades; quot fana, quot divum domos
quas magnus ille Xavier plenus deo   605
construxit, unius vertet insanus furor!
Petrus: O fulminantis diva progenies poli!
Oves Xaveri linques, quas per nives

580–4 This simile of the Libyan lion is taken word-for word (except of *ac volvit* instead of *et volvit* in 584) from Sen. *Oedipus* 919–23. In Seneca, the object of comparison is the frenzied Oedipus after the discovery of his previously unknown past transgressions.

599 This line recalls the incipits of two famous prayers, one composed by Ambrose (*aeterne rerum conditor*; *Hymns* 1.1) and another by Xavier (*aeterne rerum omnium effector deus*; see Torsellini 1596: 500).

sends them, predestined from heaven, in their own season.
Paulus: Our own eyes saw Daifusama aflame,
just like a Libyan lion that invades a field 580
shaking its yellow mane on the threatening forehead,
spreading fear with its raging face and eyes, and emitting hostile
growls and deep roars, as cold sweat
runs downs one's limbs, while it froths and redoubles its menace.
Just so does our king plan harsh trials against good 585
Christians in his mind. Recently, I saw him
thundering against Christians with flaming
eyes, face, gestures, hands, and nods,
and the nobles murmured their assent in unison for a long time.
Iohannes: Even though deep sorrow takes hold of all our bodies, 590
even though great sadness and grievous pain should ravage us,
while the noxious anger of Daifusama attempts
to destroy the Christians and prepare a thousand murders
with the flames of rage to eradicate the sacred religion
and to bury its comely name, 595
our sadness is lifted, and happiness returns to our hearts
and dances with fresh joy, as our radiant mind
rises up to starry heaven.
God, eternal ruler of all things!
Do you see how the work built up under your divine favour is collapsing? 600
Will you no longer support the pitiable
people of Arima? The tyrant of Japan looms over
our heads, and the disaster of our shared fatherland causes
great worries; how many temples, how many sacred houses,
which illustrious Xavier, filled with the divine spirit, 605
constructed, will the insane rage of one man destroy!
Petrus: O divine progeny of thundering heaven!
Are you abandoning the sheep of Xavier, which he sought out

---

600 *extinctum cadit*: A^4 has *exstructum cadat*, which changes the meaning slightly but also fits both the sense and metre.

603 *omnium*: A^4 has *plurimum*, which likewise changes the meaning slightly but fits both the sense and metre.

606–12 In A^4 as well as *B* the speaker of these lines as Matthias. But since the perturbation expressed here is inconsistent with Matthias's voice urging calm in 629–33, we follow A^5 in making the speaker Petrus.

gelidas, per amnes frigore aeterno pigros
per et diremptas Nereo toto plagas,   610
patriae, parentum, corporis et vitae immemor
quaesivit ardens? Absit, absit, mi deus!
Neophyti: O, O, dolor, dolor! Periimus, O dolor!
Paulus: Utrasque tendo, flammei numen poli,
tibi manus; vocatus adsis, gemmeo   615
miseros Olympo gratia fove tua!
Petrus: Absit nefas; me, Christiani, ut hactenus,
inter labores, inter et aerumnas viae
inter faces, interque caesorum aggeres
socium tenete! *Neophyti*: Faveat incepto deus!   620
Thomas: Dilecta Christi pignora, digna caelitum choro,
quas sic gementes funditis maesti preces?
Nostra venerando spes sit fixa uni deo;
aeterna penes quem iura liquidi poli,
ad iussa cuius condita pavent omnia,   625
facile, ubi voluerit, Daifusami truces
compescet horridi minas et impetus
sistet male sanos; supremo nil est difficile deo.
Matthias: Deo duce Iacob effugit fratris manus,
non sulferea extinxit Loth flamma devorans,   630
non spumea Nili mersit unda Moysen,
rictus leonum Daniel evasit horridos;
sic facile quaeque dissipat mala praepotens.
Thomas: Non imber obruit Susannam saxeus,
ferro tyranni sustulit Judith caput,   635
prostravit aliger Assyrios exercitus;

617–20 The text given here reflects what is in *A⁴*, except that there the first
speaker is not Petrus but Matthias. Here the speaker is changed to Petrus for
the same reason as explained in the note to 606–12. *B* also has substantially
the same text but gives them all to Matthias. *B* in 619 has *laesorum* instead of
caesorum, and in 620 has *socium tenebitis, fave incepto deus*.

629–36 In the space of eight lines, Matthias and Thomas rattle off seven
biblical (all OT) *exempla* about miraculous help from heaven. These are:
Jacob's escape from his murderous brother Esau (629, cf. *Gen.* 27.41–28.5);

through freezing snow, through rivers made sluggish with eternal ice,
and through regions cut off by the vast ocean,   610
leaving behind the care of his fatherland, parents, his own body and life,
in his burning zeal? My God, let this not be, let this not be!
Novices: O, O, painful, painful! We are lost, O painful!
Paulus: God of flaming heaven, [*Raising both arms in prayer*] I stretch
    out to you
my two arms; respond and come, from starry   615
Olympus support us poor creatures with your grace!
Petrus: May this unspeakable crime not happen; keep me, Christians, as
    before,
amidst trials, amidst the struggles of our journey,
amidst torches, amidst piled-up bodies of the dead,
as one of your group! *Novices*: May God help our resolve!   620
Thomas: Beloved children of Christ, worthy of the throng of heaven,
why do you pour out such prayers, groaning sadly?
Let our hope be affixed to venerable God alone;
the eternal laws of limpid heaven are under his control,
all creatures tremble at his command,   625
and so, when he wills it, he will put a stop to rabid
Daifusama's hostile threats, he will block his insane
impetus; nothing is difficult to God the highest.
Matthias: Jacob escaped his brother's hands under the guidance of God,
the devouring fire of sulphur did not exterminate Loth,   630
the foaming wave of the Nile did not drown Moses,
Daniel escaped the jagged jaws of lions;
thus God omnipotent dissipates all evils with ease.
Thomas: The hail of stones did not crush Susanna,
Judith cut off the tyrant's head with a sword,   635
the angel defeated the Assyrian army;

---

angels leading Lot and his family out of Sodom as it is about to be destroyed
by fire from the sky (630, cf. *Gen.* 19.12–25); baby Moses plucked out of the
Nile (631, cf. *Exod.* 2.2–10); Daniel kept unharmed in the lions' den (632, cf.
Dan. 6); Susanna saved from false accusation and consequent stoning by the
wise judge Daniel (634, cf. *Dan.* 13); Judith assassinating the enemy general
Holofernes and returning safely to her city with his head (635, cf. *Jdt.* 13.1–
11); an angel devastating the Assyrian army besieging Jerusalem (636, cf. *2
Kgs.* 19.35).

idem supremos numen tenet adhuc polos.
Petrus: Stat mente fixum dura quaeque perpeti,
obvia dare duris pectora casibus, prius
quam aeviterni numen denegem poli   640
et supplice falsos reverear manu deos.
Paulus: Stat mente fixum flammeos pati globos,
rotas, cruces, tormenta, faces, horrida,
quam degener Christicola fiam nomini.
Iohannes: Stat purpureo, Christe, tibi amorem testarier   645
cruore, nec tormenta cultus exprimet
Iovis, Xacam et nomina, testor, impia.
Omnes: Christe, tibi, numen, uni libamus; deos
non colimus, uni pectora libabunt deo.

I.9

Randus, Bardus, Mopsus, Saphioia.
Randus: Rando nec umquam cadere quidquam gratius   650
potuisset, utpote cui res nimium domi
angusta, liberius loquar, angustissima;
in Christianos persecutio pullulat
urbe modo tota, fera, gravis, atrox, horrida.
Fidi speculatores petentur, scio,   655
industrii, cauti, mihi similes; sed hos
vix novit urbs, vix imperii incolunt plagas;

---

642 *flammeos pati globos*: See note to 513.

650–713 I.9. A comic interlude in which three spies, Randus, Bardus ('stupid'
in Latin) and Mopsus compete against each other in offering their services
for the anti-Christian persecution. Randus is represented as a young
inexperienced boy, Bardus as a decrepit aged individual, and Mopsus as a
man in his prime who shows off a bird-in-a-hat trick (which he claims can be
a useful smokescreen to extricate him from danger). Safioye agrees to employ
the trio and dispatches them to sniff out the Christians. The scene is heavy
with metatheatrical humour; indeed the term *theatrum* is used twice (661,
689) to refer to the setting of this contest of spies. The mention of spies may
have also resonated (admittedly in a risky way) with the audience considering

the same Godhead is still in charge of heaven.
Petrus: I am resolved in my mind to endure every harsh trial,
to offer myself to every difficult travail, before
I deny the Godhead of everlasting heaven   640
and worship false gods as a supplicant.
Paulus: I am resolved in my mind to endure flaming bullets,
wheels, torture, horrid torments, torches,
rather than be unworthy of being called a Christian.
Iohannes: I am resolved, Christ, to testify my love to you   645
with blood, and torture will not force me to worship
Jupiter or call on Shaka, I swear, nor their impious names.
All: Christ, God, you alone we serve; we do not worship
the gods, our hearts shall be dedicated to God alone.

I.9

Randus, Bardus, Mopsus, Safioye.
Randus: For me, Randus, nothing happier could ever   650
happen, since my household finances are
in a bad, or I should speak more freely, in the worst shape;
a persecution is starting up against the Christians
just now throughout the whole city, a savage, grave, atrocious, horrid
    persecution.
Trustworthy spies are in demand, I know,   655
hard-working, careful spies, like myself; but the city hardly
knows any, few such spies inhabit these regions of the realm;

---

the rocky political drama in which the dignitaries assembled in Koblenz at this time were embroiled (see Introduction 2.2).

The sole version of this scene is found in A^5. In the manuscript it is preceded by I.8, and in the margin between I.8 and I.9 is the note: *Scena va muta/Ad exemplum regis reliqui dynastae missis speculatoribus in/Christianos Christique nomen desaeviunt./Scena via/religio pietasque* (the last two lines presumably refer to our II.1).

The metre is senarius throughout, though many lines (655, 658, 665, 670, 671, 673, 675, 677, 680, 681, 682, 683, 685, 694, 704, 708, 709, 711, 713) do not scan correctly.

651–2 *res . . . angusta*: The expression echoes Juvenal 3.165: *res angusta domi.*

rarum hoc in urbe genus et imperio rarum datur.
Bardus: Heus thraso, solus in imperio tibi vindicas
hoc munus? Notus urbecula vix altera,   660
quam bene theatro solus in hoc turgentibus
buccis operam depraedicabat is thraso?
Bene referebat qualitates muneri
huic debitas, non opere sed lingua sibi
notas. Amabo, cuius exigua genas   665
vel nulla paene lanugo tegit impias,
num creditis aptum? Parcite, ineptum dicere
parabam. At annis functus officio gravi
Bardus ego, cunctis imperii notissimus
plagis, latibula bene teneo cognita.   670
Quod si vigilans, fidus, industrius, probus,
rursus ego Bardus officio fungar meo.
Bardo favebitis, uti spero; cedet annoso mihi
Bardo iuvenalis ille Randus lacteus.
Mopsus: Quo te pedes, Barde, rapiunt, heus, tantisper   675
sistito fugaces. Munus optas pristinum?
Illene speculator eat imperio viri,
quem destituunt mancum manus, oculi, pedes,
quod mage, cerebro qui premitur phantastico?
Randus inexpers, imperitus, inscius,   680
tanto laboret officio et periculum adest
cerebri. Meum bono adhuc est loco;
quod ubi periculum (sumus homines enim),
in hunc fere modum, pilleolo de vertice
moto avolant clausae cerebro volucres;   685
sic liber urbis rursus incedo vicos.
Suffragiis ubi foret opus, mi peto dari.
Mopsum vigilem, fidum, celerem vos credite.

---

658 *thraso*: Repeated in 662, the appellation *thraso* refers to Bardus' younger
rival Randus. Thraso, from the Greek θρασύς, is the name of a character in
Terence *Eunuchus* but the word came to be used adjectivally in mediaeval
Latin meaning 'braggart' (see e.g. DMLBS s.v.).

we are a rare species in the city, and a rare one in our empire.
Bardus: [*Entering stage*] Hey, braggadocio, do you think you are the
    only one who can take on this job
in our empire? [*To the audience*] Known in hardly any other town,   660
how well was this braggadocio advertising his work
with his wagging tongue, alone in this theatre?
He listed the qualifications necessary for
this job, which he knows more in words
than deeds. Now please, do you think that the one   665
whose shameless face is covered with little or no
crop of hair is apt? Pardon, I wanted to say
inept. But I, Bardus, have been at this important job
for years, I am quite famous in all corners
of the realm, I know all the nooks and crannies well.   670
And if a vigilant, loyal, hard-working, and upright man is what you are
    looking for,
again I, Bardus, will do my job.
You will all favour Bardus, so I hope; that little baby Randus
will retreat before me, aged Bardus. [*Gets ready to leave stage*]
Mopsus: [*Entering stage*] Where are you going off to, Bardus, hey, stay   675
for just a little while. Do you want to get back your old job?
[*To the audience*] Is that man fit to be a spy under the command of a leader,
that lame one who cannot command his own hands, eyes and legs,
and what is more, has his head full of a clouded brain?
Randus lacks experience, expertise, and knowledge,   680
he would have trouble at such a demanding job, and there is danger to him
of hot-headedness. My head is still sound;
but should there be danger (for we are mere humans),
[*Starts to take off his hat*] just like this, from my head, upon the removal
    of my
hat, [*Lets go birds hidden in his hat*] birds that had been shut in my
    brain fly away;   685
thus I go on the streets of the city, free again.
If there is a need to cast a vote, I ask that it be given to me.
All you there, believe that I, Mopsus, am vigilant, loyal and quick.

---

662 *depraedicabat*: the verb *depraedico* is not attested in antiquity but appears in medieval and humanistic Latin including that of Erasmus (see DMLBS and NLW s.v.).

Saphioia: Ecquod theatro genus obgannit modo hominis?
Ecqua paratis arte frugiferum domi   690
panem? Quod artis instrumentum comprimit
latus? Otiosi forsitan urbis compita
teritis? Vacunae seduli sacrificuli?
Bardus: Ignosce, speculator ego fidissimus,
aliunde motus urbis compita subii.   695
Saphioia: Quae causa? *Bardus*: In aures fama velox detulit
nostras, ut inimica deorum gens pertinax
et stolida cultus rideat Amidae, Xacae,
Phoebique potentis, quos Daifu modo iubet
invictus orbis dominus hostiis sacris   700
et victimis honorare; quod si deneget
gens ipsa, fuso sanguine vita concidet.
At ne per ora plurima latere imperii
queat, ego speculator offero, dicoque
operam, studium, curam, laborem maximum.   705
Saphioia: Et vos quid ad haec? *Randus et Mopsus*: Quod ille, nos
    promptos habes;
iube, impera, manda, videbis ocius
Euro, volucrique per aethera iaculo
misso, patula volare per ora imperii.
Mopsus: Tigrides superabo, Pyroenta, pegasos;   710
vix ac ne vix missum, reducem dabo.
Saphioia: Gens prompta verbis, vestra celeritas dabit
fidem, ite, lubet experiri, adeste citius.

I.Chorus

O salus rerum, lacrimis precamur
mollibus, flecti facilis, rogantes;   715

---

693 *Vacunae seduli sacrificuli*: Vacuna is the Roman goddess of rural leisure. The idea that her priests are lazy is possibly a learned reference to the neglected temple of Vacuna in Hor. *Epistulae* 1.10.49.

710 *Pyroenta*: Pyrois ('fiery' in Greek) is one of the horses of the sun in Ov. *Metamorphoses* 2.153. Another learned reference.

Safioye: [*Entering stage*] What kind of people are chattering in this theatre
    now?
Are you earning your gainful bread to eat at home   690
by some profession? What instrument of work girds
your flank? Are you perhaps idling around in the streets
of the city? Does the goddess of leisure have hard-working priests?
Bardus: I beg your pardon, I, a most loyal spy
coming from elsewhere, stepped onto the streets of this city.   695
Safioye: What is your reason? *Bardus*: Swift rumour came to our
ears that a stubborn and stupid group of people, enemies
of the gods, are laughing at the worship of Amida, Shaka,
and powerful Phoebus, and that Daifu, the unconquerable lord
of the world, is ordering them to honour the gods   700
with sacred offerings and sacrifice; and that if those people
refuse, they should pour out their blood and forfeit their lives.
But lest they should be able to hide in the numerous corners
of the empire, I as a spy offer and dedicate
my energy, zeal, care, and utmost diligence.   705
Safioye: [*Turns to Randus and Mopsus*] And you, what do you say about
    this? *Randus and Mopsus*: Just as he says, so we, too, are at your service;
order, command, ask, you will see us
flying quicker than the west wind and an arrow
shooting through the air, through the open regions of the realm.
Mopsus: I will overtake tigresses, the horse of the sun-god, and Pegasus;   710
I will be back when I have hardly even been away.
Safioye: You are all quick in words; I shall trust your
swiftness, go, I want to give you a try, come back here quickly.

I.Chorus

O salvation of the world, we pray, shedding tender
tears, begging you, who respond kindly to requests;   715

714–29 I Chorus. A hymn lamenting the onset of anti-Catholic persecution
is sung or chanted. It may have been delivered by two groups taking turns by
stanza; the manuscript has *Angel. 1*; *Juv. 2*; *2 Ang. 3*; *2 Juveni 4* written in the
left margin of each stanza.
    Like the other choral passages between acts, the text here is found only at
the end of *B* and is entitled *Chorus actus primi*.

lenis exaudi, fidei ministris
    dira parantur.
Imminet saevus capiti tyrannus
Arimae nobis, meditatur omnes,
qui tuam servant bene, Christe, legem   720
    perdere ferro.
Obsident cunctos aditus viarum,
commoda observant loca, quis cruorem
funditent; Christe, heu, famulis benignus
    auxiliare!   725
Surge, conatus, pater, anteverte
impios, stratoque in humum tyranno,
nos tuos, quo nunc furit ille saevus,
    eripe ferro.

II.1

Religio, Pietas, Fides.
Religio: Sum religio, miniata Christi sanguine   730
faciem rubentem. Munus hoc perpes mihi
commisit orbis gloriosus arbiter,
ut casta cumulem altaribus donaria,
Fidem stabiliam, Romulae cauti insitam,

The metre is Sapphic. The majority of the lines copy or echo those in *BP* (see Introduction 2.4) as noted below.

714–16 *O salus . . . exaudi*: The words follow closely *BP* LI.1–3, except for *precamur* (*BP*: *precantum*), *rogantem* (*BP*: *rogantes*), and *lenis* (*BP*: levis), all slight changes to accommodate the new context.

718–19 These lines follow closely *BP* LV.9-10, except for *Arimae nobis* (*BP*: *et meae famae*) and *omnes* (*BP*: *atrox*), again changes necessitated by context.

722–3 *Obsident . . . loca*: This section is copied entirely from *BP* XVII 41–2.

726–9 These words are all copied from *BP* XVII 49–52, except for *nos tuos* (*BP*: *me tuo*), a change made to better suit the current context.

730–73 II.1. An allegorical scene in which Religion complains of being driven away from Japan by Idolomany. Faith and Piety join in her lament, and

gently give heed, cruel deeds are being prepared
    against the servants of faith.
The savage tyrant of Arima is threatening
our lives, and he plans to kill all
those who keep your commands well, Christ,   720
    by the sword.
Our enemies ambush all entryways in the streets,
and they watch out for suitable places, where they may
shed blood; O Christ, kindly help
    your servants!   725
Rise, Father, prevent their impious
attempts, and striking the tyrant to the ground,
rescue your people from the sword, with which he
    rages savagely.

II.1

Religion, Piety, Faith.
Religion: I am religion, I have my face dyed crimson-red   730
with the blood of Christ. This perpetual duty was given to me
by the glorious arbiter of the world,
the duty to heap chaste offerings on the altar
and to offer firm support for Faith, which is grounded on the rock of Rome,

---

the trio in their desperation resolve to abandon Japan and retreat to the farthest corners of the world.

    The text is extant in two nearly identical versions. In *A⁴* it is found between our I.8 and I.7 and is entitled *Actus 2dus Scena 1ma*. In *A⁶* it is entitled *Scena 4ta* and precedes our II.4. The current position is a conjectural one based on these contradictory and presumably provisional manuscript notations. The scene has substantial overlaps with *I&X* I.2–3, where Religion, Piety and Faith are represented despairing over and fleeing from Germany (*Germania*) due to the Lutheran threat.

    The metre is iambic trimetre except for 763–73 which are in anapestic dimetre. 745, 759, 760, 766, and 773 are metrically problematic.

734 *Romulae cauti*: A reference to Apostle Peter who according to tradition was the first bishop of Rome (see also note to lines 70–3) and is famously called the rock upon which the church will be built in *Mt.* 16.18.

Petrique cymbam, apostoli rectam manum.   735
En illa quondam triplicis mundi arbitra
complexa late tanta terrarum loca,
deturbor aris, Xaveri quas pietas deo
stitit dicatas; clade me hac tanta premit
Orco entheata, insana, furiata Impietas,   740
dirissimarum prima furiarum Impietas.
O India, O Iaponia! Eheu, ut iacet,
ut squalet, eheu! Perfida Impietas agit
impune choreas, exulat Fides, Pudor;
ecce fugiunt aede transfugae sacra   745
in alta regna tota virtutum cohors.
Fides: Fugiamus hinc in ultimas orbis plagas,
ubi saeva catulos lactat ursa vel tigris.
Pietas: Malim leonum degere in cubilibus
quam praeferoci iura dare Iaponiae.   750
Fides: Pietas, fuge! *Pietas*: Fuge, Fides! *Fides*: Fuge, Pietas procul!
Sed quae hic amictu puella virgo stat prope?
Scio, scio, Religio est soror mea et tua.
Pietas: Singultit intus, flebilem planctum ciet.
Religio: Periimus, O meae sorores, periimus;   755
labefacta cecidit spes meae Iaponiae.
Fides: Dolor, dolor! *Pietas*: Vix aegra nunc traho spiritum;
ita ubique coeunt spissa vitiorum seges.
Religio: Ite ergo nymphae, quocumque vos per maria
portat impetus, ite, ite celeres! *Fides*: Vah, eat Iaponia!   760
Pietas: Sit pabulum Orci! *Fides*: Foeda Ditis victima!
Religio: Quia vult perire, pereat! *Pietas*: Interea tamen,

---

735 *Petrique cymbam, apostoli rectam manum*: So both *A⁴* and *A⁶*, but . . .
manu would make the syntax less awkward. The two surviving manuscripts
of *I&X* both have *manum* written initially but later corrected to *manu*.

736 *triplicis mundi*: Tripartite division of the world is a classical trope; see
note to line 2.

as well as for the vessel of Peter and for the apostolic hand. 735
Behold, I, the erstwhile arbiter of the three-fold world,
I, who embraced such wide swaths of earth,
am being driven off the altars which pious Xavier established
and dedicated to God; with such great calamity does Impiety
oppress me, Impiety inspired by hell, the insane, raging one, 740
Impiety, the foremost of the direst furies.
O India, O Japan! Alas, look at how they lie prostrate
and how they mourn in squalid garments, alas! Perfidious Impiety freely
leads the dance, Faith and Modesty are in exile;
behold, from their sacred abode, like deserters, the entire 745
cohort of virtues flee into the realm of the deep.
Faith: [*Enters together with Piety*] Let us flee from here to the outermost
    regions of the globe,
where the savage bear, or the tigress, gives milk to its young.
Piety: I would prefer to lie in a den of lions
than to teach righteousness to untamed Japan. 750
Faith: Flee, Piety! *Piety*: Flee, Faith! *Faith*: Flee far away, Piety!
[*Catching sight of Religion*] But who is the one standing close by,
    dressed as a young maiden?
I know, I know, she is Religion, your sister and mine.
Piety: She is sobbing deeply and is indulging in tearful lamentation.
Religion: [*To Faith and Piety*] We are done for, O my sisters, we are
    done for; 755
the hope for my Japan has become weak and has fallen.
Faith: Sad, sad! *Piety*: In my grief, I can hardly breathe;
the harvest of vices comes together in such a heap, everywhere.
Religion: Go therefore, girls, wherever your impulse carries you
through the oceans, go, go quickly! *Faith*: Alas, let Japan be lost! 760
Piety: Let it be devoured by hell – *Faith*: and be shamefully sacrificed
    to the underworld.
Religion: Since it wishes to perish, let it perish. *Piety*: But in the meanwhile,

---

757 *coeunt spissa vitiorum seges*: The plural verb is used with a singular subject in construction according to sense (see e.g. Mahoney 2001: 187).

currite, lacrimae, currite, lymphae,
currite, rivi, per cava tempora.
Fides: Nunc, nunc vires exprome dolor.   765
Religio: Surungica sonent litora planctu.
Pietas: Habitansque cavis montibus Echo,
Non, ut solita est, extrema brevis
verba remittat;
totos reddat pectore gemitus!   770
Fides: Audiat omnis pontus et aether!
Religio: Ibimus ultra Thulen ultimam.
Pietas: Quo fata vocant curaque, sequemur.

II.2

Idolomania, Impietas, Crudelitas, Iuppiter, Neptunus, Ecclesia.
Idolomania: O Phlegethontis manes atros!
Megaera ferox, rector inferum!   775
Siccine Christo rapient patre
genus infandum limina superum?
Siccine clarum triviae solium
erit horroris inutile stagnum?
Pro pudor! Et tacet inferum chorus   780

763–73 These anapestic lines are written as if they were senarius in both A^4 and A^6 with line divisions coming before *rivi, exprome, litora, Echo, totos, Audiat, ultra.* The line division has been changed in this edition to fit the metrical scheme.

765–71 These lines are lifted from Sen. *Troades* (*Tr.*) 107–13 with the following minor alterations to suit the context: *Surungica* (766: *Rhoetea* in *Tr.* 108); *pectore* (770: *Troiae* in *Tr.* 112).

772 *Ibimus ultra Thulen ultimam*: A4 has *Abimus*, but A^6 *Ibimus* is metrically superior. Thule is the mythical end of the world. Cf. Virg. *Georgics* 1.30.

773 *fata*: so in A^4, A^6 has *vota*. The line recalls Virg. *Aen.* 5.709: *quo fata trahunt retrahuntque, sequamur.*

774–900 II.2 is a spectacular sung interlude in which personified vices acting together with the pagan deities Jupiter and Neptune swoop down on

run, tears, run, flow,
run as rivers through my hollow face.
Faith: Now, now, my grief, unleash your strength.   765
Religion: May the shores of Suruga resound with lamentation.
Piety: And let Echo, living in cavernous mountains,
not, as she is used to, simply repeat
the last bits of words;
let her return full groans from her heart!   770
Faith: Let all the ocean and sky hear!
Religion: We will go beyond the farthermost Thule.
Piety: Where fates and solicitude call us, we shall follow.

II.2

Idolomany, Impiety, Cruelty, Jupiter, Neptune, Church.
Idolomany: O you spirits of dark Phlegethon!
Ferocious Megaera, and ruler of the dead!   775
Shall the unspeakable tribe, with Christ as their father,
thus snatch their entry into heaven?
Shall the brilliant dominion of Hecate
thus be a useless swamp of terror?
What a shame! Yet the chorus of demons stays quiet   780

---

the sailing Church in an attempt to drive her away from Japan. Impiety first brings the good news to Idolomany, who is feeling uneasy over the progress of Christians, that Daifu has moved decisively to clamp down on these troublemakers. Cruelty then joins in with the confirmation that Buddhism is triumphant and that Japan has come back to their side. As the trio rejoice over their imminent victory, Jupiter enters the stage and promises his assistance against the Christians. Neptune then appears and expresses his displeasure over Church sailing on his domain. The vices and the pagan gods brew up a storm causing Church to call on Christ's help.

This scene is preserved in A^8 (which has lines 774–81, 803–10, 812–22, 825–35, 842–86 and 892–900) and A^9 (which has lines 774–811 and 814–93). Both A^8 and A^9 are free-standing booklets and there is no internal indication as to where this scene would have been placed. In this edition it is provisionally placed here as a carry-over of the allegorical exile of sacred forces from Japan in II.1.

nec ad arma ruit Erebi torus?
Impietas: Ecquas fundis, O Iaponum domina,
percita flammas Stygis in numina?
Comprime fulmen, fremis in vanum,
iam cito cedet genus insanum.   785
Ut pia libent Amidae thura
regia mandant fulmine iura.
Spreverit ubi gens Amidae cultum,
non scelus illud linquet inultum.
Idolomania: Quam bona portas, O soror, nuntia?   790
Valuit tantum tua potentia?
Impietas: Quid mea nequit dextera potens?
Quod gero virus, animo nocens
undique terris Iaponum saevit,
cordaque regum hominumque ferit.   795
Ad tua current sceptra potentes,
tibi se subdent regna colentes.
Idolomania: Vivat in Orco tua deinceps
virtus in astris inclyta, princeps,
si vera refers; et sine nota   800
opima feret ad tua vota
praemia sedes Erebi tota.
Crudelitas: O dies caelica, O dies aurea!
Quam bene cessit! Parta est laurea.
Io triumphent Iaponum bonzii;   805
baiula laeti propero nuntii;
resonet aether, tympana sonent;
Io triumpho, festa coronent.
Idolomania: Salve, salve, inclyta soror,
regni nostri decus et honor;   810
laeta cur edis signa triumphi,
quae nova portas iubilans tota,

The manuscripts assign voice types to some characters: Idolomany is
marked *discantus* (A^9, at 774); Impiety is *altus* (A^9, at 782); Cruelty is *tenor*
(A^9, at 803); and Jupiter is *bassus* (A^8 and A^9, at 852). Other marginal notations
that seem to relate to musical delivery are: *alternatim et simul* (842-3, A^9);
alternatim vel simul (847–51, A^8; 872–5, A^8); *repetitio omnes* (842–3, A^9; 851–
2, A^8; 873, A^9; 874–5, A^9; see also note to 894–6). The metre (except for 894–
900, on which see below) is a very loose and inconsistent approximation of

and the seat of hell does not rush to arms?
Impiety: O mistress of Japan, what flames
of Styx are you so excitedly throwing at the divine spirits?
Repress your thunder, you roar in vain,
the insane crowd will soon give way.   785
That they offer pious incense to Amida
is the thunderous command of the king.
If they should spurn the worship of Amida,
that crime will not go unpunished.
Idolomany: What good news do you bring, O sister?   790
Has your force been so effective?
Impiety: What can my powerful arm not accomplish?
The poison, harmful to the spirit, which I have with me,
ravages the land of Japan everywhere
and strikes at the hearts of kings and the people.   795
The magnates will hasten toward your sceptre
and will surrender to you, worshipping your kingship.
Idolomany: May your strength, famous among the stars,
live in hell, foremost one,
if you report the truth; and just as you wish   800
all the regions of the underworld will bring
to you plum prizes without blemish.
Cruelty: [*Arriving on stage*] O magnificent day, O golden day!
How well has this been done! The laurel has been won.
May the bonzes of Japan shout in triumph 'hurrah';   805
I hasten happily as the carrier of good news;
may the sky resound, may the drums roll;
I shout in triumph 'hurrah', may wreaths decorate the festivity.
Idolomany: [*To Cruelty*] Greetings, greetings, illustrious sister,
glory and honour of our realm;   810
why do you happily display signs of triumph,
what news do you bring, full of jubilation,

---

iambic dimitre (852–84) or anapestic dimetre (the rest). Most of the lines
have end-rhymes, another sign that the words were sung (cf. Rasch 2014:
529–30). The scene thus appears to have been an operatic interlude, a welcome
break perhaps to the audience after so many scenes of spoken or chanted
quasi-classical Latin.

801 *feret*: Corrected from *ferent* in *A*[9].

num cessit dolus ad tua vota?
Crudelitas: Vivat in annos dea Iaponiae!
Nuntia partae fero victoriae.   815
Tua iam Caesar sequitur castra,
numina patriae tollit in astra.
Adhibet omnes me duce nervos;
reprimat Christi carcere servos.
Non fluet annus, tota Iaponia   820
Amidae supplex colet imperia.
Idolomania: Quam laeta sonant pectore gaudia!
O quanto cum animi gaudio
haec nova gaudens dicier audio!
Resonet Acheron, Io triumphet,   825
io triumphent Iaponum bonzii,
undique resonent gaudia nuntii!
Pergite strenui Martis in arena,
saeviat ira, spumetque vena,
Christiadum parcatur nemini,   830
Iaponum sedi inviso semini.
Crudelitas: Non ego deses ad tua vota
ocior Euro propero tota,
proelia dabo ceu fortis murus,
sine spe victor Marte futurus.   835
Impietas: Nec ego segnis, Christi nomen
perimam ferro, si favet omen.
Idolomania: Agite ergo Marte insignes,
stringite ferrum, flammas et ignes,
numinis Amidae tollite decus,   840
trans mare pigrum pellite pecus.
Tollite Xacam, pellite Christum,
ad Stygis omnes rapite fiscum!
Impietas, Crudelitas, Idolomania: Tendite nervos, caedite servos,
tollite Xacam, pellite Christum,   845
ad Stygis istum rapite fiscum!
Idolomania: Sed quid longas trahimus moras?
Currite, furiae, currite foras,
currite, superi, rumpite moras!
Ad arma, ad arma, ad arma, ad arma,   850

---

814 *annos*: So *A⁹*, *A⁸* has *aevum* which also fits the sense.

did the trickery succeed as you prayed for?
Cruelty: Long live the goddess of Japan!
I bring news of victory accomplished.   815
The king already follows your side,
and raises the deities of his fatherland to the skies.
He exerts all of his strength under my command;
let him crush the servants of Christ in jail.
Before the year comes to an end, all of Japan   820
will grovel before and worship the power of Amida.
Idolomany: What happy joy echoes from my breast!
O with how much joy of mind
do I hear this news being spoken!
Let Acheron resound, may it shout in triumph 'hurrah',   825
may the bonzes of Japan shout in triumph 'hurrah',
let the joyful news echo from everywhere!
You all, continue strenuously in the arena of Mars,
let your anger rage, let you blood boil,
let none of the Christians be spared,   830
that progeny hateful to the land of Japan.
Cruelty: I am not lazy, upon your wish
I hasten with all my strength, faster than the west wind,
I will give a fight like a strong wall,
without a doubt I shall be victorious in battle.   835
Impiety: And I shall not tarry, I shall destroy
the name of Christ with the sword, if the omen is favourable.
Idolomany: Therefore, illustrious in battle, go, you all,
draw your swords, flames and fire,
exalt the honour of Amida's divinity,   840
drive away the useless flock across the sea.
Exalt Shaka, drive away Christ,
snatch them all away for the gain of Styx!
Impiety, Cruelty, Idolomany: Exert your strength, slay the servants,
exalt Shaka, drive away Christ,   845
snatch him away for the gain of Styx!
Idolomany: But why do we tarry for so long?
Run, furies, run outside,
run, divine beings, end your delay!
To arms, to arms, to arms, to arms,   850

cum ense et parma!
Iuppiter: Quos hic tumultus audio?
Quae bella Martis sentio?
Vibrata mittam fulmina,
ni saeva cessent odia.   855
Idolomania: Supreme rector, ausculta;
in nos furit gens male stulta
spernitque deos non sine culpa.
Iuppiter: Quae gens polorum in numina
audet movere proelia?   860
Idolomania: Audet nefanda, perfida
gens Christiadum, gens impia.
Impietas: O Iuppiter, audi, audi;
ludere Iovem ducunt laudi!
Iuppiter: Quid vana terrent somnia?   865
Iovis timete fulmina,
sub sole qui regit omnia.
Fidos clientes protegam,
hostes rebelles opprimam,
vesana sentient pecora,   870
quid mea potens valeat dextera.
Crudelitas: Io triumphet Iuppiter!
Pugnemus omnes fortiter!
Ad arma, ad arma,
cum ense et parma!   875
Neptunus: Quos hic spumantes audio?
Quas hostium classes video
remigare non sine gaudio
nostro maris in imperio?
Patiens feram? Nec exseram   880
potens in hostes dexteram?
Turbabo ventis aequora,
tonabo caelo fulgura.
Miscebo pontum et aethera.
Agite, furiae, Marte insignes;   885
stringite ferrum, flammas et ignes,
numinis Amidae tollite decus!
Trans mare pigrum pellite pecus,
tollite Xacam, pellite Christum!
Ad Stygis omnes rapite fiscum!   890
Tendite nervos, caedite servos,

with sword and shield!
Jupiter: [*Entering stage*] What tumult do I hear here?
What Martial war do I sense?
I shall shoot tremulous thunders,
unless the savage enmities cease. 855
Idolomany: [*To Jupiter*] Supreme ruler, listen;
a tribe, in their inauspicious stupidity, rails against us
and spurns the gods, not without guilt.
Jupiter: What tribe dares start a war
against the divinities of heaven? 860
Idolomany: The criminal and perfidious tribe
of Christians, the impious group dares it.
Impiety: O Jupiter, listen, listen;
they think that mocking Jupiter is praiseworthy!
Jupiter: Why do you fear meaningless dreams? 865
You all, fear the thunder of Jupiter,
who rules everything under the sun.
I shall protect my faithful followers,
I shall crush my rebellious enemies,
the insane beasts shall know 870
what my powerful arm can do.
Cruelty: Let Jupiter shout in triumph 'hurrah'!
Let us all fight bravely!
To arms, to arms,
with sword and shield! 875
Neptune: [*Entering stage*] Whom do I hear being worked up here?
[*Seeing the Church on a boat on sea*] What fleet of enemies am I seeing,
rowing not without joy
on our oceanic realm?
Shall I put up with this patiently? Shall I not stretch out 880
my arm forcefully toward my enemies?
I shall churn the sea with winds,
I shall shoot thunderbolts from the sky.
I shall mix sea with sky.
Come, you furies, illustrious in battle; 885
draw your swords, flames and fire,
exalt the glory of Amida's divinity!
Drive away the lazy flock across the sea,
exalt Shaka, drive away Christ!
Snatch all of them away for the gain of Styx! 890
Exert your strength, slay the servants,

pellite Christum, pellite Christum,
ad Stygis istum rapite fiscum!
Ecclesia: Benedicite, maria et flumina, domino,
benedicite, cete et omnia, quae moventur in aquis, domino,   895
benedicite, caeli caelorum et aquae omnes, quae super caelos sunt, domino.
O deus, O Iesu, O pater omnium,
salva, nos perimus!
O Iesu, redemptor hominum,
salva, nos perimus!   900

II.3

Daifu, miles, Matthias, Thomas, Saphioia, 3 consiliarii.
Daifu: Age nunc, satelles, numinum et nostrae manus
sistatur huc contemptor; aequati rigor
iuris tenendus; rege me, nemo nocens
in caelites erit, aut inultus criminum,
me vindice; propera! *Miles*: Ut imperasti, ocissime – .   905
Daifu: Testor verendum numen, Christum hunc exuent,
fatalis ambos vel feriet meus mucro.
Miles: Propere exsecutus iussa, sisto quos petis.
Daifu: Invisa, Matthia, tuis de moribus

894–6 These lines are cobbled together from *Dan.* 3.59, 60, 78–9 and are a part of the so-called *canticum trium puerorum*, a popular chant in Catholic liturgy; see e.g. Chaplin Child 1868. In A^8 there is a stage and musical direction preceding 894: *Ecclesia in ipsa navigatione laudat/deum. Duo discantus et instrum.*

897–900 The Church exclaims in distress as its enemies work up a storm. The picture of believers on a storm-imperilled boat calling upon Christ for help is a familiar one in Christian tradition beginning with *Mt.* 8.23–5.

901–1014 II.3. Daifu summons Matthias and Thomas to answer the charge of sacrilege against traditional Japanese religion. The brothers use this occasion to publicly expound on their Catholic belief, riling the initially lenient Daifu. The counsellors try to persuade the brothers to escape punishment by making a show of supplicating Buddhist deities, but they remain obstinate. Daifu dismisses the accused under threats of dire

drive away Christ, drive away Christ,
snatch him away for the gain of Styx!
Church: Sea and rivers, bless the Lord,
whales and all that move in waters, bless the Lord, 895
heavens, and all the waters above heavens, bless the Lord.
[*The sea begins to get stormy*] O God, O Jesus, O Father of all,
save us, we are being destroyed!
O Jesus, redeemer of humankind,
save us, we are being destroyed! 900

II.3

Daifu, soldier, Matthias, Thomas, Safioye, 3 counsellors.
Daifu: Come now, minion, let the one, who despises the gods
and us, be brought here; the strictness of my equitable law
must be upheld; with me as king, no one shall harm
the heavenly beings, nor shall anyone go unpunished for a crime,
with me as avenger; hurry! *Soldier*: As you commanded, most quickly – .
    [*Leaves stage*] 905
Daifu: I swear by the venerable spirit that they shall deny this Christ;
otherwise my fatal blade will strike them both.
Soldier: [*Returns with Matthias and Thomas*] I completed your
    command quickly and am bringing those whom you require.
Daifu: Suspicions, Matthias, are being spread among the people

---

consequences and consults with his subordinates. The hegemon expresses
reluctance on following up with his own threats, fearing the reaction of the
populace; Safioye however, persisting in his anti-Christian zeal, demands that
Daifu extirpate the brothers together with their clan. Safioye adds that he is
willing to do the dirty work by entrapping the guilty duo and Daifu acquiesces.

The text is found in A^6 and B. The two versions are nearly identical other
than minor details as noted below and the division of the scene into three in
B, in which 901–8 is II.1, 909–95 is II.2, and the rest is II.3. In A^6 the entire
scene is designated *scaena 3^(tia)* and placed between our II.1 and I.7. In B this
passage is followed immediately by our III.4. The placement in this edition
follows the general plot movement as well as the overall arrangement of B.

The scene is entirely in senarius, with the following metrically problematic
lines: 921, 937, 959, 994 (cf. note), 1005, 1009, 1010 (cf. note), 1014 (*versus
mancus*).

seruntur in vulgus, Xacam te patrium   910
magnumque passim temnere Daibut deum,
Christum cruce enectum numen proponere
rudi popello, ab illo opem, vitam, bona
manare cuncta; nil Xacam, nil ceteros,
quos vasta Iapon veneratur passim deos,   915
hominibus elargiri. Itan' se res habent?
Nunc explicato! Falsa si culpa fuerit,
patronus ero; si vera, iudex. *Matthias*: Despui ,
(non diffiteor) idola tua, Caesar. Deum
terrae polique fabricatorem colo,   920
colamque dum vita erit comes. *Daifu*: Siccine Xacae
honore tu pessumdato, regni immemor,
beneficiorum oblitus, et amoris mei
Christum interemptum praedicas urbi? Deos
deasque rides rege me, me Caesare?   925
Thomas: Non fragile colimus daemonum excordes genus,
quod stulta fingit et fabricat hominum manus.
Daifu: Quid ergo colitis impium cruciarium?
Thomas: Qui patre divo natus haud impar patri,
nec par hic idem matri, mortali satus,   930
qui patria gestans sceptra regali manu
innocuus ipse crimen humanum expiat,
ultima secutus, tractus ad saevam necem,
qui mortuis vitam, diem caecis, pedes
claudis, leprosis corpus et pellem manu   935
veterem reduxit, Caesar, hunc nos supplices
colimus, hic orbis est mundique artifex.

---

913 *popello*: So *B. populo* in A^6, which is non-metrical.

921–3 *Siccine . . . mei*: Daifu's words here echo those spoken by Constantine the Great to his falsely accused son Crispus in *C* V.69-71 (*At tu nec aequi iuris, inflexi, memor,/pudore te pessum dato, regni immemor,/oblitus aulae, iuris humani, tui,*), with minor changes to suit the context (See also Introduction 2.4).

925 *rege me, me Caesare*: Again the words echo Constantine's address to his son in *C* V.73 (*patre me, me Caesare*).

concerning your ways, namely that you show your contempt everywhere 910
for Shaka of our fatherland, and for Daibutsu, the great god,
that you propose Christ, who was killed on the cross, as a divinity
to the uncouth rabble, saying that from him comes wealth, life,
and all that is good; that according to you, Shaka, and the rest
of the gods, whom vast Japan venerates everywhere, 915
grant no benefit to humankind. Is this so?
Now explain! If the accusation is false,
I shall be an advocate; if true, a judge. *Matthias*: I rejected,
(I do not deny it) your idols, king. God,
the architect of earth and sky, is whom I worship, 920
and I shall worship him as long as I live. *Daifu*: Do you thus
despise the honour of Shaka, forgetful of this realm,
ungrateful toward my gifts and love,
and preach Christ, the murdered one, to the city? Do you laugh at
the gods and the goddesses, while I am king, while I am your ruler? 925
Thomas: We do not stupidly worship the weak tribe of demons
which the hand of ignorant humankind fashions and fabricates.
Daifu: Why then do you worship an impious gallows-bird?
Thomas: He who was born of a divine father, to whom he is not at all
    unequal,
but not equal to his mortal mother, from whom he was born, 930
who, holding his paternal sceptre in his regal hand
expiates the crime of humankind, while being innocent himself,
who underwent the extremes of fate and was dragged off to savage
    murder,
who gave back life to the dead, light to the blind, legs
to the lame and to the lepers their own bodies and pristine 935
skins with his hand, this is the one, king, whom we supplicate
and worship, he is the maker of the globe and of the world.

---

928 *cruciarium*: The adjective plays on the double significance of Jesus Christ as an executed criminal (from a pagan viewpoint) and crucified God (from the Christian one); cf. also note to *VJ* 159.

929–33 These lines are lifted from Crispus's address to Christ in *C* V.206–10, with changes of second to third person necessitated by context (*expias* (V.209)→*expiat* (932); also *es* (V.207)→*hic* (930)).

934–6 *qui ... reduxit*: These lines list some of the major miracles Jesus is reported to have performed. See e.g. *Mt.* 11.5.

Daifu: Caput scelestum, os comprimam rotis, cruce!
Matthias: Facies, opinor, quod tyrannos addecet;
patiar ego quod nobilem virum decet.   940
Saphioia: Generosa dicta! *Thomas*: Stat tamen dictis fides.
Saphioia: Libet experiri. *Thomas*: Praesto sum, quando voles.
Daifu: O contumacem spiritum! O diram fidem!
Est expiandum facinus invisum polo.
Per astra iuro, non erit inultum scelus!   945
Consiliarius 1: Tu, Thoma, sape saniora, thura fer Xacae;
fasces, domos, arces, gazas, Caesar dabit.
Exuite tantum saxeam mentem, precor;
qui pollicetur, Caesar est, Caesar dabit.
Thomas: Simulacra sunt haec levia, gloriolae leves,   950
pretiosa mundi retia, auratae cruces.
Aeterna sed nos praemia in caelo manent;
qui pollicetur, Christus est, Christus dabit.
Daifu: Quin flecte mentem, dum potes, Thoma inclyte;
prompta est volenti semper ad superos via.   955
Des thura divis; esto, tu facies metu,
veniam meretur facinus expressum metu.
Thomas: Non vasta si haec machina Christum neget suum,
ipsum relinquam; falsus tuus Daibut,
est fictus Amidae cultus et vanus Xacae.   960
Daifu: O exsecrandum iure caelitibus caput!
Testor verendum numen aeternum Xacae,
fatalis ambos hauriet meus mucro.
Vos respuistis Caesaris dona et minas;
iam non minari, non placet donis agi;   965
vobis parantur monstra supplicii nova.

939–42 The exchange between noble martyrs and a determined persecutor
here copies what is in *T* (see also Introduction 2.4) 285. The words of Boethius
in *T* are given here to Matthias (with the change *quicquid senatorem
decet→quod nobilem virum decet* (938)), those of Theodoric the Great (454–
526) to Safioye, and those of Boethius' father-in-law Quintus Aurelius
Memmius Symmachus (?-526) to Thomas. See also note to 1216.

943 This line copies an exclamation by a Roman praetor concerning the
stubborn martyrs Boethius and Symmachus in *T* 287, with a modified end (*O
laevum nefas→O diram fidem*). Cf. also 996 which repeats most of this line.

Daifu: Criminal fellow, I will crush your mouth with wheels and torture!
Matthias: You will do, I believe, that which is fitting to tyrants;
I will endure what is fitting to a noble man.   940
Safioye: [*In a mocking tone*] Magnificent words! *Thomas*: But they are
   trustworthy.
Safioye: Let us put them to the test. *Thomas*: I am here, whenever you wish.
Daifu: O stubborn spirit! O detestable religion!
The crime hateful to heaven must be punished.
I swear by the stars, this guilt shall not go unavenged!   945
Counsellor 1: You, Thomas, think more wisely and bring incense to Shaka;
the king will give you insignia, houses, castles, treasures.
Just get rid of your rock-hard mind, please;
the king is the one who promises you, the king will grant these gifts.
Thomas: Those are but fleeting images, small and light fragments of glory, 950
costly snares of this world, golden gallows.
But eternal prizes await us in heaven;
Christ is the one who promises us, Christ will grant these gifts.
Daifu: But change your mind, while you are able, renowned Thomas;
the way to heaven is always open for those who wish it.   955
Just give incense to the gods; supposing you do this out of fear,
a deed that is forced upon by fear merits forgiveness.
Thomas: Even if this vast universe should deny its own Christ,
I will not leave him; your Daibutsu is false
and the worship of Amida and Shaka is an empty fiction.   960
Daifu: O fellow rightly detestable to the heavenly beings!
I swear by the venerable and eternal spirit of Shaka,
that my fatal blade shall strike at them both.
You have rejected the favours and threats of your king;
it no longer pleases me to threaten or to propose favours;   965
a new and monstrous punishment is being prepared for you.

954–7 Daifu's exhortation for apostasy here copies a passage in *F* (see Introduction 2.4) 242, where Publius, the (likely legendary) Prefect of Rome, urges Ianuarius, one of the sons of the title character, to abandon the faith. There are two minor changes to suit the context: *flecte O puer*→*Thoma inclyte* (952); *epulare*→*Des thura* (954).

964–6 Daifu's threatening words are again lifted from Publius's warning toward the martyr Felicitas in *F* 212, with the following modifications changing the addressee from the singular to plural: *Tu respuisti*→*Vos respuistis* (964); *In te parantur*→*vobis parantur* (966).

Matthias: Propone ferrum, laminas, tela, et faces,
caput revellas, in lucris haec deputo.
Non me movebis, nam dei fulcit manus.
Eripere mentem non potes, vitam potes.   970
Stat gloriose pro dei causa mori.
Consiliarius 1: Truculentus hostis tu tibi fieri potes;
quo mens recessit? Vivere datur, emori
cur destinasti? Quis iubet, quis imperat?
Quis hominum adigit hanc ante condictam diem   975
resecare lucem? *Consiliarius 2*: Si voluntati sedet
numquam litare diis, nec inflecti potest,
esto! Modicum tamen hocce thuris accipe
et te litasse simula, ut astantem tibi
supra caput pestem vel hac fugias via.   980
Simulare tantum suadeo; quid hic mali?
Consiliarius 3: Ne sperne monita; tempori aptari decet.
Patientia regis ne abutere, si sapis.
Matthias: Vah, daemonum mancipia! Mene quidpiam
simulare facto, quod animo nolim? Deum   985
silentio premam? Diabolo supplicem?
Dum terra caelum media libratum feret,
dum sempiternas Phoebus evolvet vices,
numerusque arenis deerit et solem dies,
noctem sequentur astra, dum vivet deus,   990
numquam mea morietur in deum fides,
ut illud amens mente concipiam nefas.
Daifu: Sat est, sat altos pertuli fastus tuos;
moriere vecors, si cupis, moriere, Thoma.
Cedite, scelesta capita, ex aula cedite!   995

967–9 967 and 969 copy two consecutive lines spoken in defiance by the martyr Felicitas to Marcus Aurelius in *F* 193.

971 This line is repeated by Iustus in 1213.

983 The line is recycled (with change of *ne* to *non*, likely by error as it unhinges the metre) in 1470.

984 *mene*: So B; A⁶ has *mens* which makes little sense.

Matthias: Try out your iron instruments, red-hot plates, weapons, and
    torches,
chop off my head; I consider all this to be my gain.
You will not move me, since God supports me with his hand.
You cannot change my mind, though you can end my life.   970
I am determined to die gloriously for the sake of God.
Counsellor 1: You could become your own worst enemy;
where has your mind taken off to? You are allowed to live, why
are you determined to die? Who orders, who commands you?
Who of all the humans is forcing you to leave the light of day   975
before your settled destiny? *Counsellor 2*: If it should never be
your wish to sacrifice to the gods, nor can this be changed,
let it be so! [*Offering a piece of incense*] But just take this little bit of incense
and pretend that you have sacrificed, so that you may escape
the calamity that hangs over your head even in this way.   980
I suggest that you only pretend; what evil is there in this?
Counsellor 3: Do not spurn our admonition; you should accommodate
    yourself to the times.
If you are sane, do not abuse the patience of your king.
Matthias: Alas, you slaves of demons! Should I pretend
anything in deed, what I do not wish in mind? Should I   985
keep silent about God? Shall I supplicate the devil?
As long as the earth at the centre holds the sky in balance,
as long as Phoebus goes round in his eternal gyrations,
as long as the sand is numberless, and day comes with the sun,
and night with the stars, as long as God lives,   990
my faith in God shall never die
and I shall never entertain such an insane crime in my mind.
Daifu: This is enough, I have put up with enough of your haughtiness;
you will die an insane man, if you wish, you will die, Thomas.
Leave, criminal fellows, leave this court! [*Thomas and Matthias leave stage*] 995

986–90 These lines echo Sen. *Med.* 401–4 (*dum terra* .... *feret/nitidusque
certas mundus evolvet vices/numerusque arenis ... dies/noctem sequentur astra,
dum siccas polus/*), where the title character expounds on her enduring rage.

994 *moriere vecors, si cupis, moriere*: The metre could be easily emended if
the second *moriere* is changed to *mori*. The words up to *cupis* are copied from
the line in *F* 194 (*Moriere vecors, si cupis, sed non semel*) where Marcus
Aurelius is threatening the title character.

O contumacem spiritum! O dirum nefas!
Quid consili tuo, Phanes, das Caesari?
Consiliarius 3: Quid dubius haeres? Quidve consilium diu
tam facile torques? Debita extinctos nece
vis esse barbaros hos? Nil perspectius.   1000
Saphioia: Caesar, scelesta capita ferro decute.
Malo mederi dum potes, ferrum occupa.
Neglecta crescunt per suos gradus mala.
Addas parenti liberos, simul cadant.
Daifu: Ex tripode loqueris, Saphioia.   1005
Ast est timendus plebis insanus furor,
si luce cernat una proceres Iaponum
altissimae stirpis ruere. *Saphioia*: Caesar potens,
has mitte curas in mare Creticum.
Dolus an virtus, quis in hoste requirat?   1010
Incauta sternetur vinclis suis fera;
inter scyphos et amicos mortem invenient.
Tu tutus interim dapes, Caesar, pete.
Daifu: Placet, eamus intro.

II.4

Saphioia, Fingi, gubernator.
Saphioia: Infame abesset tale vellem hominum genus,   1015
quocumque se pars fundit orbis ultima,

---

996 Cf. note to 943.

997 *Phanes*: This appears to be the personal name of counsellor 3. Phanes is
a Greek name, most famously that of the counsellor to the Egyptian pharaoh
Amasis II (570–526 BCE) (cf. Herodotus 3.4.1).

1002–3 These lines are lifted from an official's suggestion to Thedoric the
Great concerning punishment to be meted out to Boethius and Symmachus
in *T* 287.

1004 The first half of this line echoes Theodoric's threat to Boethius' wife
concerning her children in *T* 310 (*Addam parenti liberos, non est satis*).

1005 *ex tripode*: A proverbial expression referring to the ancient oracle of
Delphi. See e.g. Erasmus 1703: 297–8.

O what stubborn spirit! O terrible crime!
What counsel do you give to me, your king, Phanes?
Counsellor 3: Why do you doubt and hesitate? And why do you torture
    yourself about
such an easy decision for a long time? Do you want these barbarians
to be killed in the way they deserve? Nothing is clearer.   1000
Safioye: King, strike off the criminal heads with the sword.
Take up your arms, while it is still possible to counter evil.
Evils grow on their own when they are neglected.
Add the children to their parent, let them die together.
Daifu: You are my Delphic oracle, Safioye.   1005
But I fear the raging anger of the populace,
if they should see leading Japanese nobles from the most ancient lineage
fall on a single day. *Safioye*: Powerful king,
throw away those worries into the Cretan sea.
Who worries whether to use strength or trickery against an enemy?   1010
The beast will be brought down unawares in its own snares;
they will meet their doom amidst wine-cups and friends.
You in the meanwhile, king, go to your supper secure.
Daifu: That is good, let us go inside. [*They all leave stage*]

II.4

Safioye, Fingi, governor.
Safioye: I wish that such an infamous tribe of men would go off   1015
to wherever the end of the world stretches itself out,

1009 *in mare Creticum*: A proverbial expression meaning 'far away'. See e.g.
Hor. *Carmina* 1.26.2 and Erasmus 1703: 814.

1010 *Dolus ... requirat?*: This line is lifted from Virg. *Aen.* 2.390, where
Coroebus, the suitor of Cassandra, encourages Trojans to don on captured
Greek armour during their final desperate struggle to save the city.

1015–44 II.4. Safioye, in pursuit of his plan to murder Thomas and Matthias,
commands his subordinate Fingi to summon the governor of Arima. While
the latter is being awaited, Belial reminds the audience that Safioye is his
special agent charged with the task of leading Daifu and the Japanese people
to perdition (cf. 105–6). Upon the governor's arrival, Safioye asks him to
prepare a feast on the following day for the brothers and the official agrees.
Though not told of the plot, the governor suspects from Safioye's demeanour
that the feast will be a cover for some nefarious trap.

quod vulgus impellit alienis legibus
vitam trahere, quod exprobat Xacae fidem,
quod frena naturae soluta comprimit.
Quid Christus ad nos, quem crucifixum serit,   1020
quem praedicant temerarie beare nos?
Quantum beet suos, fratres Iendonii
mox sentient; nam festivas inter dapes
ferro cadent, solvent poenas proterviae.
Ades Fingi! *Fingi*: Praesto sum; quid iubes? *Saphioia*: Tibi   1025
heri quae dixi, differemus omnia;
sed intra subito et praefectum castri voca!
Fingi: Vin' Arimensem? *Saphioia*: Ipsus quem volo; citus vola!
Fingi: Ipsos praevertam Zephyros – .
Belial: Hic vir, hic est tibi quem promitti saepius audis,   1030
est hic est hominum divum contemptor; ad Orcum
Iaponidum ducet gentes regemque Daifu.
Gubernator: Vocatus adsum. Quid me vis? *Saphioia*: Iam iam scies.
Gubernator: Effare, quid est? *Saphioia*: Proceres animo Iendonios
stat luce crastina dapibus lautissimis   1035
excipere. Tu, fac mensa ferculis crepet.
Gubernator: Muneris erit mei curare ista, at tuum

The text is found in A^6 and *B*, which contain nearly identical lines except that *B* divides it into two scenes (between 1032 and 1033). In A^6 it is found between our I.7 and III.1, and in *B* between our II.3 and III.2. The placement in this edition is based on the arrangement in the manuscripts as well as the general plot movement.

The metre is senarius except for Belial's pronouncement in dactylic hexametre (1030–2). Problematic lines are 1029 (*versus mancus*), 1041, 1043, 1044.

1020 *Quid*: So *B*, A^6 has *Quod*, presumably an error induced by the repeated use of this word in previous lines.

1020–1 The verb agreeing with *genus* changes from *serit* to *praedicant* in construction according to sense (see e.g. Mahoney 2001: 187).

this tribe that forces our people to trudge through life
under alien rules, abuses the faith of Shaka
and draws tight the loose rein of nature.
What does Christ, whom they claim was crucified,   1020
who, they say, blesses us randomly, have to do with us?
What blessings he gives to his followers, the Yendono brothers
will soon find out; for during a merry feast
they will fall by the sword and pay the penalty for their impudence.
Come, Fingi! *Fingi*: [*Enters stage*] I am here; what is your command?
    Safioye: What   1025
I said to you yesterday, all of that we shall delay;
but go in at once and call the commander of the fort.
Fingi: Do you mean the one of Arima? *Safioye*: He is the very one I
    want; go quickly!
Fingi: I shall outrun even the west wind – . [*Leaves stage*]
Belial: [*Aside, standing apart from human figures and pointing out Safioye*]
    This, this is the man
whom you heard promised to you more than once,   1030
he is the one who despises humankind and the gods, and to hell
he shall bring the people of Japan as well as king Daifu.
Governor: [*Entering stage*] I am here at your command; what is your wish?
    Safioye: You will know right away.
Governor: Speak, what is it? *Safioye*: It is my decision to invite
the Yendonos, the nobles, tomorrow to a most lavish   1035
feast. You, take care so that the table groans with dishes.
Governor: It will be my task to take care of that, but yours will be

---

1025 *Fingi*: A personal name invented for the moment possibly from *Fingo*, the early modern transliteration for Higo, a region that roughly corresponds to the modern Kumamoto prefecture.

1030 This line copies Virg. *Aen.* 6.791, there used by Anchises in the underworld to designate the future Augustus Caesar.

1031 *divum contemptor*: Another Virgilian echo, recalling the designation of Mezentius, the mythical villain and Aeneas's archenemy, as *contemptor divum* (Virg. *Aen.* 7.648).

1037 *Muneris...ista*: So B. A⁶ has *Muneris mei erit ista curare*, which is metrically problematic.

vocare convivas. *Saphioia*: Fiet voto satis – .
Gubernator: Dum se malus bonum simulat, malum parit
maius. Tuam, Saphioia, teneo probe indolem;   1040
monstri quid alis? Anguis in spinis latet.
Timeo, dapum ne extrema luctus occupet.
Quae causa subsit, perspicere facile queo.
Sed ego domum propero, cruentas ut parem dapes.

II.Chorus

Quam diu stultum, truculente, frustra   1045
cum deo bellum geris, O tyranne?
Nil agis. Temet crucias tuorum
     funera acervans.
Non minae terrent, flagra non cruenta,
nec rogi, stricti neque fulgor ensis,   1050
sive tortorum madidae recenti
     sanguine dextrae.
Promoves poenis generosioris
pectoris robur, cumulasque Christi
pro fide multa nece, provocasque   1055
     stultus athletas.
In gregem Christi, furibunde latro,
tu licet totum moveas furorem;
opprimes numquam, velut icta ferro
     palma resurget.   1060

1040 *maius*: So *B*, the word is not found in *A⁶*.

1041 For *B alis*, *A⁶* has *alas*, but the indicative fits the syntax better. The snake-in-the-grass motif echoes Virg. *Eclogues* 3.93 (*latet anguis in herba*).

1045–60 II chorus. This is a hymn directed toward the agent in charge of anti-Christian persecution (i.e. Daifu and/or Safioye), berating the addressee for his impious and ultimately fruitless attack. The content is generic but unlike the chorus for I seems to be original, with just one Horatian tag in 1059.

to invite the guests. *Safioye*: As you wish – . [*Leaves stage*]
Governor: When an evil man pretends to be good, he brings forth
a greater evil. I know your character well, Safioye; 1040
what monster are you nurturing? A snake hides in the bush.
I fear that, at the very end of the feast, grief will come.
I can easily see through what purpose is behind this.
But I shall hurry home, so that I may prepare the bloody feast.

II.Chorus

How long will you wage your stupid war in vain 1045
against God, O cruel tyrant?
You accomplish nothing. You are tormenting yourself, piling up
    the dead bodies of your own people.
Neither do your threats hold any fear, nor the bloody scourge,
nor the pyre, nor the gleam of the drawn sword, 1050
nor the hands of torturers, drenched
    with recent bloodshed.
With your punishment, you are increasing
the strength of the noble heart, you are gathering more athletes
for the Christian faith with your many murders, and you are foolishly 1055
    challenging them.
Against the flock of Christ, raging bandit,
you may apply your insanity in full force;
you will never crush them, they will rise up again
    like a palm struck by the sword. 1060

Like I chorus, it is in Sapphic stanza and is found only toward the end of
B, where it is entitled *Chorus Actus idi* (*sic*) and is placed after the text of I
chorus. It may have been delivered by alternating groups, as each of the first
three stanzas have the following notation in the left margin: *1 Ang.*; *2 Juv.
Chr.*; *2. Ang.*

1059 *velut icta ferro*: The tag is from Hor. *Carm.* 4.6.9, where the referent is
Achilles struck dead at a young age.

III.1

Symposiarcha, Chera, archimagirus, Benzelo.
Symposiarcha: Heus, Chera, Chera! *Chera*: Domine, quid vis? Impera!
Symposiarcha: Repente properare propere te volo.
Chera: Quid, here, festinas adeo? Quid rogas?
Symposiarcha: Volatum Pegasi, aut deorum interpretis
talaria opto nobis, Briarei manus   1065
centenas, oculos Argi; velocissime
ornanda sunt convivia iussu principis.
Chera: En me paratum, quaevis iussa ut exsequar.
Symposiarcha: Archimagiro nuntia, ut sese paret,
ne quid in opimo minus sit convivio.   1070
Chera: Faxo lubens. Holla, magire, holla, resera
fores! Moraris? Pande tecti limina!
Archimagirus: Quis me vocat? Tu, Chera, quid fers nuntii?
Chera: Ut regium celer pares convivium!

1061–155 III.1. A final comic interlude centred on the preparation of the feast at the governor's. The symposiarch sends Chera, a young boy-servant, to the *archimagirus* (chief cook) with the command to prepare a sumptuous banquet. The master chef, upon hearing the message, rattles off a list of delicacies, some of them extremely learned and obscure. The cook then seems to call on a parasite by the name of Benzelo, though what the latter says or does is unclear presumably due to be a lacuna at this point (see note to 1118–20). The impatient symposiarch reappears, berates their idle chatter and attempts to send the boy away with instructions to properly salute and notify the guest. Chera pretends to misunderstand the directions in a final roundup of this raucous scene.

Much of III.1 is cribbed from *P*, as pointed out below (see also Introduction 2.4). The cribbing presumably happened indirectly through *CB*, as its V.2 and 3 overlap substantially with our scene (see Introduction 2.3).

The text is found twice in *A*. The shorter and cleaner *A⁶* has only 1061, 1069–86, 1094–5, 1104–10, 1122–45, 1147–51, and 1153–5. *A⁷* on the other hand, which has all lines except 1075 and 1079, is clearly a developing draft

III.1

Symposiarch, Chera, chief cook, Benzelo.

Symposiarch: Hey, Chera, Chera! *Chera*: [*Running onto stage*] Master,
    what do you want? Give your command!
Symposiarch: I want you to suddenly hurry up hurriedly.
Chera: What are you hurrying about so much, master? What do you want?
Symposiarch: The flight of Pegasus, or the winged sandals of the messenger
    of the gods are what I want, or the hundred hands   1065
    of Briareus, or the eyes of Argus; with the greatest speed
    we must prepare a feast by the command of our prince.
Chera: Look, I am ready; whatever you order, I will do.
Symposiarch: Give word to the chief cook that he should see to it
    that nothing must be amiss in the sumptuous feast. [*Leaves stage*]   1070
Chera: I shall gladly do so. [*Runs to the front of a house and knocks*]
    Hello, cook, hello, open
the door! Are you taking your time? Open the entrance to the abode!
Chief cook: [*Opens the door and comes out*] Who calls me? You, Chera,
    what news do you bring?
Chera: The news that you must prepare a regal feast quickly!

---

with many lines crossed out or scribbled in margins (see Figure 3). All of these lines are restored in our edition, as noted in the commentary below. In A^6 the scene is found between our II.4 and III.2, whereas A^7 is a free-standing draft containing only this scene. The current placement follows that of A^6.

The scene is mostly delivered in senarius. As usual there are metrically problematic lines (1062, 1063, 1069, 1070, 1079, 1080, 1102 (*versus mancus*), 1124, 1128, 1153, 1154). Furthermore, 1087–93 are cribbed from a prose source and only provisionally divided into a rough equivalent of senarius here.

1062–8 These lines are crossed out in A^7 and were probably meant to be replaced by 1061 and 1069–75, which are found in A^6 as well as the left margin of A^7. The crossed-out lines are notable for the mythological barrage mentioning the flying horse Pegasus (1064), the winged sandals of the messenger-god Mercury/Hermes (1064–5), the hundred-handed Briareus (1064–6) and the similarly-many-eyed Argus (1066). The production team may have decided in the end this display of erudition to be excessive.

Archimagirus: Ego in culina, scilicet regno in meo   1075
habeo apparata cuncta festivissime.
Veniret a se rex vel alter principum,
posset epulari hic ille quam largissime.
Quin immo, quae dicam tibi attende;
nec spernes facile mea fercula.   1080
Modico calentes igne porcellos dabo,
lardi nitentis ustulatos guttula
assabo. Deinde condiam cuniculos,
pingues sagina proferemus anseres,
turdos, palumbes, turtures, passerculos,   1085
villaticaeque cortis insignes aves.
Pavos e Samo, Phrygias attagenas,
grues mellitas, haedos recentes, pelamides
Chalcedonias, murenas Tartesias, pectunculos
Chios, Rhodios helopes, scaros Cilices,   1090
nuces Thasias, phasianorum et pavonum cerebella,
linguas phoenicopterorum, murenarum lactes,
ceterasque patinae Vitellianae cuppedias – .
Chera: Sic est agendum. Perge modo, perge acriter,
dapes para, renuntiabo hero id meo.   1095
Archimagirus: Sed heus, hero commender ut magis tuo,
et hoc renuntiabis: Ita facio, lego
arietis unam vel duas pernas, bene
concido, lardi misceo quod satis puto,
deinde piperatas condio, limonii   1100
mali saporem spargo quam gratissimum.
Gustent sepulti, vivent.

1075–8 *Ego . . . largissime*: These lines copy much of *P* 1635-9, where a cook
by the name of Phaedromus is boasting of his culinary kingdom. The
following are slight changes to accommodate the new context:
Venisset→Veniret, *Asiae→a se*, *aut→vel* (all *P* 1637 and *JM* 1075); *P* 1638
(*Quorum tyrannis orbem saeva territat*) is omitted entirely.

1081–6 These lines are lifted entirely from *P* 1289–94, where the cook
Phaedromus triumphantly lists his recipes.

1087–93 These lines are scribbled in the right margin of *A⁷*. They are all
taken from the prose dialogue between *Fortuna* and *Aulicus* in Tixier's school

Chief cook: In my kitchen, that is to say in my kingdom,   1075
I have everything prepared in a most merry way.
Should a king come from his own home, or some one of the high nobles,
that one would be able to feast here most magnificently.
Come now, listen carefully to what I tell you;
and you will not carelessly cast aside my dishes.   1080
I will make suckling pigs warm with fire,
and roast them, singeing them with droplets of
sparkling lard. Then I will spice up rabbits,
we will serve up plump, fattened geese,
thrushes, woodpigeons, turtle-doves, sparrowlets,   1085
and outstanding birds from our villa's pen.
Samian peacocks, Phrygian meadow-birds,
honeyed cranes, fresh young goats, Chalcedonian
young tuna, Tartessian eels, small Chian
scallops, Rhodian sturgeons, Cilician wrasses,   1090
Thasian nuts, brains of pheasants and peacocks,
tongues of flamingos, milk of eels,
and other dishes of Vitellian delicacies – .
Chera: [*Preparing to leave*] Go on in this way. Go on, go on busily,
prepare the feast, I will report back to my master.   1095
Chief cook: But wait, so that I may be more pleasing to your master,
you will report this back as well; I am doing this, I am picking
one or two mutton legs, I chop them up
neatly, I mix in what I think is enough fat,
then I spice it up, and I sprinkle on   1100
the tangiest juice of lemon.
Let the dead taste it, they will come back to life again.

---

text (Tixier 1615: 179v.; see also Introduction 2.4) and inflate the already
considerable list of obscure delicacies. *patinae Vitellianae* (1093) refers to the
infamous gourmand emperor Vitellius (15–69) (cf. Suetonius *Vitellius* 13,
where some of the delicacies mentioned here also appear).

1094 *Sic est agendum. Perge*: These words copy the exhortation of the
gourmand Archedonus in *P* 1295.

1097–101 *Ita facio … vivent*: The words here again repeat those of
Phaedromus in *P* 1717–1722, except for the change of *Sic* (*P* 1717) to *Ita*
(1097) which saves the metre in the new context.

Chera: Recreabitur herus nuntio tali meus.
Archimagirus: Sed quorsum abis? Plura audias! Cuniculos
transfigo verubus, asso sit quantum satis,   1105
in praeparato iure mergo postea,
addo cochleari zingiberi, lectum piper,
garioque philon Indicum, exploro meis
naribus odorem, sentio postquam mihi
placuisse, ab ipso amoveo tantisper foco.   1110
Chera: Sed quid opus est verbis? Inani illa stomacho
gustare, quam audire, cupio egomet edepol.
Valeto – . *Archimagirus*: Specto hoc diligentia mea
nunc lautius coquendo; si possum, mihi
muneribus hospitum parabo pallium,   1115
item lacernam, qua profestis in forum
diebus ibo, quam soleo, spectatior.

–   –   –

Archimagirus: Encomia ista fac sint vera, Benzelo.
Benzelo: Verissima hodie efficiam, quodque iusseris
et plura quam tu iusseris, faciam lubens.   1120
Archimagirus: At ecce adest mensae strategus aulicus.
Symposiarcha: Quid sic loquendo tardas innectis moras?
Num sic culinae fervet occupatio?

1104–10 *Cuniculos . . . foco*: The cook's final culinary comment is again lifted
from Phaedromus's recipe in *P* 1756–64. *JM* here shortens the original
somewhat, omitting *P* 1757 and part of *P* 1762–3 (*mox . . . labiis*). In *A*[7],
1109–10 are added in the right margin. *garioque philon* (1108, *P* 1761) is
presumably derived from *garyophyllon* which refers to some kind of Indian
spice (see L&S s.v.); Fernandes 1989: v.2 129 translates the phrase as *cravo da
índia*.

1111–17 These lines are added in the right margin of *A*[7]. 1114–17 (*si possum
. . . spectatior*) are partly lifted from *P* 1722–5 where the cook Phaedromus
expresses his fond hope of buying a new set of shopping attire from the

Chera: My master will be refreshed by such a message. [*Begins to leave*]
Chief cook: But where are you taking off to? There is more! I affix
rabbits on spits, I roast them until it seems enough, 1105
then I dip them in a prepared sauce,
I add ginger with a spoon, choice pepper
and spice of the Indies, I check the smell
with my nose, and after I feel it is good enough
as far as I am concerned, I move them away from the fireplace a
little bit. 1110
Chera: But what need is there of words? My stomach is empty
and I crave more to taste them than just to listen, really.
Goodbye. [*Leaves stage*] *Chief cook*: I watch over this with my due
diligence,
doing my cooking rather carefully; if I can,
with the tips from our guests I will get a coat 1115
and likewise an overcoat, and better dressed in these than before,
I will go on working days to the market.
— — —
Chief cook: Make sure that those encomiums are true, Benzelo.
Benzelo: I will make sure that they will be most true today, and
whatever you wish
and more than you wish, I will do willingly. 1120
Chief cook: [*Seeing the symposiarch entering stage*] But look, the courtly
commander of the table is here.
Symposiarch: Why do you keep on delaying so leisurely here with your
talking?
Do I see the kitchen cooking up busy work now?

---

earnings of an upcoming feast. *pretio epularum* (P 1723) is changed into
muneribus hospitum (1115).

1118–20 The character Benzelo appears here out of the blue. Some statement
made by Benzelo, perhaps a praise of the dishes being prepared, must have
dropped out from the manuscript immediately prior to 1118. Benzelo is the
name of a gluttonous parasite in the German Protestant humanist Philipp
Nicodemus Frischlin (1547–90)'s historical drama *Hildegardis Magna* (see
e.g. Kaminski 1995: 52, 67).

1122 *innectis*: In A^7 this word is written above *nectitis*, which is also found in
A^6. The singular is adopted here in view of *move* in 1124.

Ocius move hinc gradum, iussa principis
Perage. Heus, Chera, quid agis? Heus, Chera, advola!   1125
Audisne, puer? *Chera*: Here, acriter certe audio;
ad audiendum aures habeo acutissimas,
pedes ad volandum velocissimos,
os ad loquendum falsa felicissimum.
Symposiarcha: His nemo puerum dotibus laudandum habet,   1130
te praeter unum. Nae, tu te laudas nimis.
Velox ad aedes principum excurras Cami.
Caput, antequam loquare, totum detege.
Me, me tuere. Retro deduces pedem,
mandata tunc ordire nostro nomine: 1135
'Per me salutat', inquies, 'herus, tuam,
huiusce princeps urbis, excellentiam,
oratque suo intersit hodie convivio'.
Didicisti? *Chera*: Didici. *Symposiarcha*: Finge te cum illo loqui.
Quae mando, repete. *Chera*: Detegam imprimis caput,   1140
pedem reducam retro, mox sic ordiar:
'Per me salutat urbis moderator tuam,
huiusce regni princeps, insolentiam'.
Symposiarcha: Dixi 'insolentiam', puer? *Chera*: 'Excellentiam'
dixisse volui. *Symposiarcha*: Lapsus in una syllaba   1145
corrupit omnem pessime sententiam.
Chera: Sine, meo more ut fecerim quae praecipis.
Capite retecto stabo, tunc retro pedem
ago sinistrum, aut si libebit, dexterum,

1124–5 *Ocius ... advola!*: So A^7, A^6 has *Ocius hinc vos abripite et iussa principis/peragite. Heus, Chera, Chera, quid agis?* The reading of A^7 is adopted here for the sake of consistency in number.

1126–55 *audio ... modo*: Most of the comic dialogue between Chera and the symposiarch here copies the exchange between the boy-servant Anarchus and the glutton Archedonus who wants to invite his friends Pamphagus and Gastrophilus to dinner in *P* 1351–82. The following are the differences: *concurrendum* (P 1353)→*volandum* (1128); *salsa* (P 1354)→*falsa* (1129); *At curre velox extra muros oppidi* (P 1357)→*Velox ad aedes principum excurras Cami* (1132; corrected in A^7 from *... ad aedes excurras ducis Iaponii* (*Cami* or *Kami* is the early modern Jesuit regional designation corresponding to the

Quick, get your legs moving, do as our prince
commands. [*The Chief cook and Benzelo go into the house*] Hey,
    Chera, what are you doing? Hey, Chera, come here quickly!   1125
Are you listening, boy? *Chera:* [*Reenters stage*] Master, I certainly
    hear you loud and clear;
my ears are very keen at hearing,
my legs are very quick at running,
my mouth is very skilled at spewing lies.
Symposiarch: No one has any boy, other than you, who is praiseworthy   1130
for these skills. Really, you praise yourself too much.
Quick, run off to the abode of the princes of Kami.
Before you speak, uncover your head completely.
Look at me, me: You will draw one foot behind,
then, begin the message in our name;   1135
'through me', you will say, 'my master,
the prince of this city, salutes Your Excellency,
and begs you to join his feast today'.
Did you get it? *Chera:* I got it. *Symposiarch:* Imagine that you are
    speaking with him;
repeat what I am telling you. *Chera:* I shall uncover my head,   1140
I shall draw my foot back, soon I shall begin thus:
'through me, the governor of the city salutes, O prince
of this realm, Your Insolency'.
Symposiarch: Did I say 'Insolency', boy? *Chera:* 'Excellency'
I meant to say. *Symposiarch:* A mistake in one syllable   1145
skewed the whole sentence really badly.
Chera: Let me do what you told me in my own way.
I will stand with my head uncovered, then I push my left
foot back, or if you like, my right foot back,

---

present-day Kansai area (i.e. the cities of Kyoto, Osaka and the surroundings),
from where Thomas Heibyōe himself is said to have come, see Trigault 1623:
46); *hospes* (P 1362)→*herus* (1136); *civis* (P 1363)→*princeps* (1137; in A^7 left
margin also *huiusce regni princeps* written in as an alternative); *veniat in suam
si vult domum* (P 1364)→*suo intersit hodie convivio* (1138; but the same words
as in *P* also written in A^7, then crossed out); *hospes Archedonus* (P 1368)→*urbis
moderator* (1142); *huiusce civis urbis* (P 1363)→*huiusce regni princeps* (1143;
in A^7 in the main text and the margin *invicte princeps* and *praefectus urbis* are
also scribbled in as alternatives; A^6 omits *urbis . . . princeps* (1142–3) entirely);
fecerim (P 1373)→*faciam* (1147); *celebri convivio* (P 1381)→*iucunde excipere*
(1154; so A^7, A^6 has *herus, parato ut cras intersis convivio* for the entire line).

et semiridens hisce oculis pellucidis,   1150
et tam venustis: 'Caelites', dicam, 'te ament,
ipsique ubique gentium te sospitent,
O vir virorum maxime; exspectat te meus
herus, parato te, iucunde excipere'.
Symposiarcha: Amplector, isto potius occuras modo!   1155

III.2

Matthias, Thomas.
Thomas: Frater, repente venit optatus dies,
quo nos tyrannus feriet in causa dei.
Mentem tyranni nosco, nosco et indolem.
In corde fel, mel in lingua viri latet
pransosque sanguinaria prehendens manu   1160
deducet in macellum, ut sparso sanguine
nostro ferales epulas foedemus; hoc, frater, placet?
Matthias: Frater, placet vel millies sic emori!
Ego parricida non moriar nec proditor.
Beatus ille, qui reponit spem in sinu   1165
summi tonantis, nec sibi fidit nimis.
Innixus illi non timebo mala omnia,
quaeque Orcus, aether et tellus parat;
nec lividorum me quassabunt spicula.
His gloriosum linguis est pati famam.   1170
Tu mihi salutis una spes, una fiducia;

1156-83 III.2. Matthias and Thomas rejoice at the prospect of being
entrapped and murdered for the sake of their religion. They pray jointly for
strength to be able to undergo the trial successfully until their pious exercise
is interrupted by the arrival of Thomas's children.

The scene is preserved in two nearly identical versions, namely A^6 and *B*.
In A^6 this scene is merged with III.3, but our edition follows *B* in making a
break at 1183. The metre is the usual senarius, with a few problematic lines
(1162, 1167, 1168, 1170, 1171).

1159-62 In *B*, these lines are added after 1166. *In corde fel, mel in lingua*
(1159) recalls the popular medieval quatrain *Annis mille iam peractis,/nulla
fides est in pactis;/mel in ore, verba lactis,/fel in corde, nil in factis* (see e.g.
Strigel 1565: 239).

and smiling lightly with [*Rolling his eyes*] these my sparkling, and
  such enticing   1150
eyes: 'May heavenly beings' I shall say, 'love you,
and wherever in the world you are, may they keep you safe,
O greatest of all men; my master looks forward,
should you be ready, to welcome you'.
Symposiarch: [*Embracing Chera*] I embrace you, approach him rather
  in this manner of yours.   1155

III.2

Matthias, Thomas.
Thomas: Brother, the day that we wished for has come suddenly,
the day on which the tyrant will strike us down for the sake of God.
I know the mind of this tyrant, and I know his character.
Bile is hidden in his heart and honey in his tongue,
and after we have eaten, he will grab us with his bloody hand   1160
and drag us to the butcher's stall, so that we may shed our blood
with which to sully the hellish feast; brother, does this seem good?
Matthias: Brother, it seems good to die even a thousand times in this way!
I shall die neither a parricide nor a traitor.
Blessed is he, who places his hope on the bosom   1165
of God the highest and does not trust himself too much.
Relying on God, I shall be fearless against all evils
or against what hell, sky and earth bring forth,
and the darts of the envious shall not shake me.
It is glorious to have one's reputation tarnished by such tongues.   1170
You are my only hope of salvation and my only trust;

1163 *Frater, placet*: In *B*, these words are written above *Ex corde iuvat*; A6 has
Ex corde placet. The current reading is the only metrically correct one.

1165 The line combines elements from Hor. *Epod.* 2.1 (*Beatus ille, qui procul
negotiis*) and *Ps.* 72.28 (*mihi autem adhaerere deo bonum est, ponere in domino
meo spem meam*). *A⁶* has *spem suam in sinu*, which is metrically problematic.

1170 The line echoes Cruz *Sedecias* 2012 (*His gloriosum manibus est mortem
pati*) where the prophet Jeremiah (*c.* 650–*c.* 570 BCE) is provoking king
Zedekiah (*c.* 597 BCE–?) with his dire prophecies. The next line of *Sedecias*
(*necat innocentem nemo, si non est nocens*: 2013) is echoed (with *necat
innocentem* changed to *nocet innocenti*) in 1175 below.

tu me, deus, si protegas clipeo tuo,
contra impios animo imperterrito viros
securus ibo, hostesque non stabunt mei.
Nocet innocenti nemo, si non est nocens.   1175
Thomas: Flagris, catastis, bestiis, flammis, rotis,
Christum tyrannus numquam de corde exuet.
Tu, qui nitentis astra moderaris poli
et picta mundi frena moliris manu,
da, Christe, menti robur, invicti, precor,   1180
da, nos tenaces esse propositi viros!
Sed quid tumultus per viam subito audio?
Matthias: Ipsa est tuorum clara natorum cohors.

III.3

Thomas, Matthias, Iacobus, Iustus, Famulus, Iusta (muta).
Thomas: Verbum est vetus, quandoque pueris et suus
est nasus, ante pilos subit prudentia,   1185
quandoque †mentem†, cum minus rere. Quid opus

1175 See note to 1170.

1178–9 This appellation of God as the one who rotates the universe echoes *C* IV.556-7 (*At, o nitentis astra qui torques poli/et picta mundi frena moliris manu*), where Ablavius, a benign courtier, laments the fall of the title character. *T* 321, where Theodoric's daughter Amalasuntha (*c.* 495–535) is lamenting her father's death, also uses similar phrasing (*tu, qui nitentis frena moderaris poli*).

1184-1261 III.3. Thomas's two children Iustus and Iacobus, accompanied by a servant and perhaps their mother Iusta (who never speaks but may be present as a silent character; see 1246), appear on stage. Iacobus tells Thomas and Matthias that the city is rife with rumours concerning a plot against their lives. The news predictably increases Thomas and Matthias's joy, which is however tempered by anxiety as to whether the children can withstand a similar trial in a worthy manner. To test their resolve, Thomas orders Iustus to grab burning coals, which the latter promptly begins to obey but is stopped by the father's countermand before actual injury occurs. The latter part of the

if you, God, protect me with your shield,
I shall go without fear against impious men
with my mind unshaken, and my enemies shall not stand.
No one harms an innocent one, unless the latter be harmful oneself. 1175
Thomas: With his lashes, scaffolds, beasts, flames and wheels,
the tyrant will never remove Christ from my heart.
You, who control the stars of resplendent heaven
and govern with your hand the brilliant celestial signs of the universe,
give, Christ, strength to our mind; I pray, may you allow 1180
us to be men who hold on to our invincible proposition!
[*Hears the sound of people approaching*] But what commotion do I hear
    suddenly sounding through the street?
Matthias: [*Seeing Iustus, Iacobus and Iusta approaching with a servant*]
    None other than the illustrious band of your children.

III.3

Thomas, Matthias, Iacobus, Iustus, servant, Iusta (mute).
Thomas: There is an old saying that, when boys have their own
noses, wisdom comes before the beard, 1185
and sometimes †the mind†, when you expect it less. What need

---

scene is devoted to the two parties' sentimental parting from each other. Renewed statements of resolve from Thomas and Matthias to face their upcoming trial conclude the scene. Many lines in the scene are cribbed from Caussin's martyr plays as pointed out below.

The scene is found in A^6 and B, which are basically identical except that only the latter has 1260–1. The placement of this scene follows that in the manuscripts.

The metre in this scene is the usual senarius. The following lines are metrically problematic: 1202 (cf. note), 1212 (cf. note), 1218, 1222, 1238, 1243, 1245.

1184–6 *Verbum . . . rere*: Although the first part of the sentence suggests that the whole is a proverbial expression, the sense (especially around †*mentem*† (1186)) remains obscure. The phrase *ante pilos subit prudentia* (1185) may well echo Pers. 4.4–5 (*scilicet ingenium et rerum prudentia velox/ante pilos venit*), which is in fact an ironic statement referring to the precocious but ultimately disastrous prodigy-politician Alcibiades of Athens (*c.* 450–404 BCE).

exempla petere remota? Iam Iustus meus
mihi fidem fecit, hodie dum nescio
quid de ferali prandio ferat puer.
Matthias: Amabo, parvulos excute. *Thomas*: Fili, quid est?   1190
Iacobus: O genitor, O miserande natorum parens
nimis duorum, quanta te clades manet!   ·
Thomas: At quae clades? *Iustus*: Saphioia tibi struit necem.
Thomas: Ain'? *Iacobus*: Pater, nunc rumor urbem pervolat.
Matthias: At causa tanti quae mali? *Iacobus*: Christi fides.   1195
Thomas: O filii partes mei, venit dies
sancto petitus ambitu et longa prece
expressus astris, venit innubis dies,
qui nos beatos martyres sistat polo!
Cervicibusque vestris et ferrum imminet.   1200
Quae vestra mens? An verear, aut sperem haud scio.
Iacobus: Si Marte nostro, pater, hoc nobis foret
bellum gerendum, nonnihil certe mihi
fratrique Iustulo timerem; sed nihil,
Christo auspice, pavesco. Suis aderit deus.   1205
Thomas: Quam me sagace, quam venustulo patrem
superi bearunt filio! Si masculum
decus parentum prolis heroicae solet
vulgare virtus et polo facere palam,
quid est quod addi possit optatis meis!   1210
Sed, Iuste, tu quid? An fugies? *Iustus*: Numquam, pater!

1188 *mihi fidem*: So A^6, B has *fidem mihi*, which also fits the sense and metre.

1194 *Pater*: So correctly in B, the word is missing in A^6.

1196–9 *venit . . . polo*: The words copy those in F 195, where the title character encourages her sons to undergo martyrdom in a worthy manner; *vos* in F is changed to *nos* (1199) to suit the context. *innubis* in F and B (1198) is *optatus* in A^6.

is there to seek examples from far away? My Iustus has already
made me believe this, while he brings today some news
or other about our fatal supper.
Matthias: Please, ask the little ones. *Thomas*: Son, what is it?   1190
Iacobus: O father, O most pitiable parent
of your two children, what a great disaster awaits you!
Thomas: But what disaster? *Iustus*: Safioye plans to murder you.
Thomas: Really? *Iacobus*: Father, now the rumour flies through the city.
Matthias: But what is the reason for such a great evil? *Iacobus*: Your
     faith in Christ.   1195
Thomas: O my sons, part of myself, the day has come,
the day that was sought with holy ambition and intoned to the stars
with long prayers, that cloudless day has come,
which will place us in heaven as blessed martyrs!
And a sword threatens your necks, too.   1200
What are your thoughts? I am not at all sure if I have something to
     fear, or to hope for.
Iacobus: Father, if this war had to be fought
with our own strength, I certainly would have some fear
for myself and my brother, little Iustus; but with Christ leading me,
I am afraid of nothing. God will help his own.   1205
Thomas: With what a wise and what a pleasing son have the heavenly
     beings
blessed me, his father! If the virtue of a heroic progeny
often advertises the masculine honour
of parents and makes it visible to heaven,
what more can be added to my wish?   1210
But Iustus, what about you? Will you flee? *Iustus*: Never, father!

1201 The line also copies a part of Felicitas's exhortation in *F* 195.

1202–5 *Si . . . pavesco*: These words closely follow the reply of the boy-martyr
Martialis to his saintly mother Felicitas in *F* 196, with the following changes
to suit the context: *mater*→*pater* (1202; the change unhinges the metre); *et
tibi timere, sed nihil, Christo auspice*/*video timendum*→*fratrique Iustulo
timerem; sed nihil*/*Christo auspice, pavesco* (1204–5).

Non imbellem feroces progenerant aquilae columbam;
stat gloriose pro dei causa mori.
Matthias: Quid si tyrannus flammas, ignes inferat?
Iustus: Favente numine, has cordate perferam.   1215
Thomas: Animosa dicta! *Iustus*: Sed stabit dictis fides.
Thomas: Stabit fides, si prunas has prendas manu.
Iustus: Fiet, pater, tentabo. Caelum, fave!
Thomas: Horrore quatior, artubus totis tremo;
Iustus tenellus ignes viventes premit.   1220
Animose fili, facis, ut Iaponem decet;
depone, mentem agnosco masculam.
Matthias: Estote fortes, regium est Christo pati,
qui vos relictos curet affectu patris.
Thomas: Perstate, pueri, patrias vobis opes   1225
virtutem habete, figite in vestro gradum,
nec vos supino tramite adversus ferat
potentis aulae fulgor et mundi bona;
humana cuncta parva sunt et vilia.
Valete, dulces liberi, partes mei!   1230
Iustus: Ah, ah, pater! *Iacobus*: Mi, mi pater! *Iustus*: Dulcis pater!
Thomas: Hoc nunc supremum, filii, capite osculum
paterni amoris, filii, ah, ah, filii!
Iacobus: Pater, O pater, quis hoc tribuat mihi, O pater!

1212 The words in this line copy Hor. *Carm.* 4.4.31–32 (except for the change of the opening *neque* to *non*) which is part of the praises heaped on Nero Claudius Drusus (38–9 BCE) as a progeny worthy of Augustus. A more immediate source for *JM* however was probably Trigault 1623: 72, which quotes these Horatian lines in relation to the son of *kirishitan* in Arima who reportedly displayed fortitude worthy of his father in insulting his own uncle (who was publicly urging him to apostatize) and calling him the son of a devil (*cacodaemonis filium*).

1213 See note to 971.

1216 The exchange between parent and son here echoes that between Safioye and Thomas in 939 and demonstrates Iustus's similarity to his about-to-be martyred father.

Brave eagles do not beget a tame dove;
I am determined to die gloriously for the sake of God.
Matthias: What if the tyrant threatens flames and fire?
Iustus: With divine favour, I shall judiciously bear them.   1215
Thomas: Brave words! *Iustus*: But they are worthy of trust.
Thomas: Your words will be trustworthy, [*Gesturing to a burning
    brazier*] if you grab these red embers with your hand.
Iustus: They will be, father, I will try. May heaven help me! [*Stretches
    out his hand to the brazier*]
Thomas: I am shaken with terror, I tremble in all my limbs;
Iustus, the tender boy, is grabbing burning fire.   1220
Brave son, you are doing what is fitting for a Japanese;
let it go, I recognize your masculine spirit.
Matthias: Be brave, it is a regal thing to suffer for Christ,
who will take care of you as orphans with a father's love.
Thomas: Persist, boys, keep hold of virtue   1225
as your paternal wealth, fix your steps in your own path,
and do not let the glory of courtly power or the riches of the world
come against you and carry you off on a downward path;
all human things are small and worthless.
Goodbye, sweet children, part of myself!   1230
Iustus: Ah, ah, father! *Iacobus*: My father, my father! *Iustus*: Sweet
    father!
Thomas: [*Embracing and kissing his sons*] Now, sons, take this last kiss
of fatherly love, sons, ah, ah, my sons!
Iacobus: Father, O father, who would grant us this, O father!

1217–21 Stories of Japanese child converts willingly grabbing burning coals
and red-hot iron to demonstrate their resolve are told in Trigault 1623: 174
and 208, respectively.

1219 The same line is recycled in 1325.

1224 The line copies the martyr Boethius's exhortation to his sons in *T* 290.

1225–9 These lines also copy Boethius's exhortation to his sons in *T* 290,
with the following minor changes: *aversos→adversus* (1227); *magni
lares→mundi bona* (1228); *lubrica→vilia* (1229).

Thomas: Animae innocentes, parcite dolori meo!   1235
Vos flere iniquum, sed rogo, veniam date;
non flere durum est, nescit hic frenum dolor.
Iustus et Iacobus: O pater, pater, sic nos linquis, pater?
Thomas: O cara lecti pignora, O lumen patris,
vos forte in ulnis ultimum amplector meis.   1240
Valete, dulces liberi, partes mei!
Matthias: Valete, dulces animulae, memores mei!
Iustus et Iacobus: O pater, pater, sic nos linquis, pater?
Famulus: Abite, pueri, quid parentem lacrimis
gravatis? *Iustus et Iacobus*: O pater, sic nos linquis?   1245
Thomas: Valete, dulces liberi, coniunx, vale,
vos flere iniquum, sed tamen cogor; date
veniam, rogo, nati mei. Est durus nimis
qui vult habenis stringere undantes aquas.
Moderator orbis summe, qui vasto cies   1250
mundum rotatu, saecla qui condens ducum
maior minores territas reges metu,
si prole tanta videar indignus pater,
hoc vile potius verberet fulmen caput!
Matthias: Compone mentem; restat actus ultimus   1255
utrique simul aeque elaborandus. *Thomas*: Placet,
utut volet deus; dulcis frater, veni.
Matthias: Moriemur una fortiter, primam deus
fortunet aciem martyrum; restat mori.

1235–7 These lines copy the lament of Boethius's wife over her dead husband and father in *T* 310.

1239–40 The words here are again lifted from Boethius's address to his sons in *T* 290.

1246 The line is copied from Boethius's farewell to his family in *T* 291.

1247–9 These lines again echo the lament of Boethius's wife in front of her husband and father in *T* 287, with the following change to suit the context: *lugere iniquum est, fateor, et cogor tamen./Hoc vestra virtus prohibet, at→vos flere iniquum, sed tamen cogor, date/veniam, rogo, nati mei. Est* (1247–8).

1250–4 Thomas's wish to be struck dead by lightening should he be found unworthy of his progeny copies that of Constantine (expressed in relation to

Thomas: Innocent souls, forgive my grief. 1235
It is wrong to weep over you, but I ask you, forgive us;
it is hard not to weep, this grief cannot be reined in.
Iustus and Iacobus: O father, father, do you leave us like this, father?
Thomas: O dear progeny of my marriage, O light of your father,
perhaps I embrace you for the last time in my arms.
Goodbye, sweet children, part of myself!
Matthias: Goodbye, sweet little souls, remember me! 1240
Iustus and Iacobus: O father, father, do you leave us like this, father?
Servant: Go away, children, why do you burden your parent
with tears? *Iustus and Iacobus*: O father, do you leave us like this?
  [*Iustus, Iacobus and the servant begin to leave stage*] 1245
Thomas: Goodbye, sweet children, wife, goodbye,
it is wrong to weep over you, but I am forced to do so; forgive,
I beg you, my sons. If anyone wishes to constrict
with reins these flowing streams, that one is too harsh.
You, supreme ruler of the world, who move 1250
the globe in its vast gyration, who establish generations of rulers
and threaten the smaller kings, yourself being greater, with fear,
if I should seem to be an unworthy father of such a worthy progeny,
may a thunderbolt rather strike my worthless head.
Matthias: Keep your mind in good order; the final act remains, 1255
which must be acted out equally by both of us. *Thomas*: It seems good,
whatever God wills; sweet brother, come.
Matthias: We will both die bravely, may God give good fortune
to the front line of martyrs; what is left is to die.

---

his still favoured son) in *C* I.409–14, with the following changes: *orbes* (*C* I.410)→*mundum* (1251); *videor* (*C* I.412)→*videar* (1252); *nimiumque* ... *tonas* (*C* I.413)→omitted.

1255 *compone*: So *A⁶*, *B* has *compesce*, with little difference in meaning or metre.

1255–6 *restat... elaborandus*: Perhaps an instance of metatheatrical humour, as *actus* can mean both generic 'action' and 'act' (in a play) and III is indeed the penultimate act. But for Matthias and Thomas, to whom the statement applies (*utrique*: 1256), III is actually the final act, since they are going to be killed at its end.

Nunc tu, pudicae mentis inspector deus,   1260
coram labores aspice, et praesens ades.

III.4

Matthias, Saphioa.
Matthias: Sed quis loquenti sese obviam praestat mihi
ora referens amore laetiora? Quid
struat, quid intendat, facile coniecero.
Dux magne, salve! *Saphioa*: Vos salvete, nobiles.   1265
Accede, frater, propius, amplexum cape,
habeto amoris osculum pignus mei.
Subite tectum, genio conseremus hunc
diem; Falerni pocula mensam pervolent
et vos, periti musices plausum date.   1270
Favete nostro gaudio cantu, lyra;
hilaritas sit hodie atque delectatio.

III.5

Saphioia, Thomas, famulus, 2 milites.
Saphioia: Animose caede, occide, caede, percute,
occide Thomam, percute, obtrunca, feri!
Thomas: Occidimus, occidimus! *Famulus*: Mea ut praecordia 1275
transfigit ille clamor! *Saphioia*: Invade, irrue!
Iendonico squaleant sanguine nostrae dapes!

1262–72 III.4. In this short scene, Safioye comes to meet Matthias and Thomas, who are fully aware of the nefarious plot, and invites them to the murderous feast. Two virtually identical versions of the scene are found in A^6 and B. In B, the stage direction *canitur* follows 1272, perhaps indicating that some music or song took place here to mark the beginning of (what turns out to be murderous) feasting. The metre is the usual senarius. 1262 is metrically problematic.

1273–80 III.5. Another short scene in which Thomas is killed during a feast. Given the minimalist nature of the dialogue, it is likely that the murder scene

Now, God, you who know chaste minds well,   1260
look at our labours taking place before you, and come, be present.

III.4

Matthias, Safioye.
Matthias: [*Seeing Safioye approaching*] But as I am speaking, who
     comes to meet me
with a face lit up with love? I would have easily guessed
what he plans and what he intends.
Hello, great leader! *Safioye*: Hello, you noblemen.   1265
Come closer, brother, let me embrace you, [*Embracing and kissing Matthias*]
and take my kiss as a sign of my love.
Come into the house, we will spend this day together
in conviviality; let cups of Falernian wine fly about over the table,
and you, connoisseurs of music, do give applause.   1270
Add to our joy with song and lyre;
let there be laughter and rejoicing today. [*All go inside a house*]

III.5

Safioye, Thomas, servant, 2 soldiers.
Safioye: [*From inside the house*] Slaughter bravely, kill, slaughter, strike,
kill Thomas, strike, lop off, slash!
Thomas: [*From inside the house*] We are dead, we are dead! *Servant*:
     [*Standing outside the house*] How that shouting pierces through   1275
my heart! *Safioye*: Assault, attack!
Let our feast turn squalid with the blood of the Yendonos!

---

was not acted out but hinted at by the clamour coming from behind the
façade, to which the servant in 1275–6 seems to be reacting on stage. The
murder of Matthias is not represented in our manuscripts at all (cf. note to
IV.1), but presumably was understood to take place in a manner similar to
Thomas's. Safioye is shown here being present and giving orders during
Thomas's murder, an arrangement which contradicts his later asking the
soldiers how he died (see note to 1347).

   Like the previous one, this scene is found in two nearly identical versions
in A^6 and B and concludes the act in both. The metre is the usual senarius.
1279 is metrically problematic.

Miles 1: Io, Io, cecidit, cecidit perfidus! *Miles 2*: Io,
tollere gentem ita perfidam est datum mihi!
Miles 1: Sic, sic pereat omnis, quisquis temnit Xacam!   1280

III.Chorus

Ecclesia, alii.
Ecclesia: O lux principibus sperata diu!
1: O luce dies gratior omni!
Mittant oculi fundere fletus;
miscere iuvat gaudia gaudiis.
2: O lux nobilibus funesta nimis!   1285
O lux tenebris tristior omni!
Largos fundant oculi fletus;
miscere iuvat lacrimas lacrimis.
3: Quis enim digne deflere queat?
Squalet gentis gloria nostrae;   1290
lugeat aether, lugeat orbis,
lugeat Arima funera tanta!
4: Quis enim digne gaudere queat?
Fulget gentis gloria nostrae;
gaudeat aether, gaudeat orbis,   1295
Arima laudet sidera tanta!
1: Gaudeat aether, gaudeat orbis,
2: Lugeat aether, lugeat orbis,
3: Arima laudet Feibioium genus,
4: Arima plangat Feibioium genus,   1300
1: totaque plangat Iaponum tellus!
2: totaque laudet Iaponum tellus!

1281–1304 III.Chorus. The church and several others (possibly arranged
into choral groups) alternately rejoice and mourn over the fate of the martyrs.
It is a mixed chorus in which divinely inspired voices express joy at the
outcome of the drama, while their pagan and earthly counterparts are
saddened and dismayed over the same event.

The lines are preserved in A^6 and *B*. A^6 identifies it as *CHORVS IV* and
places it after the epilogues. *B* identifies it as *Chorus actus 3tii* and places it at
the very end of the manuscript together with the choruses of the other acts.
The content of this chorus is of such a generic nature that it could conceivably

Soldier 1: Hurrah, hurrah, he fell, the traitor fell! *Soldier 2*: Hurrah,
I was permitted to destroy such a treasonous lineage!
Soldier 1: Thus, thus may all those who despise Shaka perish!　　　　1280

III.Chorus

Church, others.
Church: O light, long hoped for by the princes!
1: O day, more grateful than every light!
Let eyes forget to shed tears;
　　　it is good to mix joy with joy.
2: O light, so inauspicious to the nobles!　　　　　　　　　　1285
O light, sadder than shadows to all!
Let eyes shed abundant tears;
　　　it is good to mix tears with tears.
3: For who can mourn worthily?
The glory of our nation lies squalid;　　　　　　　　　　　　1290
let the sky mourn, let the world mourn,
　　　let Arima mourn such great deaths!
4: For who can rejoice worthily?
The glory of our nation shines;
let the sky rejoice, let the world rejoice,　　　　　　　　　　1295
　　　let Arima praise such great stars!
1: Let the sky rejoice, let the world rejoice,
2: Let the sky mourn, let the world mourn,
3: Let Arima praise the lineage of Feibyoe,
4: Let Arima mourn the lineage of Feibyoe,　　　　　　　　　1300
1: and let all the land of Japan mourn them!
2: and let all the land of Japan praise them!

---

be for IV (after the death not only of Thomas and Matthias but also of
Thomas's children); but here I provisionally follow the placement of *B*.

　　The metre is anapestic dimeter. The initial *O* in 1281 and 1285 are
metrically redundant.

1299–1300 Both lines end with *Feibioium genus* in *A⁶* but *B* has *Iendonium
genus* written above *nobiles martyres*. For *Feibioium* and *Iendonium* see notes
to 281 and 1488.

3: gaudeat aether, gaudeat orbis!
4: lugeat aether, lugeat orbis!

IV.1

4 famuli Thomae et Matthiae.

Famulus 1: Sol, qui per alti fervidas caeli plagas   1305
flammas micantes fervidus radio explicas,
quam malum iniquo et adverso omine
terris coruscum lumen ostendis tuum?
Famulus 2: Non fugis et atris splendidum tuum caput
involvis umbris? Cernere haec oculis potes   1310
patiens apertis scelera nec vultus tegis?
En, immerentes hospites hospes necat
flammatus ira, interque festivas dapes
crudele atroci stringitur ferrum manu,
mutatur ense patera, mugitu horrido   1315
maestoque tota contremit planctu domus
stupefacta. Saphioiae diras hospitis
in hospites innoxios fraudes, dolos
natura damnat ipsa, cunctarum parens
altrixque rerum assueta iam tot cladibus   1320
invita tantum sustinet tellus nefas.
Famulus 3: Haec ultionis saepe quaesitae dies,
O proditor Saphioia? Numquam ultio est,
nisi inter epulas, foederis pignus sacri?
Horrore quatior, artubus totis tremo.   1325
Vix credo in hominem cadere tantum nefas,
ut quis homini, quam non dedit, per vim auferat
rapiatque vitam, quam semel raptam, nequit
revocare ab Orco et reddere aethereis plagis.
Famulus 4: Quis nos per avias et liquidi poli vias   1330

1305–34 IV.1. Four servants of Thomas and Matthias are represented speaking about Safioye's dastardly offence against hospitality. They decide to go off and report the crime to Thomas's children.

3: let the sky rejoice, let the world rejoice!
4: let the sky mourn, let the world mourn!

IV.1

4 servants of Thomas and Matthias.
Servant 1: O sun, who through the high regions of fervid heaven   1305
spread out your flashing flames, fervid with rays,
what an evil scintillating light, with an inequitable
and adverse omen, do you show to the earth!
Servant 2: Do you not flee and hide your shining head
in black shadows? Are you capable of seeing these crimes   1310
patiently, with eyes open, and not cover your face?
Look, a host kills innocent guests,
a host inflamed with anger, and in the midst of festive dishes,
the cruel sword is drawn by the deadly hand,
the cup is exchanged for the blade, and at the horrid   1315
and grievous groans, the astonished house trembles
in mourning. The atrocious trickery of Safioye,
the host, against innocent guests, and his trap
are condemned by nature itself, and the parent and caretaker
of all things, earth, who is accustomed already to so many   1320
calamities, puts up with such a nefarious crime unwillingly.
Servant 3: Was this the day of your oft-sought revenge,
O Safioye, you traitor! Does it not count as revenge to you,
unless you act it out in a feast, an occasion for sacred truce?
I am shaken with terror, I tremble in all my limbs.   1325
I can hardly believe that such a great crime can come upon a person,
so that any one would take away and rob life, which one did not give,
   from another
human, which, having been once robbed, no one can
recall from the underworld and restore to the light of day.
Servant 4: What storm will carry us through trackless ways   1330

The scene is found in *A*[6] and *B* with no substantial difference. Both identify
the scene as IV.1. The scene is in senarius, with two metrically problematic
lines (1307, 1326).

1325 See note to 1219.

procella saevis ocior ventis feret?
Fugiamus hinc, quocumque satis est, si modo
fugiamus atri conscias sceleris domos,
natisque nuntiemus tam dirum scelus.

IV.2

Saphioia, 2 milites.
Saphioia: Iam, iam iuvat vixisse, iam votis meis   1335
superior adsum, parta iam, parta ultio est!
Iam sat furori est, iam sat est etiam mihi.
Hucusque lenta per biennalem moram
vindicta crevit et tulit tantum malum.
Vindicta non est sera, quando sic venit,   1340
sed paenitebit forte, paeniteat volo;
en, paenitet fecisse sed factum iuvat,
quod nullus immutabit in melius dies.
Sic odia pono. Nequis invictos asperet
deos Daifu, gens haec exemplum dedit.   1345

1335–59 IV.2. Safioye exults over the murder which he had long planned, and his elation increases upon hearing from the soldiers that Thomas breathed his last in great and prolonged agony (though he should have witnessed Thomas's death himself; cf. 1347 with III.5). One of the soldiers asks what should be done with the sons, and Safioye replies that they are to be killed if they refuse to abandon Christianity, but that the final decision rests with Daifu.

The text here is found in two nearly identical versions in A^6 and *B*. The metre is senarius. Metrically problematic lines are 1344, 1346 (cf. 1484), 1352, and 1355.

1336 *parta ... est*: The entire phrase copies Sen. *Medea* 25, where the title character ruminates on possible ways to hurt her husband Jason.

1337 *iam ... mihi*: Another Senecan tag, this time copied from *Thyestes* 889, where Atreus triumphantly reminds himself that he has killed his hated brother Thyestes's sons.

of limpid heaven, more swift than savage winds?
Let us flee from here, wherever there may be enough distance
to escape the house that was party to the atrocious crime
and let us announce this dire deed to the children. [*The servants run
   off stage*]

IV.2

Safioye, 2 soldiers.
Safioye: [*Coming out of the house*] Now, now I am glad to have lived,
   now I have more than   1335
what I prayed for, now my revenge has been done, done!
Now my rage is satisfied, now even I am satisfied.
Up to this point, through a two-year interval
my vengeance has grown and resulted in such a great crime.
Vengeance is not slow, when it comes in this way,   1340
but perhaps I will regret it, I wish I regretted it;
look, I regret that it is over, but the accomplished deed gives me joy,
which no day will change for the better.
But I make an end to my enmity. Lest anyone should provoke the
   invincible
gods of Daifu, this clan has provided an example.   1345

1338 *biennalem moram*: The two-year delay mentioned here may refer
loosely to the long-standing trap that Safioye weaved patiently (according to
the Jesuits) against the young dynast Naozumi in order to annex his territory
(see Trigault 1623: 119–21, cf. Introduction 2.1), or to the multiple summons
and threats that had been issued by the authorities to Thomas and Matthias
over at least two years (see Trigault 1623: 123–4), or a combination of both.

1340 The first half of this line is lifted from Stefonius *Flavia* 1170, where
John the Apostle (*c.* 6–100) warns the pagan philosopher Apollonius of Tyana
of the slow but sure vengeance of God. *quae tandem venit* in the original is
changed here to *quando sic venit*.

1344 *Sic . . . pono*: The words echo Sen. *Thyestes* 1025 (*Sic odia ponis?*), where
the title character addresses his triumphant brother after the latter's
unspeakable act of revenge.

1345 *Daifu*: Here genitive; cf. note to 186.

Adeste, properate, fida famulantum cohors!
Ubi Thomas efferus? *Miles 1*: In domo truncus iacet,
cum fratre debitas scelerum poenas luens.
Saphioia: Anne una taetrum spiritum plaga expulit?
Miles 2: Non, sed tenacem et diu reluctantem egredi   1350
per frusta tandem corde transfosso impiam
vitam revellit vulnus. *Saphioia*: Hoc deerat adhuc
plenae ultioni, hoc gaudio cumulum facit,
periisse misere perfidos. *Miles 1*: Sed filii
superstitesne vivent? *Saphioia*: Ambo cadent,   1355
ni supplices tendant nostris palmas diis.
Sed ista Caesari divo committimus;
vos excubantes socios petite milites
fortique dextera divos defendite.

IV.3

Iacobus, Iustus, famuli 3, angelus.
Iacobus: Miserande genitor! *Iustus*: O pater! *Iacobus*: Pater, O pater!   1360
Iustus: Ah occidis tali fato, mi, mi pater!
Iacobus: Iam iam cruento sanguine piae fluant
per ora lacrimae et dextera vellat comas!
Iustus: Haec festa, perfide, convivia, Saphioia?
Haec ego videre, haec debeo natus pati?   1365
Iacobus: O caelum, O astra, O crimina, O scelera, O nefas!
Heu, fata Christiadum talia, numen, vides?
Famulus 1: Miserande iuvenis, tristium mentem obrutam
pelago dolorum exsuscita ac nimiis modum

1360–90 IV.3. Iacobus and Iustus lament the death of their father while two servants try to soothe them. An angel brings spiritual consolation to the weeping boys with a reminder that great rewards await martyrs. A servant comes to tell the youngsters that their mourning mother is summoning them, and they exit the stage.

Come, hurry, faithful attendants!
Where is savage Thomas? *Soldier 1*: [*Coming out of the house*] He lies
    inside the house, cut down,
Having suffered the penalty that he deserved for his crime, together
    with his brother.
Safioye: Did a single wound drive out his unholy spirit?
Soldier 2: No, but his life was tenacious and resisted going out for a
    long time; 1350
and after his heart was pierced, little by little, at last his impious spirit
was finally wrenched away through the wound. *Safioye*: This was the
    last missing piece
for my full revenge, this is the summit of my joy,
the fact that the traitors perished miserably. *Soldier 1*: But
    shall the sons
survive and be kept alive? *Safioye*: Both shall fall, 1355
unless they stretch out their hands as supplicants to our gods.
But we will entrust this issue to our divine king;
you, seek out your fellow soldiers who are standing guard
and defend the gods with your mighty arms.

IV.3

Iacobus, Iustus, 3 servants, angel.
Iacobus: Poor father! *Iustus*: O father! *Iacobus*: Father, O father! 1360
Iustus: Ah, you die by such a fate, my father, my father!
Iacobus: Now, now, let pious tears for the cruel
bloodshed flow across my face and let my hand tear out my hair!
Iustus: Was this the convivial feast, you traitor, Safioye?
Must I see this, must I as a son suffer this? 1365
Iacobus: O heavens, O stars, O crime, O evil deed, O unspeakable deed!
Alas, God, do you see these sufferings of Christians?
Servant 1: Poor young man, raise up your mind which has been
buried under a sea of painful grief, put a limit on your excessive

---

Two nearly identical versions of the text are found in A^6 and B, where they
are both identified as IV.3. The metre is in senarius, except for the angel's
pronouncement in dactylic hexametre (1380–3; lifted from Caussin, see
note). Metrically problematic lines are 1362, 1363, 1374, 1379, and 1390
(*versus mancus*).

impone lacrimis et manu frenum attrahe   1370
animoque forti turbidum pectus doma!
Iustus: Meum paternus pectus occludit dolor
maestique verbis transitum gemitus negant.
Famulus 2: Estote fortes, iuvat afflictos deus.
Iustus: Ah, ah, pater mi, da tuis tecum mori!   1375
Iacobus: Te flere iniquum est, non flere est durissimum;
ah, quis mihi dabit causa pro numinis
tecum mori? Sine te nolo vivere, volo
mori! *Iustus*: Tu nunc mihi pater et mater, O Iesu, eris!
Angelus: Pergite magnanimi iuvenes; vos inclyta caelo   1380
palma manet, sedes hic vobis fata quietas
ostendunt, texuntque piam per dura salutem
funera; sic crescit pulchro de vulnere virtus.
Iustus: Nostris benignus votis aspiret deus!
Iacobus: Per acerba, dura et aspera invicto pede   1385
deum sequamur; haud molli virtus via
rosisque strata ad caelitum ducit domos.
Sudoribus caelum emitur et doloribus.
Iustus: Ita est! *Famulus 3*: Parens vos advocat maestissima.
Iacobus: Praei, sequemur.   1390

IV.4

Daifu, Saphioia.
Daifu: Quem di supremis imperii rebus ducem
nuper locarunt, civium et patriae patrem,
partes in omnes semper intentum addecet

1380–3 These dactylic lines are lifted from F 234, where an angel consoles
the children of the title character before their martyrdom. *sedes . . . ostendunt*
(1380-1) also recalls Virg. *Aen.* 1.205–6 (*sedes ubi fata quietas/ostendunt*),
where Aeneas soothes his followers with the hope of the promised land.

1391–1425 IV.4. Daifu justifies his actions against Thomas and Matthias by
citing his need to defend the law of the land without partiality, though he

tears, pull in the rein with you hand   1370
and subdue your turbulent heart with a stout mind!
Iustus: Grief for my father blocks up my heart
and my grievous groans deny passage to words.
Servant 2: Be strong, God helps the afflicted too.
Iustus: Ah, ah, my father, grant that your family may die with you!   1375
Iacobus: It is wrong to weep over you, but it is most difficult not to weep;
ah, who will allow me to die with you
for the cause of God? I do not wish to live without you, I want
to die! *Iustus*: You will now be my father and mother, O Jesus!
Angel: [*Appearing above*] Go on, magnanimous young men; the
        renowned victory-palm   1380
awaits you in heaven, the fates display for you quiet stations
here, and they fashion pious salvation through harsh
deaths; virtue thus grows out of a beautiful wound.
Iustus: May God kindly favour our wish!
Iacobus: Through rough, harsh and rocky trials let us follow God   1385
with our invincible footsteps; virtue leads us to the home of heavenly
        beings
through a path that is not at all easy, nor strewn with roses.
Heaven is won by sweat and pain.
Iustus: Yes! *Servant 3*: [*Entering stage*] Your most mournful mother
        summons you.
Iacobus: Go ahead, we will follow. [*They all leave stage*]   1390

IV.4

Daifu, Safioye.
Daifu: The one, whom the gods recently placed on the summit
of imperial command as the father of citizens and of fatherland,
must apply his care always in every direction

---

grants that if he were a private person he might have preferred not to proceed
in such a draconian fashion. When Safioye reminds him that something must
be done with Thomas's children, Daifu expresses his hope that they can be
persuaded to abandon their paternal obstinacy and be allowed to live and
continue the family line. While they wait for the children to appear, Safioye
cites their mother's strict religious education as a possible obstacle to Daifu's
planned tactic, but the latter remains hopeful that the children would relent.

versare curas; temere ut attentet nihil
animus, in alios asper, in quosdam levis.   1395
Aequalis esse quisquis in cives potest,
hunc esse summum civium merito decet.
Si mihi liceret arbitrio curas meas
componere et, quo vela, quo venti ferunt
dirigere cursum, teste nec mundo ac Xaca,   1400
domum, fidem, consilia, mores, vel genus
Iendonii palam probarem forsitan;
impune iuvenes possent protervi suo
parere Christo. Nunc alia regni mihi
tenenda ratio; nostra praestanda est fides,   1405
praestanda vita. Lege nunc peccat mea,
ubique quicquid peccat imperium meum.
Proinde ne, me rege, permissum scelus
putet esse quisquam, regis oppositu nefas
arcebo. Sit quodcumque cuiusvis, ubi   1410
libet; una iuris aequitas par omnibus.
Saphioa: Auguste, sensit hoc hodie gens perfida
Iendoniorum, ferro persolvit fides.
Sed tulit Thomas progeniem vitiosiorem.
Daifu: Malum ovum mali corvi.   1415

A⁶ and *B* have the scene in two nearly identical versions but only *B* has 1421. In *A⁶* the scene continues without a break into IV.5 and is labelled *scaena 5ta & 6ta*, while *B* labels it as in our edition. The scene is in the usual senarius; 1414, 1415 (*versus mancus*), 1422, and 1424 are metrically problematic.

1391–1411 This nuanced speech by Daifu in which he shows himself to be a moderate at heart is mostly cobbled together from the words of Constantine that open the final act of *C*, where he addresses his son and title character whom he falsely believes to be plotting against him and with utmost reluctance prepares to hand out the death sentence. The correspondences, sometimes exact and sometimes approximate, are as follows: *Quem praesidere rebus humanis deus/iussit et ad arces civium accersit salus* (*C* V.1-2)→*Quem di supremis imperii rebus ducem/nuper locarunt, civium et patriae patrem* (1391–2); *partes ... curas* (*C* V.3-4)=*partes ... curas* (1393–4); *temere decernat nihil/anulus, in alios ... levis* (*C* V.13-14)→*temere ut attentet nihil/animus, in alios ... levis* (1394–5); *Aequalis ... decet* (*C* V.7-8)=*Aequalis ... decet* (1396–7); *Si mihi ... mundo, domum/consilia, mores et fidem et vitam et genus/Romae*

with diligence; so that his mind would attempt nothing
heedlessly, being harsh to some, but lenient toward others.   1395
Whoever can be equitable to citizens,
that one deservedly ought to be the greatest of the citizens.
If I could conduct my affairs using my own
judgement and steer my ways where the sails
and the winds carry, and the world and Shaka were not my witnesses, 1400
perhaps I could openly approve of the lineage, faith,
plans, character, or family of the Yendonos;
the wilful young men could without penalty obey
their own Christ. Now I need to apply a different manner of thought
to my kingdom; I have to maintain my faith   1405
and must preserve my life. That trespass is committed under my law,
if any trespass is committed anywhere against my command.
Accordingly, lest anyone think that a transgression is permitted
under me as king, I shall keep the wrongdoing in check
with regal intervention. Whatever belongs to anyone, let it be as   1410
it pleases; the justice of law alone must be equal to all.
Safioye: August king, the treasonous lineage of the Yendonos sensed this
today; their religion paid its due to our sword.
But Thomas brought forth a more vicious progeny.
Daifu: Bad egg from a bad crow.   1415

---

probarem, iuvenis infelxi, quaeas/uti licenter moribus quondam tuis; (*C* V.23-
28)→*Si mihi ... mundo ac Xaca,/domum, fidem, consilia, mores, vel
genus/Iendonii* (cf. note to 281) *palam probarem forsitan;/impune iuvenes
possent protervi suo/parere Christo* (1390–1404); *Nunc alia regni ratio. Nunc
tecti nihil,/exposita cuncta, nostra praestanda ... peccat humanum genus* (*C*
V.35-8)→*Nunc alia regni mihi/tenenda ratio; nostra praestanda ... peccat
imperium meum* (1404-7); *decet esse, ne me rege ... quisquam. Regis ... arcebo,
sit ... libet. Una ... omnibus* (*C* V.53-6)→*Proinde ne, me rege, ... quisquam,
regis ... arcebo. Sit ... libet: una ... omnibus* (1408–11).

1414 For *Thomas* in *A⁶*, *B* erroneously has *Matthias*. *progeniem vitiosiorem* is
a Horatian tag from *Carm.* 3.6.48, a lament on the decline of morals in the
current generation.

1415 *Malum ovum mali corvi* is a common proverb since antiquity and
popular among humanists; see e.g. Erasmus 1703: 343–4. In the right margin
of *B* is the stage direction *abit quidam vocatum*, indicating that a minion
leaves the stage to summon the boys.

Ducantur huc coram; facile tenuis manu
flectetur arbos; vivat in natis parens.
Saphioa: Auguste Caesar, falleris; citius tigres,
ursos, leaenas flecteres, credo, prece
quam filios Iustae; Christum non auferes.   1420
Hos mater insana animat ad tantum scelus.
Daifu: O Iusta, Iusta, quid stulta actitas?
Cur parvulos perdis, quos aeternum potes
servare? Sed ferunt huc gradum parvuli;
Sermone blando mulcebo mentes – .

IV.5

Daifu, Iustus, 3 consiliarii, Iacobus.
                               Puer   1425
dilecte caelo, salve! Tu, Iustule, Xacam et
Amidam deos nosti? *Iustus*: Novi, Caesar, deum,
qui vasta caeli templa dextra condidit
et patria gestans sceptra regali manu,
innocuus ipse, crimen humanum expiat,   1430
ultima secutus, tractus ad saevam necem,
quem genitor olim coluit in terris meus;
molitor orbis Christus et caeli artifex.
Consiliarius 1: Ut fascinavit perditos matris furor!
Iacobe, tu patriis lita nostris diis!   1435
Quid immoraris? Adimple iussum Caesareum,
si vivere iuvat! Ne morere tam turpiter!
Miserere pueritiam tuam; attentus vide,

1425–83 IV.5. Daifu, together with three of his counsellors, attempts to soothe Iustus and Iacobus and persuade them to apostatize and live, but the two persist in their exemplary Catholic fortitude. The exasperated Daifu orders them in the end to be led away in chains and commands Safioye to execute them.

*A⁶*and *B* have virtually identical versions of the text. *B* identifies the scene as IV.5, while in *A⁶* it is written continuously from the previous scene. The metre is the usual senarius; metrically problematic lines are 1441, 1457, 1470.

Let them be brought here before me [*a messenger leaves to summon*
   the boys]; a tender tree will be bent
easily by the hand; let the parent live in his children.
Safioye: August king, you are deceived. You would sooner persuade
tigers, bears, and lionesses with your prayer, I believe,
than the sons of Iusta; you will not take their Christ away.   1420
Their raving mother urges them on toward this great crime.
Daifu: O Iusta, Iusta, what do you keep on stupidly doing?
Why do you destroy your little ones, whom you can keep
for eternity? [*Seeing Iustus and Iacobus approaching*] But the little
   ones are coming this way;
I will soothe their minds with kind words. –

IV.5

Daifu, Iustus, 3 counsellors, Iacobus.
                                   Boy   1425
beloved of heaven, greetings! Do you, little Iustus, know Shaka
and Amida, the gods? *Iustus*: I know, king, God
who created with his hand the vast temples of the sky
and holding his paternal sceptre in his regal hand,
expiates the crime of humankind, while being innocent himself,   1430
who underwent the extremes of fate, and was dragged off to savage murder,
whom my father once upon a time worshipped on earth;
Christ is the maker of the globe and of the world.
Counsellor 1: How has the madness of the mother enchanted the lost boys!
You, Iacobus, sacrifice to our paternal gods!   1435
Why do you delay? Fulfil the king's order,
if you want to live! Do not die so disgracefully!
Have pity on your own childhood; consider carefully

1429–32 *patria . . . necem* (1429–31) repeats Thomas's declaration of faith in
front of Daifu in 931–3, and shows Iustus to be a good pupil of parental
catechism (1432).

1437 So A[6], B has *Quid horruisti? Fac iussum Caesareum* which is metrically
inferior.

quonam ruas! *Daifu*: Thus offer, et vitam offero.
Iacobus: Quod tantopere mea te iuventus commovet,   1440
grates ago, misericordia haud utor.
Cum luce stabilem sancient umbrae fidem,
cum morte vita, flamma cum fluctu, prius
quam mortuis mutisque diis ego perlitem.
Non mihi iuventus, non opes, Caesar, tuae   1445
antiquiores Christo erunt meo, suo
qui nos cruore lactat et vitam dedit.
Daifu: Miserande iuvenis, sceptra quo reus trahis?
Tene ego trucidem? Fluctus incertum rapit,
iramque pietas, ira pietatem fugat.   1450
Sed, Iuste, tu quid? An fratrem libet sequi?
Eia age, puer, tenerae istiusmodi tuae
aetatulae stat parcere et benefacere.
tantum hoc agas, facillimum, levissimum;
lita Daibudo nostro et diis patriis!   1455
Iustus: Non hoc ab incunabulis mater mea,
non morte parens Thomas docuit sua.
Crudelis in patriam, in parentes impius,
ero sepultus, tale si admittam scelus.
Consiliarius 1: Audite, iuvenes, mittite hoc stolidum nefas,   1460
parete monitis; dulcis est vita et brevis.
In flore primaevo vitam cur funditis?
Iustus: Maturus aevi est, qui potest Christo mori.
Iacobus: Quicumque caelo nascitur, vixit satis.
Deo refundam, quam dedit vitam deus.   1465

1440–1 These two lines echo those in *E* (see Introduction 2.4) 535, where the title character, an aged martyr, is arguing with the persecutor Antiochus IV Epiphanes (215–164 BCE), with the following modifications: *te mea senectus→mea te iuventus* (1440); *eiusque causa velle dicis parcere→*omitted.

1444 *perlitem*: So *A⁶*, *B* has *litem* which is metrically inferior.

1449–50 *Fluctus . . . / . . . fugat*: Daifu's words echo those of Constantine as he wonders whether to execute his son or not in *C* V.245–6, with the initial *aestus* changed to *Fluctus* for the sake of metre. The lines also echo Medea's agonizing internal debate on whether to murder her children in Sen. *Med.* 939–44 (*anceps aestus incertam rapit; . . . ira pietatem fugat/iramque pietas*).

where you are headed to! *Daifu*: Offer the incense, and I offer you life.
Iacobus: For the fact that my young age moves you so much,   1440
I give you thanks, but I have no use for mercy.
Shadows will conclude an enduring peace with light,
life with death, and flame with waves, before
I make auspicious sacrifices to gods who are dead and deaf.
Neither my youth nor your riches, king,   1445
shall be more precious than my Christ, who
nurtures us with his blood and has given us life.
Daifu: Pitiable young man, to what extent are you, as a defendant,
    provoking my sceptre?
Should I strike you down? A wave is dragging me, as I am undecided,
and affection drives away anger, anger, affection.   1450
But Iustus, what do you say? Do you want to follow your brother?
Come now, boy, it is my decision to pardon your young age,
so tender, and to treat it well.
Just do this, this easiest and tiniest thing;
sacrifice to our Daibutsu and our paternal gods!   1455
Iustus: My mother did not teach this from our infancy
nor our father Thomas with his death.
I will end up having been cruel against my fatherland
and impious against my parents, if I should commit such an offence.
Counsellor 1: Listen to me, young men, let go of this stupid crime   1460
and listen to our advice; life is sweet and short.
Why do you waste your lives in the flower of youth?
Iustus: The one who can die for Christ is old enough.
Iacobus: Whoever is born for heaven has lived enough.
I shall give God back my life which he has given me.   1465

1457 *Thomas*: So *A⁶*, *B* erroneously has *Matthias*.

1459 *scelus*: So *B*, *A⁶* has *nefas*, with little difference in meaning or metre.

1460 *stolidum*: So *B*, *A⁶* has *solidum*, but *B* makes better sense.

1463–4 These two lines copy those spoken by Ianuarius, a young martyr, to a Roman judge in *F* 243. See also Introduction 2.4.

1465 This line recombines what is divided into two lines in *F* 242 in Ianuarius's statement to the Roman judge (*quam dedit vitam deus/deo refundam*).

Consiliarius 2: Depone iuvenilem proterviam, miser!
Ridere supplicia potes cum haud sentias;
cum senseris, tum cantilenam aliam canes.
Non tu ex chalybe, non ex silice compositus es.
Consiliarius 3: Patientia regis non abutere, si sapis;   1470
demitte Christum, et tempori expergiscere!
Iacobus: Non dormio, sed omnem in deo fiduciam
vigilans repono. Christe, regnorum metus,
tibi vivo, tibi morior, tibi uni servio!
Iustus: Nihil agis; ad omne me offero mortis genus.   1475
Daifu: Etiamne nobis parvus insultet puer?
Quid ais, nefande? Hocne voluit mea lenitas?
An quia ego placidus, tu ferox es factus? Huc,
huc, milites, adeste, constringite scelus
in compedes, in carcerem retrudite!   1480
Iustus: O sancta vincula, suaviter vos osculor!
Iacobus: Dulces catenae! *Daifu*: Tu, Saphioia, verticem
ferro revellas impiis! *Saphioia*: Ut tu iubes – .

IV.6

Saphioia, 4 milites, Iacobus, Iustus, lictor.
Bene habet, peractum est, divos defendi meos;
haec una lux iuvenes protervos auferet.   1485
Adesto, propera, fida famulantum cohors!

1467–9 The lines copy those of *E* 537, where a torturer threatens the title character in vain.

1470 See note to 983.

1481 *osculor*: So *B*, *exosculor* in *A*⁶ which is metrically inferior.

1484–1545 IV.6. Safioye, together with four soldiers, leads Iacobus and Iustus to their execution. Before striking the final blow, the persecutors try for one last time to force them to apostatize but fail; with the result that Iacobus

Counsellor 2: Poor fellow, put away your youthful impudence!
You can laugh at the punishment when you have not felt it at all;
when you have felt it, then you will sing another song.
You are not made of steel or stone.
Counsellor 3: If you are wise, do not abuse the patience of your king;   1470
put Christ away and wake up to the times!
Iacobus: I am not asleep, but am wide awake and place
all my trust in God. Christ, fear of the realms,
I live for you, I die for you, I serve you alone!
Iustus: You are wasting your time; I offer myself up to all kinds of death.
    1475
Daifu: Should the small boy continue to insult us?
What do you say, criminal? Did my leniency call for this?
Or, because I have been gentle, you have become aggressive? *[Calling
on the soldiers]* Here,
here, soldiers, come, bind these wrongdoers
in shackles and throw them into prison!   1480
Iustus: [*While he is being bound in chains*] O sacred fetters, I kiss you
with love!
Iacobus: Sweet chains! [*The soldiers leave with Iustus and Iacobus in
chains*] *Daifu*: You, Safioye, chop off
the heads of the impious ones with the sword! *Safioye*: As you
command. – [*Daifu and the counsellors leave*]

IV.6

Safioye, 4 soldiers, Iacobus, Iustus, executioner.
This is good, now it is finished, I have defended my gods;
this single day will get rid of the impudent young men.   1485
Come, hurry, faithful attendants!

---

and then Iustus are decapitated. From the surviving script and stage directions
it seems that their execution was acted out (presumably with the use of
appropriate props).

The text is found here in two virtually identical versions in A^6 and B, except
that only B has 1523. *B* identifies the scene as IV.6 and A^6 as IV.7. The metre
is the usual senarius except for 1503 on which see note. Metrically problematic
lines are 1509, 1519, 1538 (see note), 1540–4 (adapted from a prose source,
see note), 1545 (*versus mancus*).

Milites: Tui sumus, nos utere atque abutere!
Saphioia: Adducite huc Feibioicum ducum genus!
Caeleste testor numen et avorum sacra,
vos, astra, testor, vosque, dominorum metus,   1490
qui regna terrae, regna qui caeli manu
torquetis aequa, dii deaeque, gratiae
omnem futurae obsaepiam iratus viam!
De stirpe sed fert huc gradum durum genus.
Agedum efferatam pone iam mentem, puer,   1495
et disce tandem regis imperia pati!
Iacobus: Infracta virtus non pedem retrahit retro.
Miles 1: Cogere. *Iacobus*: Cogi qui potest, nescit mori.
Miles 2: Iuvenem stolidiorem esse vix quemquam reor.
Miles 3: Puerile, vitam tam gravi perdere malo.   1500
Iacobus: Virile, vitam tam levi capere bono.
Miles 4: Orbari amico Caesare nonne miserrimum est?
Iacobus: Orbare seipsum deo nonne est miserius?
Saphioia: Furentis est, spontaneam ruere in necem.
Iustus: Sapientis est, in astra sic conscendere.   1505
Saphioia: Ergone mea monita nihil apud vos valent?
Iacobus: Nihil. Dei quoniam valet vox omnia.
Saphioia: Bullata dicta iam crepare desines!
I, lictor, expedito ferrum; cervix cadat!
Lictor: Abominandum divis, huc prodi, caput!   1510
Propera, scelus, Xacae temptor! Propera, ducis

1488 *Feibioicum*: B has *Iendonicum* here and A⁶ has *Feibioicum* above
Iendonicum. *Feibioicum* comes from *Feibioye*, the early modern transliteration
of Thomas's personal name Heibyōe (see Introduction 2.1). See also note
to 281.

1490–2 Safioye's address to the gods echoes Constantine's call on God before
giving the death sentence to his son in *C* V.63–5, with the following
modifications: *haec astra testor, teque* (V.64)→*vos ... vosque* (1490); *caeli
moves,/arbiter et aequa cuncta moderaris manu* (V.64-5)→*caeli manu/torquetis
aequa, di deaeque, gratiae* (1491–2).

Soldiers: [*Coming on stage*] We are yours; use us and abuse us!
Safioye: Bring here the family of Feibyoe, the family of leaders! [*The soldiers leave again*]
I swear by the heavenly spirit, the spirits of my ancestors,
by you, I swear, O stars, and by you, whom our lords fear,   1490
you, who turn around with your equitable hands the realms of earth
and the realms of the sky, O gods and goddesses, that I shall
in my wrath block up every path of future pardon!
[*Seeing the soldiers bringing Iustus and Iacobus*] But the obstinate
    family of that lineage are coming their way here.
Come now, abandon at last your unbridled intention, boy,   1495
and learn in the end to endure the command of our king!
Iacobus: My unbroken strength does not step back.
Soldier 1: You will be forced to. *Iacobus*: Only someone who does not
    know how to die can be forced.
Soldier 2: I do not think that there is another youth more stupid.
Solider 3: It is childish to lose one's life in such a seriously evil way.   1500
Iacobus: It is manly to receive life in such an easy and good way.
Soldier 4: Is it not most miserable to be robbed of your king as your friend?
Iacobus: Is it not more miserable to rob yourself of God?
Safioye: It is a sign of madness to rush into spontaneous death.
Iustus: It is a sign of wisdom to climb into heaven in this way.   1505
Safioye: So is my advice worth nothing to you two?
Iacobus: Nothing. Because God's word is worth everything.
Safioye: It will be time now for you to stop playing around with your
    puerile proverbs!
Go, executioner, unleash your blade; let his head fall!
Executioner: Come forth here, you fellow, abominable to the gods!   1510
Hurry, you criminal contemptuous of Shaka! Hurry, the command

---

1498 The exchange copies that between Lycus, the king of Thebes, and Hercules's wife Megara in Sen. *Hercules Furens* 426.

1502 *nonne est miserius*: So B, A^6 has *nonne miserius est* which is metrically inferior.

1511 *temptor*: In the sense of *contemptor*. The noun *temptor* is not attested in classical Latin but was current in the humanistic variety in this sense, possibly due to the misreading of some mediaeval manuscripts (see Forcellini s.v.).

nos urget imperium! *Iacobus*: At dei me caritas.
Exuite, trahite, rapite, vellite, caedite,
ut lubet; Iesu propius accedam meo,
quo plus dolorum verberumque corpore   1515
excepero. *Saphioia*: Tu, miles, in turbam coi;
peltis, sarissis, bombardis iuvenes tene,
ne Christianorum rapiat eos furor.
Milites: Prompti sumus. *Iacobus*: O magne terrarum sator
caelique, Christe, iam, precor, tandem tibi   1520
adiunge Iacobum; nam quae mortis mihi
causa sit, et ipse cernis et caelum videt
aliquisque nostram conscius deflet vicem.
Sum Christianus, Christianus emori
amore tui amo. Perge, lictor, hoc tuae   1525
iugulum machaerae, spiritum addixi deo.
Maria, mater gratiae etc.
Saphioia: Dilecte caelo pariter et terris puer,
vides furore percitum fratrem tuum
solvisse crimen capite; tu melius sape!   1530
Iustus: Hoc, Saphioia, crimen est, ob quod reus
triumphet, astra gaudeant, ipsi incolae
Stygis tremescant, cuius accusans reo
placet, refellens displicet, cuius luit
quicumque poenam, computat lucri loco.   1535
Saphioia: Ah, flecte mentem, dum potes; serus dolor
manes sepultos urget! At lentus, puer,
occludis aures? Capite damnatus cede!

1522-3 *et ipse ... vicem*: These words copy those spoken by the falsely
accused Crispus to his father Constantine in *C* V.221-2.

1527 *Maria, mater gratiae* is the first line of a popular mediaeval Marian
quatrain, the rest being *mater misericordiae,/tu nos ab hoste protege/et hora
mortis suscipe*. The lines are mentioned on some occasions as deathbed
prayers; see e.g. Monte Simoncelli 1614: 4 and Jesuits 1604: 293. In the right
margin of *B* is the stage direction *decollatur*, suggesting that the beheading
was somehow shown on stage.

1531-4 These lines are a loose verse rendition of a prose passage from *H* (see
Introduction 2.4) 388 (*Hoc nempe crimen est ex quo reus gaudet, pallet iudex,*

of our leader urges us! *Iacobus*: God's love on the other hand urges me.
Strip, drag, snatch away, torment, and strike me
as you like; I will approach my Jesus all the closer,
the more pain and blows I receive   1515
upon my body. *Safioye*: You, soldiers, come together in formation;
keep the young men with your shields, swords, and guns,
lest the frenzied Christians snatch them away.
Soldiers: [*Coming together in a formation*] We are ready. *Iacobus*: O
   great founder of the lands
and of the skies, Christ, now at last, I pray, join your Iacobus   1520
to you; for you yourself see what the reason
for my death is, and heaven sees it
and some sympathetic person is weeping over our fate.
I am a Christian, and I long to die a Christian
in love for you. [*Stretches out his neck*] Go on, executioner, I have
   given over this,   1525
my neck, to your sword, and my spirit, to God.
Mary, mother of grace, etc. [*He is beheaded*]
Safioye: You, boy, beloved equally of heaven and of earth,
you see that your brother, incited by madness, has paid
the penalty with his life; you should be wiser!   1530
Iustus: This, Safioye, is the crime, on account of which the accused
would triumph, heaven would rejoice, and the very inhabitants
of hell tremble, of which the accuser does favour
to the defendant, and does a disfavour, if he denies it, and the one who pays
the penalty for it considers it to be for his own benefit.   1535
Safioye: Ah, change your mind while you can; regret comes
too late to those who lie buried! Yet, boy, you stubbornly
close your ears? Go away, condemned to death!

---

*caelum laetatur, terrentur daemones, contremiscunt inferi, cuius accusatio
votum est et poena felicitas*), where the title character and martyr is shown
arguing against his heretic father Liuvigild (*c.* 519–86).

1536–40 *Ah … aures*: This admonition of Safioye echoes one made by a
Roman judge to the martyr Ianuarius in *F* 241–2, with the following
modifications: *Adverte→Ah flecte* (1536); *At lentas ferus→At lentus, puer*
(1537).

1538 *cede*: So *A*⁶ and *B*; *cade* would fit both the sense and the metre better.

Iustus: Pro hac fide obire paratus sum, pro hoc numine
vel mille mortes oppetere non recuso;   1540
concide corpus, pelles lania, tot ora videbuntur
esse quot erunt guttae, et per sanguinis rivos
effusus spiritus, pupurata in caelum via
quamprimum evolabit. En, cervicem praebeo; feri!
Mater dei, iuva!   1545

Epilogus 1

Spectantium corona spectatissima,
finem putas fortasse, quod modo ultimus
finierit actus atque miserando exitu
cum filiis pater diem extremum egerit;
sed aliud est, quod Confluae nostrae inclyta   1550
iuventa anhelat, nempe honores publicos
et praemia eroganda doctioribus.
Agite ergo, ferte parvulam, sultis, moram,
dum nominatim doctiores proferam.
Nec dubito, vester grande conspectus dabit   1555
momentum honoribus hisce et adolescentiae
nostrae excitabit studia. Iam dixi satis.
Namque audio, immo cerno properantes foras

1539–44 *Pro . . . evolabit*: Like 1531–4, these lines attempt to render in verse
the prose passage spoken by the title character in *H* 388 (*Cuperem equidem
centies si liceret pro hac nominis gloria emori. Iam enim ad dei laudes
praedicandas unum os nimis angustum videtur; concide corpus, velle, lania, tot
ora videbuntur esse quot erunt vulnera, et per sanguinis rivos effusus spiritus
purpurata in caelum via quamprimum evolabit*) but are metrically less
successful.

1545 After the final words of prayer spoken by Iustus, the stage direction
plectitur is given in the right margin of *A*[6], suggesting that his execution too
was acted out on stage.

1546–62 Epilogue 1. A single actor delivers a humorous epilogue to the
effect that even though the play is over, there is one important business

Iustus: I am prepared to die for my faith, and for my God
I do not refuse to die even a thousand deaths;   1540
chop up my body, lacerate my skin, there will seem to be as many
    mouths
as there are droplets of blood, and my spirit, poured out
in rivers of blood, will fly off to heaven
on a red carpet. [*Stretching out his neck*] Look, I offer my neck; strike!
Help, mother of God! [*He is beheaded*]   1545

Epilogue 1

Most spectacular circle of spectators,
perhaps you think that this is the end, since the last act
just ended, and the father with his sons
saw the last light of day in a pitiable denouement;
but there is another thing, which the illustrious youth   1550
of our Koblenz are striving for, namely public honours
and prizes to be awarded to those who are most learned.
Come now, put up, please, with a very small delay,
while I introduce the names of the learned ones.
Nor do I doubt but that your presence will give   1555
great momentum to these honours and will incite
the zeal of our youth. Now I have said enough.
For I hear, or rather I see people rushing out

---

remaining, namely the distribution of prizes (*honores publicos/et praemia*: 1551–2). Annual plays in Jesuit schools were typically staged on so-called prize-days, when awards would be distributed to students who had distinguished themselves in specific subjects (see e.g. Yanitelli 1949: 140). The speaker mentions other actors leaving the theatre with prizes, says that he himself has waited for one in vain, and concludes his speech with a customary final request for kind judgement addressed to the audience.

The epilogue survives in both A^6 and *B*. Only the latter has 1558–62. The metre is senarius: 1562 is a *versus mancus*.

1550 *Confluae*: So A^6. This is presumably Koblenz for which the Latin names *Confluentes, Conbulantia, Confluencia, Confluens, Confluentes Rheni et Mosae, Confluentia, Cophelenci, Covelence* are known (see Plechl 1972: 563). *B* has *Cobringae*, which is not a known Latin geographic name.

cum praemiis; consisterem, si praemium
etiam mihi annuerent, sed annuunt nihil.   1560
Ergo valete; errata pueris parvulis,
viri graves, ignoscite.

Epilogus 2

Impulsa ventis lenibus per aequora
ad portuosum litus accessit ratis.
Portum tenemus, spectatores optimi,   1565
principibus faventibus,
martyribus annuentibus.
Cum fratre spectastis Thomam, Iaponum ducem,
inter dapes et gaudia exstinctam lucem,
cum matre spectastis filios pro fide acriter,   1570
pro caelitum numine cecidisse fortiter.
Quid amplius moramur?
Quid anxii iactamur?
En, vos martyrum laurea,
en, vos principum aurea   1575
expectat polo purpura.
En, praetulit facem,
adferet et pacem
Matthias invictus,
Thomas haud unquam victus,   1580

1563–1600 Epilogue 2. After a remark celebrating the conclusion of the play and a very brief (but not entirely accurate; cf. note to 1570) summary of the play, the singer or group of singers turn to an exhortation to piety after the example of the martyrs shown on stage. This epilogue concludes with the customary excuse for any errors made by the dramaturge or the actors and a final call for applause directed at the audience.

The first three lines of this prologue up to 1565 are in senarius, but the rest are in mostly rhyming verses (which were thus likely sung to the accompaniment of music). Otherwise they follow no clear metrical principle, accentual or quantitative. Tiny numbers written before some of the lines (*1* before 1576, *3* before 1577, *2* before 1581) may also be an indication of musical delivery.

with prizes; I would stay, if they give me
a prize, too, but they are giving me nothing.   1560
So, goodbye; please forgive the errors
of small boys, grave men.

Epilogue 2

Pushed on by gentle winds through the seas,
the raft has reached the hospitable shore.
We are now at the port, most noble spectators,   1565
with the support of princes,
with the approval of martyrs.
You have watched Thomas, the leader of the Japanese, together with his
    brother,
you have watched his life extinguished in the midst of the joys of festive
    table,
you have watched the sons keenly die for their faith with their mother,   1570
and bravely for the divine spirit of heavenly beings.
Why should we delay further?
Why do we tarry with anxiety?
Look, the laurel of martyrs,
look, the gilded purple of the princes   1575
await you all in heaven.
Look, invincible Matthias
preceded with his torch
and will also bring forth peace.
So will Thomas, who was never quite defeated,   1580

This epilogue is found only in *A⁶*, where it is marked *Epilogus 2us* and is
written immediately after Epilogue 1 (which is simply marked *Epilogus*).
From the manuscript it appears as though both were intended for delivery in
the present order (but perhaps without the last five lines of Epilogue 1, which
is found only in *B*).

1570 *cum matre*: Iusta, the mother of Iustus and Iacobus, is martyred neither
in this play nor in the original account of Trigault (see Introduction 2.1).
matre here may be a careless error for *patre* or may indicate that Iusta's death
was also part of the play in its planning stage.

martyrum decus et gloria.
Colite caeli numen,
petite fidei lumen,
ut caelesti sorte,
nec non felici morte,   1585
vos beent divum numina!
Nunc satis est, abunde est.
Agit poeta gratias,
grates ex corde maximas.
pro tam benigna   1590
omni laude digna
honoris et amoris tessera.
Si quid forte choragus
actorve erravit ignarus,
parcite!   1595
In oculis amoena,
si pia et sine poena,
si placuit Camoena
nec displicuit scena,
favete, avete, valete!   1600

the honour and glory of martyrs.
Worship the spirit of heaven,
seek the light of faith,
so that with a heavenly fate,
and also with a happy death,   1585
the spirits of those above might bless you!
Now this is enough, much has been done.
The student says thanks,
and gives the greatest gratitude from his heart,
for such a kind   1590
token of honour and love
that is worthy of every praise.
If the author in any way
or the actor in his ignorance erred,
please forgive!   1595
If the muse was comely to the eyes,
if she was pious and without blame,
if she was pleasing,
and if our staging did not displease,
applaud, be well, goodbye!   1600

Victor the Japanese: Latin Text

Prologus

Nautae Batavi multa de Victore falso iactantis fraude detecta litteris
   argumentum dramatis explicatur.
Nauta Batavus, Prologus.
Nauta: Mater beatum quidquid abscondit sinu
spatiosa tellus, quidquid aequorei vehunt
fluctus, videre cuncta contigit mihi
sorte invidenda. Classe lustravi vaga
quidquid latebat abditum. *Prologus*: Scaenae locum   5
quis fastuosis occupat clamoribus?
Nauta: Nihil videndum video; nisi iuvet rate
et iam nitentes siderum flammis vias
tentare et inter astra cursui meo
statuere metam. *Prologus*: Mira, nisi fallit, refert.   10
Exquirere libet. Optime vir, edic, quis es?
Nauta: Navita Batavus. *Prologus*: Dic, quibus ab oris solum
hoc attigisti? *Nauta*: Ab omnibus. *Prologus*: Quibus? *Nauta*: Omnibus.
Prologus: Omitte nugas; unde, sine ioco, venis?
Nauta: Venio undequaque. Crede, sunt verissima –   15

1–68 The play opens with a Dutch sailor's monologue who reminisces about
his recent voyage followed by the entry of the Prologus. From the ensuing
dialogue the audience learns that this is a play about Japanese Catholic
converts by the name of Victor and Andreas. As a subtext to the prologue one
may discern an attempt to shore up Jesuit authority (as opposed to that of the
Dutch East India Company) as purveyors of accurate knowledge of the
world, especially the Far East (see also Introduction 1.1 and 3.2).

The metre of the prologue (as well as in other scenes, unless otherwise
noted) is iambic trimetre except for lines 57–64 which are in prose. The
scenery presumably represents a shore or a port.

1 *abscondit sinu*: A Senecan tag (Sen. *Phaedra* 1205). Declamation on the
vastness of the ocean at the beginning of a tragedy is a classical *topos*; cf.

Victor the Japanese: Translation

Prologue

After the untrustworthiness of the Dutch sailor, who spews out many lies
  concerning Victor, is uncovered, the argument of the play is explained
  through an epistle.
Dutch sailor, Prologus.
Sailor: Whatever riches our wide mother earth hides in her bosom
and whatever floats on ocean waves,
it has been my good fortune to see them all
by my enviable luck. I have surveyed with my wandering fleet
whatever used to lie hidden. *Prologus:* [*Aside*] Who fills the stage   5
with his boastful shout?
Sailor: I do not see anything unless it is prohibited; unless it gives me
  pleasure
while I explore with my ship paths which shine with sidereal flames
and place the limit of my course
among the stars. *Prologus:* [*Aside*] He reports wondrous things, unless
  I am mistaken.   10
I want to ask. [*To the Sailor*] Good man! Tell me, who are you?
Sailor: A Dutch sailor. *Prologus:* Say, from which shores
do you come to this land? *Sailor:* From all shores. *Prologus:* Which?
  Sailor: All.
Prologus: Let go of your nonsense; jesting aside, where do you come from?
Sailor: I come from everywhere. Believe me; my words are most truthful. 15

Euripides *Medea* 1, Sen. *Phaedra* 85. The identity however of the speaker, a
contemporary Dutch sailor, presents a humorous contrast to this classical
touch.

7 *Nihil videndum video*: The Dutch sailor, like the typical Senecan hero-
villain, delights in breaking taboos which keep ordinary mortals in check (see
e.g. Gunderson 2015: 127–8).

12 *Navita Batavus*: From here on the Dutch sailor with his boastful tales of
questionable veracity becomes a combination of the braggart soldier of
ancient comedy (see e.g. Barsby 1999: 157, 264–5) and the lying traveller in
early European modern literature (see e.g. Eckert 2012: 14–16).

Prologus: figmenta. Sed age, quid rei hic loci geris?
Nauta: Quae rara mecum huc attuli, num salva sint,
cuncta explicare placuit hic. *Prologus*: Etiam mihi
expone. *Nauta*: Faxo, monstra conspicies nova.
En, quid recondit vitreus vasis sinus?   20
Prologus: Hic, credo, laticem continet. *Nauta*: Recte autumas.
Aenigma penitus solve; quem laticem putas?
Prologus: Conicere nequeo. *Nauta*: Si nequis prodam. Latex
e capite Nili est. *Prologus*: Fabula est – *Nauta*: verissima.
Quid hic reclusum? *Prologus*: Nil video. *Nauta*: Propius vitrum   25
bene intuere. *Prologus*: Nil video. *Nauta*: Necdum? *Prologus*: Nihil.
Nauta: Metuenda ratibus aura Typhonis latet
hic clausa. Credis? *Prologus*: Teste nil opus est, tuus
ventum latentem prodidit satis tumor.
Sed unde Typhon? *Nauta*: Quando Iaponum extimis   30
redux ab oris vela converti retro
et saevientis irruens aurae furor
agitavit aequor turbine et classem prope
gyro procella rapuit, e periculo
haec spolia retuli victor. *Prologus*: Hic nefarii   35
dolus patebit. Classe Iaponum quoque
terras obiisti? *Nauta*: O simplicis hominis caput!

18–19 *explicare ... expone*: A play on words. Both *explico* and *expono* can mean 'to put out in the open' (to sort out, dry etc.) as well as 'to explain' (see e.g. L&S s.v.).

24 *e capite Nili est*: The source of the Nile, imperfectly understood until the nineteenth to early twentieth century, was a favourite topic of controversy in classical and later Western cultures. The Spanish Jesuit Pedro Páez (1564–1622) may have been the first Western European to see Lake Tana, the source of the Blue Nile, and his testimony was first brought to the public's attention by the Jesuit polymath Athanasius Kircher (1602–80) in 1665 (see Kircher 1665: 72–3). This little detail may thus be seen as a triumphal display of the newest Jesuit geographical discovery of the day.

Prologue: They are lies. But come now; what are you doing here?
Sailor: So that I can check if the rare objects which I brought here are safe,
I decided to lay them all out here. *Prologus*: Explain what they are
to me, too. *Sailor*: You will indeed see strange portents.
[*Holds out a glass vial to the Prologus*] Look, what does the glassy
    bosom of this container hold?   20
Prologus: I think it contains a liquid. *Sailor*: You judge correctly.
Solve the riddle completely; what do you think the liquid is?
Prologus: I cannot guess. *Sailor*: If you cannot, I will say it: The liquid
is from the source of the Nile. *Prologus*: That is a tall tale! *Sailor*: A most
    truthful one.
[*Shows another vial*] What is contained here? *Prologus*: I see nothing.
    Sailor: Look more closely   25
at the glass. *Prologus*: I see nothing. *Sailor*: Not yet? *Prologus*: Nothing.
Sailor: The wind of Typhon, fearsome to ships, lies hidden,
shut up here. Do you believe it? *Prologus*: There is no need for any witness.
Your bloated self is enough sign of a hidden wind.
But where do you have the Typhon from? *Sailor*: From the place where,
    during my return from the farthest   30
shores of Japan, I turned my sails back,
and the furor of savage wind, rushing forth
stirred up the sea with its whirlwind, and the storm almost snatched away
the fleet with its gyration. But I survived and
took away these spoils out of the peril. *Prologus*: [*Aside*] Here, the trickery   35
of this nefarious one will be revealed. [*To the sailor*] Did you also visit
the lands of Japan with your fleet? *Sailor*: Oh you simpleton!

28–9 *Tuus/ventum latentem prodidit satis tumor*: A play on words, as *tumor*
here can refer both to the sailor's pot-belly and his bombastic speech. The
actor playing the sailor may have had a protruding stomach as part of the
stage costume, a common prop in classical comedy (see e.g. Csapo 2014: 56).
ventus here could also allude both to the sailor's boastful talk and flatulence
hinted at by the aforementioned prop (see L&S *ventus* and *ventosus* s.v.).

27–35 The Dutch sailor boasts that he brought the spirit of *Typhon* (typhoon,
attested with this meaning since antiquity; see e.g. Valerius Flaccus 3.130–2)
back from Japan. The idea that the sea around Japan is infested with typhoons
is commonplace (see e.g. Sacchini 1652: 201).

Me praeteriisse regna Iaponum putas?
Omitte dubia! *Prologus*: Quid geritur illic novi?
Nauta: A gente quidquid barbara geri potest.   40
Prologus: Ut Christianum nomen his terris viget?
Nauta: Non aliter optes, si queas. *Prologus*: Nihil movet
rex Taicosama turbinis? *Nauta*: Potius favet.
Prologus: Iam fraus liquescit. Andream nosti? *Nauta*: Andream?
Quis ille? *Prologus*: Nobilis vir, Ozacae incola.   45
Nauta: Describe. *Prologus*: Cuius est pater Victor senex.
Nauta: Utrumque novi. *Prologus*: Quid gerunt ambo? *Nauta*: Senem
tumulo propinquum morbus invasit gravis.
Prologus: Non erubescis, impudens doli artifex?
Nauta: Quid erubescam nescius fraudis malae?   50
Prologus: Linguam procacem! *Nauta*: Ficta si putas, proba;
aut ego refellam, quidquid obiectas probri.
Prologus: Vide, quid ista contineat epistola?
Nauta: Epistola? Unde? *Prologus*: Ex Iapone; legam, si placet
Nauta: Sine; longiores imminens iter moras   55
hic trahere prohibet. Abeo. *Prologus*: Siste! Quid fugis?
Nauta: Non fugio. *Prologus*: Siste, dum legam partem;
          Epistola
"His diebus Victor octogenarius senex neophytus
Christianus in pium errorem incidit. Saeviente enim

---

40 *A gente quidquid barbara*: The Dutch sailor seems dismissive of the
Japanese, unlike the Jesuits who often depicted them as exemplary believers;
see also Introduction 1.1 and 1.2.

43 *rex Taicosama*: This is the infamous Taicosama in Jesuit accounts, known
today as Toyotomi Hideyoshi (see Introduction 1.1). By the 1660s he had
long been dead and his dynasty dethroned.

44–6 *Andream nosti?...Cuius pater Victor senex*: The two main characters
and the setting of the following action are introduced here. For the characters'
historical identity see Introduction 3.1.

Do you think I neglected to visit the realms of Japan?
Have no doubt about that! *Prologus*: What new thing is happening there?
Sailor: Whatever can be done by a barbarous race.   40
Prologus: How strong is the Christian sect in these lands?
Sailor: In a way that even if you could, you would not wish otherwise.
   Prologus: King Taicosama
stirs up no storm? *Sailor*: Rather, he is favourable.
Prologus: Now the lie is becoming clearer. Do you know Andreas? *Sailor*:
   Andreas?
Which one? *Prologus*: The noble man, the inhabitant of Osaka.   45
Sailor: Describe him. *Prologus*: His father is Victor, the old man.
Sailor: I know them both. *Prologus*: How are they both doing? *Sailor*: A
   grave illness
has caught hold of the old man, and he is close to the grave.
Prologus: Are you not ashamed, you impudent artisan of trickery?
Sailor: Why should I be ashamed, unconscious as I am of malicious lies? 50
Prologus: What an insolent tongue you have! *Sailor*: If you think I
   am lying, prove it;
or I will refute whatever blame you throw at me.
Prologus: [*Takes out a sheet of paper*] Look, what does this letter contain?
Sailor: Letter? From where? *Prologus*: From Japan; I shall read it, if you let me.
Sailor: Let me go; my imminent journey   55
prohibits me from tarrying longer here, I am leaving. *Prologus*: Stop!
   Why are you leaving?
Sailor: I am not leaving. *Prologus*: Stop, while I read a part of it;
      Epistle
During these days, Victor, an octogenarian Christian
neophyte, fell into a pious error. For as Taicosama was raging

---

53–4 Against the Dutch sailor's glass bottles with their obviously fake contents, the Prologus triumphantly shows an authentic (presumably Jesuit) letter from Japan. Much of the news about Japan in Europe up to the early seventeenth century was supplied by the Jesuits (see Introduction 1.1).

58–64 These are the only lines in this play delivered in prose. The text tagged as *epistola* recalls the numerous Jesuit missionary reports sent from the East to Europe and widely disseminated both inside and outside the order (see Introduction 1.1).

in Christianos Taicosama, arma, quibus mortem non   60
inultus exciperet, frustra dehortante filio Andrea
et amicis, rursus induit. Correctus demum est hic
error a duobus nepotibus, quibuscum inermem se
hostibus sistere statuit. Ozacae Id. Ian. 1595." – Doli
nunc machinator impudens effer pedem   65
aut irrogabo crimini poenam tuo!
At vos, amicae litis et sacrae in patrem
pietatis este iudices! En, ipse adest.

I.1

Victor Christianis adscriptus Iaponum sectas exsecratur. Famulum ad
   vocandum Andream filium mittit.
Victor, Theodorus.
Victor: Tandem beatus sidere secundo dies
mihi renidet. Aureis dies notis   70
signanda! Qua mi summa votorum obtigit,

---

63 *a duobus nepotibus*: Meant here are Victor's two grandsons Modestus and
Narcissus, who manage to make their grandfather lay down his arms in
III.2–3. In the Jesuit accounts of Bartoli and others (see Introduction 3.1)
Ogasawara Ginsei's unnamed daughter-in-law (Andreas's wife) takes the lead
along with similarly anonymous family members including her sons. In
keeping with the Society's prohibition against staging women (or rather boys
dressed as women; see Jesuits 1600: 22) on school stage, *VJ* substitutes them
with these grandsons.

64 *Ozacae Id. Ian. 1595*: Place and date of dispatch, a standard closing
formula for a letter. The manuscript erroneously has *Ien.* for *Ian.* The events
on which the play is based in fact took place around January 1597 (see
Introduction 3.1).

67–8 *amicae litis ... et sacrae in patrem/pietatis*: *amica lis* is an unusual
oxymoron but the phrase appears in the title of a book published in 1665
which Wiestner likely saw (Rhay 1665; the copy in BSB (BV001511097) has
a contemporary inscription on the frontispiece indicating ownership by the

against the Christians, he took up arms   60
with which he would not have been unwilling to face death, although his
    son Andreas
and his friends tried to dissuade him. This error was in the end corrected
by his two grandsons, with whom he decided
to face his enemies unarmed. Osaka, Ides of January 1595." Now, you
    impudent
crafter of trickery, scurry out,   65
or else I will exact punishment for your crime! [*The sailor leaves*]
[*To the audience*] Be judges of this amicable debate and of the sacred
piety towards one's father. [*Points to Victor entering the stage*] Look, he himself
    is here. [*The Prologus leaves the stage while Victor and Theodorus enter*]

I.1

Victor, having joined the Christians, denounces the Japanese sects.
    He sends his servant to summon his son Andreas.
Victor, Theodorus.
Victor: At last, the blessed day with its favourable star
shines upon me. A day to be decked out with golden   70
signs! On this day, the sum of my wishes has been attained;

Munich college library). The subject of the play is indeed going to be Andreas's
friendly but firm correction of or resistance against his father's error.

68 *este iudices* is addressed to the audience. Appeal to the audience's goodwill
by the speaker of the prologue is a common feature of Roman comedy (see
e.g. Plaut. *Amphitryo* 151–2, Terence *Hauton Timorumenos* 1-52).

68 *En ipse adest*: Pointing to Victor, who is presumably already stepping onto
the stage and is the first speaker in the following scene.

69–122 I.1. Victor and his servant Theodorus, having just been baptised, are
ecstatic over their entry into Catholicism and openly contemptuous of their
native religious traditions. Victor dispatches Theodorus to summon his son
Andreas, but while on his way the latter espies a group of Buddhist priests
approaching and decides to listen in to their conversation.

60–71 *beatus . . . signanda*: here and elsewhere (see also 75–80) *dies* is used
both in the masculine and the feminine, even within the same sentence. Such
switching of gender in close proximity, while rare, is attested in classical texts;
see e.g. Livy 34.35.

qua nube mentis liber haurio iubar,
auramque vitae caelitis, qua me beat
aether favore maximo, sacra fide.
Theodorus: O auspicatum numinis summi diem   75
honore, qua te meque gaudiis favens
inundat aether! Ipse vix modum meae
felicitatis aestimo. *Victor*: O niveum diem
quae nos tenebris eximit, vitae dies
quae prima nostrae contigit! *Theodorus*: Salve, dies   80
desiderata, qua salutifer latex
labem expiavit mentis et pestem mali!
Victor: O Christe, salve! O anchora! O lux! O salus
spesque una, salve! Vivere et tecum mori
stat mente fixum. *Theodorus*: Vota respice, O deus!   85
Victor: Et vos, magistri lucis ac vitae duces
salvete, cara capita terris et polo!
O quas feremus muneri tanto vices,
quod Christianis imbuistis nos sacris
subolesque genitas Taenaro aetheris viam   90
docuistis ultro? Tramitem auspiciis semel
vestris prehensum perfidus non deseram.
At vos, valete, stipites! Rerum pudor!
Xacae pudendum nomen, et regni lues,
Amida, facessite! Exsecror natos Stygi   95
deos. *Theodorus*: Superba capita! Si nostra piget
lingua lacessi, vindices proterviae

---

76 *te meque*: emended from *teque meque* in the manuscript.

79–80 *vitae . . . contigit*: What is meant here that this is the first day of true
life for them, i.e. as baptised Catholics.

81 *salutifer latex*: This phrase may refer to both the water of baptism and the
blood of Christ, which wash away the sins of humankind. See e.g. *Eph.* 5.26
and *Rev.* 1.5.

86–7 These words are ostensibly an apostrophic address to the Jesuit fathers
and catechists who prepared Victor and Theodorus for baptism.
Metatheatrically they may also have been directed to the Jesuit teachers in the
audience.

on this day I, freed from my mental fog, am imbibing the sunlight
and the breeze of divine life, with which heaven,
showing its greatest favour, blesses me; namely with sacred faith.
Theodorus: O day made fortunate by the honour of God   75
the highest, on which auspicious heaven inundates you and me
with joy! With difficulty can I ascertain the limit
of my happiness. *Victor*: O snow-white day,
which takes us out of shadows, day which chances upon us
as the first of our life! *Theodorus*: Greetings to you, O wished-for   80
day, on which salvation-bearing water
expiated the wrongs of the mind and the contagion of evil!
Victor: O Christ, greetings! O anchor, O light, O salvation,
and our only hope, greetings! To live and to die with you
is the fixed resolve of my mind. *Theodorus*: Oh God, look upon our
      prayers!   85
Victor: And you, masters of light and leaders of life,
greetings, faces dear to earth and to heaven!
Oh, what return shall we give for such a great gift,
the gift of imbuing us with Christianity,
and teaching us, a progeny destined to hell, the way to heaven,   90
of your own accord? I shall not perfidiously desert the path
which we began to follow under your auspices.
[*Turning to pagan statues*] But you, useless blockheads, goodbye! O disgrace!
You, shameful name, Shaka, and you, disease of the realm,
Amida, go away! I curse the gods born   95
to hell. *Theodorus*: [*Toward the statues*] Heads full of pride! If you hate being
taunted by my tongue, exact punishment from me

---

90 *subolesque genitas Taenaro*: The Council of Trent (1545–63), which solidified counter-Reformational Catholic doctrine, taught that due to original sin all humankind regardless of age or race was destined to hell without the sanctifying grace imparted chiefly through the guidance of the true and single church (see e.g. Wiley 2002: 99–100).

93 *At vos valete, stipites*: There were likely some stage props representing pagan Buddhist statues which the actors proceeded to abuse both verbally and physically.

exigite poenas! Amida, lentus haec vides,
lentusque pateris! Vindica! Taces, Xaca?
Iniurioso numen impeto tuum   100
pede. Ultor esto, si potes. *Victor*: Telis carent
di bonziorum. Heu, quanta caecitas gravat
mentes profanas Iaponum! In parem trahunt
gentes ruinam perfidi regni popae.
Theodorus: Faex exsecranda, pestilens ulcus! Dies   105
quod refugus horret pondus invisum soli!
Victor: Peritura tandem fraudibus plebes suis.
Theodorus: Quos non scelesta machinabitur dolos?
Tartarea pubes conscias in nos Styge
umbras vocabit. *Victor*: Evocet, spiret minas;   110
numquam pavebo. Strage compellam lares
repetere nigros. In suam rursus crucem
tenebrasque pergent Taenaro exciti greges
crucis fugati luce. Sed age, mihi manus,
Theodore, fida, protinus natum mihi   115
huc advocato. *Theodorus*: Quo tuum imperium vocat,
abeo. *Victor*: Citus fac adsit. *Theodorus*: Ut iubes, citus
huc advolabit Andreas. Proh, quis gradum
citatus infert? Video; scelerosum genus
huc bonziorum properat. Heu, quanta popae   120
flammantur ira perfidi! Exploro sagax
quid moliatur stygia faex terris mali.

I.2

Bonzii Christianae rei incrementa dolent.
2 bonzii, Theodorus.

Bonzius 1: Extincta necdum Christianorum lues

100–1 *Iniurioso ... pede*: The actor playing Theodorus is probably meant to kick or trample on one of the statues here. Early modern Jesuit accounts do report instances of Japanese converts, driven by religious ardour, attacking and destroying Buddhist images and temples (see e.g. Hesselink 2016: 28).

and avenge my insults. Amida, do you passively look at this
and passively endure? Take revenge! You are quiet, Shaka?
[*Proceeds to kick a statue*] I attack your godhead with my injurious   100
foot. Exact revenge, if you can. *Victor*: The gods of the bonzes
lie powerless. Alas, how much blindness weighs down
the profane minds of the Japanese! The perfidious priestlings of the realm
drag our pagan fellows down toward equal ruin!
Theodorus: Execrable dreg, pestilent everywhere! The sun   105
flees, because it does not want to see their hateful weight on earth!
Victor: These people will in the end be destroyed by their own lies.
Theodorus: What tricks do these criminals not invent!
The hellish race will call their allied spirits from the underworld
against us. *Victor*: Let them summon them, let them threaten;   110
I will never tremble. I will force them by their defeat to return again
to their black homes. The crowds summoned from the underworld
will again go on their way to their own gallows and shadows,
put on the run by the light of the cross. But come now, Theodorus,
my faithful right-hand man, straightaway summon my son here   115
for me. *Theodorus*: I speed away, whither your command
calls me. *Victor*: Make sure he is here quickly – . [*Leaves stage*]
     Theodorus: As you command, quickly
will Andreas fly here. [*Sees two Buddhist priests entering the stage*] Alas!
     Who steps in here
in a hurry? I see; the criminal race
of the bonzes are hastening this way. Alas, with how much anger   120
are the perfidious priestlings inflamed! [*Takes cover so as to spy on the
     conversation of the priests*] Keenly will I search out
what evil the dregs of hell are preparing for this land.

I.2

The bonzes grieve over the growth of Christianity.
Two bonzes, Theodorus.
Bonze 1: The Christian pest, not yet extinct, sprouts forth

---

110 *spiret minas*: Cf. *Acts*. 9.1 *spirans minarum* (referring to Saul of Tarsus
(*c.* 5–64/65)).

nostris ruinis pullulat. Crescit malum
pubetque damnis in dies semper novis.   125
Bonzius 2: Ni praedometur gnaviter serpens malum,
grassante peste, Iaponum periit vetus
religio. *Bonzius 1*: Populis perditis, virus nocens
confundet astra; faciet et deos nocens
secum nocentes. *Bonzius 2*: Erebus in pestis necem   130
est concitandus; comprimet labem soli.
Bonzius 1: Tentata per me cuncta; prastabat tamen
tentasse numquam; saeviit malum magis,
in me retorsit fortior praestigiis
praestigiatrix turba constructos dolos.   135
Theodorus: O crux salutis, tessera et vindex mali!
Bonzius 1: Neque lene pretium fascini infelix tuli.
Bonzius 2: Periclitatur omnium pariter salus.
Bonzius 1: Deum iacebunt fana funditus, suis
vagi exsulabunt sedibus. *Bonzius 2*: Nosque exsules   140
spretosque patrio perfidi eicient solo.
Bonzius 1: Periimus! *Bonzius 2*: Ecce, flectit huc praetor gradum
omine secundo regius. Spirat minas
rapidisque fervet aestibus.

124–44 I.2. As Theodorus watches secretly from the side, two bonzes spew
forth a litany of complaints about the growth of the Catholic church in Japan.
Their conversation takes a different turn when they see a highly placed official
approaching, displaying signs of anger that they guess (correctly) to be
directed at their enemy.

The substance of the bonzes' complaint is a standard trope reported in
Jesuit literature and reflects to some extent genuine anti-Catholic sentiments
expressed in early modern Japan (see Introduction 1.1).

134 *praestigiis*: emended from *praestigiatrix* in the manuscript.

to our ruin. The evil grows
and ripens every day, causing new destruction.   125
Bonze 2: Unless the slithering evil is diligently forestalled,
with the growth of the pest, the ancient religion of Japan
will be done for. *Bonze 1*: With the people lost, the noxious disease
will destroy heaven; noxious in itself, it will make the gods
noxious too. *Bonze 2*: The underworld must be aroused   130
to kill off the pest; it will put an end to the sin of the land.
Bonze 1: I have tried everything; but it would have been better
never to have tried; the pest became more furious,
and the deceitful crowd threw back at me
with a force superior to my trickery, the traps that had been set up
    for them.   135
Theodorus: [*Aside*] O cross of salvation, our token and avenger of evil!
Bonze 1: And unhappily, I received not a small recompense for my
    witchcraft.
Bonze 2: Everyone's safety is at stake.
Bonze 1: The temples of the gods will lie low on the ground, they
will wander off as exiles from their homes. *Bonze 2*: And the perfidious
    ones will   140
throw us out as exiles and rejects from our paternal soil.
Bonze 1: We are lost! *Bonze 2*: [*Sees the royal praetor entering the stage*]
    Behold, in a favourable omen
the royal praetor comes his way here. He breathes out threats
and is boiling over with rabid rage.

---

142 *praetor* in classical Latin is a magistrate holding a high office, and the
term could be applied loosely to various positions such as that of a dictator,
consul, or proconsul (see L&S s.v.). Here, some kind of representative or chief
delegate of the person holding the supreme military and civil command of
Japan (Taicosama/Hideyoshi in this case) is envisaged, as becomes clear in
the following scene.

143 *Spirat minas*: see note to 110.

I.3

Praetor superveniens decretam persecutionem nuntiat et satellites ad
    Christianos indagandos mittit, omnia spectante Theodoro.
2 bonzii, praetor regius, 4 satellites, Theodorus.
    Bonzius 1: Causam libet
noscere furoris. Quis furor mentem occupat   145
flammaque rodit vivida? *Praetor:* Poenas gravi
sceleri parare regii nutus iubent.
Bonzius 1: Cuius quiescit strage mucronis rigor?
Praetor: Cum proditorum sanguinem hauserit satur.
Bonzius 1: Quae monstra narras? *Bonzius 2*: Crimen avertant dii   150
regique firment sceptra. *Bonzius 1*: Quis turba recens
regem inquietat? *Praetor*: Pessimum regni nefas.
Bonzius 1: Ferro rebelles concidant. *Bonzius 2*: Tantum luant
scelus nefanda capita. Quod nomen reis?
Praetor: Nomen pudendum, nomen indignum die,   155
oblitterandum; nosse quod noxa haud caret.
Bonzius 2: Ambage missa pande; quos sontes notas?
Praetor: Sunt Christiani, turba contemptrix deum,
et quae profanis plausibus crucem colit.
Bonzius 2: Portenta rerum! *Bonzius 1*: Damna publicae rei!   160
Theodorus: Res Christiana nutat. O Christe, hoc malum
averte! *Bonzius 1*: Nullus carnificis irae modus
sit, donec omnem destinet caedi luem.
Bonzius 2 : Haec amputanda est antequam radicem agat.

144–201 I.3. The bonzes are joined by the praetor and his four subordinates
as Theodorus continues to eavesdrop. The praetor reveals that Taicosama has
issued a decree to arrest and execute all Christians as traitors to their land
and religion. He further orders his subordinates to enforce the decree, much
to the delight of the Buddhist priests (and to Theodorus's consternation).

146–57 The praetor, with his ambiguous language, keeps the bonzes in
suspense and builds up the climax for the revelation: For Japan, the number
one enemy now are the Christians.

158–70 The anti-Christian decree of Taicosama/Hideyoshi described here is
a dim reflection of the edict issued in late 1596 (see Introduction 1.1). This

I.3

The praetor joins the scene and announces that the persecution has been
    decreed, and sends his minions to search out the Christians, while
    Theodorus is watching everything.
Two bonzes, royal praetor, Theodorus, 4 minions.

Bonze 1:   I want to know
the reason for his anger. [*To the praetor*] What anger fills up your mind   145
and gnaws at it with a burning flame? *Praetor:* The royal will
commands me to prepare a punishment for a grave crime.
Bonze 1: By whose destruction will your rigid sword be satisfied?
Praetor: When it shall have taken its fill of the blood of traitors.
Bonze 1: What monstrosities do you mean? *Bonze 2:* May the gods avert
    their crime   150
and strengthen our king's sceptre! *Bonze 1:* Who disquiets the king lately
with worries? *Praetor:* The worst evil of the realm.
Bonze 2: May the rebels fall by the sword! *Bonze 2:* May the evil ones
pay for such a great crime! What is the name of the accused party?
Praetor: A shameful name, a name unworthy of the light of day,   155
one that should be obliterated; even getting to know it is harmful.
Bonze 2: Let go of the riddle and be straightforward; whom do you
    denote as guilty?
Praetor: They are the Christians, a crowd contemptuous of the gods,
and one which worships a cross with profane applause.
Bonze 2: Evil portent! *Bonze 1:* Destruction of our country!   160
Theodorus: [*Aside*] Christianity is in danger. Oh Christ, avert this
evil! *Bonze 1:* The executioner should put no limit to his rage
until he should consign the entire pest to death.
Bonze 2: It should be lopped off, before it takes root.

---

edict was announced in the Kyoto/Osaka region in the beginning of
December and led immediately to the arrest of some Catholics, mainly
Franciscans and their flock (for more details see e.g. Hesselink 2016: 111).

159 *crucem colit*: The Christian practice of venerating an instrument of
torture and execution has been a source of scandal for unbelievers since
antiquity. This sense of scandal also at times hindered Jesuit proselytization
in early modern Japan (see e.g. Hesselink 2016: 120 and note to *JM* 928).

164 The speaker of this line is simply named *Bonzius* in the manuscript, but
overall context suggests that he must be the second one.

Praetor: Per sceptra iuro Taicosamae, per deum   165
numen verendum; hoc conscium sceleris caput
supplicia pendat, si datam fallo fidem.
In proditores regis et deum feror
carnifice ferro. Hoc fulgur incussam metet
pubem. Peribunt dira Iaponiae probra.   170
Bonzius 2: Novis struenda monstra sceleribus nova.
Bonzius 1: Debent necari mortibus, quotquot queunt
excogitari. *Praetor*: Quidquid in reos potest
excogitabo. *Theodorus*: O Christe robora tuos!
Praetor: Ades satelles! *Satellites 4*: Promptus impera! *Praetor*: Neces   175
celerate mille sontibus! *Satellites 4*: Quotquot voles.
Praetor: Vobis agetur praeda; latibula anxii
excutite; dirum Christianorum pecus
onerate ferri mole, nexilibus plagis
mandate vinctos carceri! *Satellites 1 et 2*: Ut, praetor, iubes.   180
Praetor: Vos expiandae congruas pesti neces
fabricate: Tela, cuspides, flammas, cruces,
et quod nocentum sanguinem totum potest
elicere, ferte, victimas Diti dabo.
Satelles 3: Imus, crucesque noxias cruciariae   185
genti paramus. *Satelles 4*: Sentiet flammas rogi
pubes rebellis. *Theodorus*: O tuos, Christe, adiuva!
Praetor: Hostes deorum nesciant clementiam!
Bonzius 1: Cultor deorum perge et ultor; pecus
in Christianum saevias; caelo inferet   190
te tanta pietas. *Praetor*: Pergo. Iaponiae sacris

185–6 *crucesque ... paramus*: Cf. note to 159.

Praetor: I swear by Taicosama's sceptre, by the venerable spirit   165
of the gods; may my head, conscious of guilt,
be punished, if I betray the trust given to me.
I rush to the traitors of king and of the gods
with an executioner's sword. This thunder will sweep off
the stricken progeny. The dire shame of Japan will perish.   170
Bonze 2: New monstrosities must be prepared against new crimes.
Bonze 1: They ought to be killed off with as many deaths as can be
contrived. *Praetor*: Whatever is possible, I shall contrive
against the guilty ones. *Theodorus*: [*Aside*] Oh Christ, give strength to
   your followers!
Praetor: Come, minion! [*The minions come on stage*] *Four minions*:
   Command us promptly. *Praetor*: Hasten up   175
a thousand deaths against the guilty ones. *Four minions*: However
   many you shall wish.
Praetor: You shall hunt down the prey. Carefully search out
their hiding places. Weigh down the dire flock of Christians
with heavy iron, throw them, bound with
clinging chains, into prison. *Minions 1 and 2*: Praetor, as you command.
   [*Minions 1 and 2 leave stage*]   180
Praetor: [*Speaking to minions 3 and 4*] You, contrive suitable deaths
   for the evil
that is to be expiated: Missiles, spear-points, flames, crosses
and whatever can drain all the blood of the harmful ones,
bring them. I will give them over as victims to Hades.
Minion 3: We will go and prepare painful crosses against the people   185
who are fit for the cross. *Minion 4*: The rebellious progeny
shall feel the flames of their funeral-pyre. [*Minions 3 and 4 leave stage*]
   Theodorus: [*Aside*] O Christ, help your own people!
Praetor: May the enemies of the gods not receive clemency!
Bonze 1: Go on as follower and avenger of the gods; vent your wrath
on the flock of Christians; such great piety   190
shall bring you to heaven. *Praetor*: I shall go on. Spirits of Japan, be
   favourable

---

189 *ultor; pecus*: Metre indicates that there must be one long or two short
syllables missing after *ultor*. There are many possibilities including *iam, nunc,
tu, hoc* and *proh*.

favete coeptis numina, ut ferro malum
hoc praesecetur! *Bonzius 2*: Fausta res agitur. Pavor
animumque curis lancinans cessit dolor.
Bonzius 1: Totus revixi, clade cum fausta cadent				195
infausta capita. Leniam hoc spectaculo
exaestuantes pectore impetus meo.
Theodorus: Heu! Quas procellas nimbus hic atrox aget?
Heu, dira sitis, heu, dira sanguinis calet
animis cupido! O numen, adiuva, gregis				200
miserere sancti!

I.4

Victor, intellecta ex Theodoro in Christianos persecutione, armis se
	accingit et exercet vires.
Victor, Theodorus.
	Victor: Fare; quis mentem pavor
subito inquietat? *Theodorus*: Periimus! *Victor*: Salvi tamen
superamus ambo. *Theodorus*: Periimus! *Victor*: Dubios metus
excute. *Theodorus*: Periimus! Omnium ambigua salus
rapitur procella. Periimus! *Victor*: Tanti mali				205
causam recense. *Theodorus*: Proxima ruina labat
res Christiana. *Victor*: Dubia pro certis tenes.
Theodorus: Heu, dubia non sunt, certa quae probat fides.
Heu, dura fata! *Victor*: Pectus in fata explico.
Effare, quaenam. *Theodorus*: Regio iussu tumet				210
aulae satelles. Marte truculento calens
ruit huc et illuc; aestuans neces struit
in Christianos. *Victor*: Qua cohors causa cadet,

201–29 I.4. Theodorus comes back to Victor with the news of the anti-Christian decree. Victor immediately works himself up into a paroxysm of rage and begins to swing his old sword in mock-battle.

206 *ruina*: To be scanned as two syllables (long-long), with synizesis in -*ui*-. For synizesis in Seneca see e.g. Fantham 1982: 237.

to our sacred attempts, so that this evil
may be lopped off with the sword! [*Leaves stage*] *Bonze 2*: Pious business
    is being done. My fear
and pain, which were tearing apart my mind with anxiety, are gone.
Bonze 1: I feel completely revived; with this auspicious catastrophe,
    inauspicious   195
heads will fall. With this spectacle I shall assuage
the rage boiling in my heart.
Theodorus: [*Aside*] Alas! What storm will this thundercloud bring?
Alas, a dire thirst, alas, a dire wish for blood
burns in their hearts! O divine will, help! Take pity on   200
your sacred flock!

I.4

Victor, being informed of the persecution of the Christians from Theodorus,
    girds himself with arms and exercises his strength.
Victor, Theodorus.
    Victor: [*To Theodorus, rushing onto the stage*] Speak, what sudden fear
disturbs your mind? *Theodorus*: We are done for! *Victor*: Nonetheless we
    are both
safe and sound. *Theodorus*: We are done for! *Victor*: Shake off
your uncertain fears. *Theodorus*: We are done for! The safety of all
is being snatched away in the confusing storm. We are done for! *Victor*:
    Explain the reason   205
for such a great evil. *Theodorus*: Christianity is tottering,
its ruin coming close. *Victor*: You are confusing uncertain things with
    certain ones.
Theodorus: Alas! What solid truth demonstrates is not uncertain.
Alas! Harsh fate! *Victor*: My heart is open to fate.
Speak out, what this fate is. *Theodorus*: The minion of the court   210
is puffed up with royal command. Heated up with rabid Mars,
he rushes hither and thither; boiling over, he plots death
against Christians. *Victor*: Speak, for what reason will our innocent

---

213 *cohors*: The manuscript has *genus* instead, which is emended here to
match the gender of *perosa* in line 215.

dic, innocens? *Theodorus*: Quod impios Christum colit
perosa ritus Iaponum. *Victor*: Certo caret   215
haec scelere causa! *Theodorus*: Bonzii affigunt scelus,
odisse quotquot criminis labem vident.
Victor: Fingant scelesti crimen et vitam exigant.
Non timeo fata. Fortiter possum mori,
sed non inultus occidam; manibus cadent   220
meis litandae victimae; hauriet latus
pugio rebelle; sanguinem hauriet virum.
Theodorus: Solus et inermis ruis in armatos globos?
Victor: Ruo per catervas funerum et similis mei
ista refellam dextera immeritam necem.   225
I! Posita fesso Marte mihi citus refer
huc arma! Inerme patrius mucro latus
firmet; supremum victor hac actus manu
bibet cruorem. *Theodorus*: Nobilis leti comes
tibi futurus refero. *Victor*: Quis animi vigor,   230
effeminati sentient palmam greges.
Non sic abibunt odia. Funestum ferent
pretium cruoris. Christe, te in caedes duce,
intrepidus ibo. Citus ades? Mecum obvius
victoriarum nobiles palmas leges?   235
Theodorus: Legam, paratus vivere et tecum mori.
O Victor, ensem rursus emeritum cape!
Victor: O mucro felix, sequere felicem manum!
I, perque cuneos hostium intrepidus vola.

---

217 The manuscript has *sceleris* for *criminis*; I have emended the line *metri causa*.

227 *patrius mucro*: the Jesuits often noted the Japanese attachment to their native sword (see e.g. Reff 2014: 44–5). The status of the Ogasawara clan as teachers of traditional Japanese martial arts (see Introduction 3.1) is also alluded to here. The Jesuit authors including Bartolii mention that Ogasawara Ginsei, with whom Victor is conflated, habitually carried with him a short

group fall? *Theodorus*: The reason is that it worships Christ
in hatred of the impious rites of the Japanese. *Victor*: Surely this is　　215
not a crime! *Theodorus*: The bonzes allege criminality
against whomever they see to be unfavourably disposed to sinful crimes.
Victor: Let the criminals make up accusations and let them take away
　　my life.
I am not afraid of death. I can die bravely,
but I shall not die unavenged; victims shall be doomed,　　220
sacrificed by my hands; my dagger will hack off
the rebel flank; it will draw the blood of men.
Theodorus: Are you rushing, alone and unarmed, into armed formations?
Victor: I rush through an army of deaths, and true to myself
I shall fend off my unmerited death with this right hand.　　225
Go! Quickly, here, bring back my arms which I put down
when my martial spirit was exhausted. Let my ancestral blade gird
my flank; the weapon shall, driven by this hand, imbibe in its victory
blood for the last time. *Theodorus*: [*Heading off stage*] I am bringing it
　　back to you, and I will become
a companion to your noble death. *Victor*: The crowd with their effeminate　　230
hands will feel what vigour is in my mind.
Their enmity will not come off scot-free. They will pay a grievous price
for our blood. Christ, with you as leader into the slaughter
I shall go without fear. [*To Theodorus, who returns on stage*] Are you
　　coming swiftly? Will you, facing the enemy with me,
take up the glorious victory-palm of our triumphs?　　235
Theodorus: I shall do so, I am prepared to live and die with you.
[*Handing Victor his sword*] Oh Victor, take up your retired sword again!
Victor: [*Takes up and swings around his sword*] O happy blade, follow my
　　lucky hand!
Come, fly without fear through enemy formations!

---

sword in accordance with Japanese custom (see Yūki 1994: 89 and Scioli
2013: 306).

232 *non sic abibunt odia*: A tag from Sen. *Hercules Furens* 27, where Hera is
plotting yet another catastrophe for the title character.

233 *Christe, te in caedes duce*: The idea that Christ should lead one to murder,
directly contradicting the fifth commandment (*Exod.* 15.13) epitomises the
profane fortitude which has taken hold of Victor.

I.5

Leo et Quirinus Christiani rident senem arma tractantem, et se ad
   martyrium animant.
Victor, Theodorus, Leo, Quirinus.
Victor: Ades, satelles! Praesto sum. Ferrum rota!   240
Non segnis ictus dextera haec ludet tuos.
Ades, experire, ut conscium sortis suae
senium triumphet. *Leo*: Quis furor senem entheat?
Quirinus: Similis furenti est. *Victor*: Ense sic fissum caput
nocens hiabit. *Leo*: Mentis, ut video, impotens   245
sibi bella fingit. *Victor*: Colla sic gnarus metam
manusque sontes. Viscera hoc rimas agent
impete reclusa. *Quirnus*: Ore fulminat minas
caedesque. *Victor*: Sic per agmina et densos globos
semita patescet. *Quirinus*: Hosti imaginario   250
lymphatus instat. *Victor*: Victor, aspicies suo
artus cruore perlitos, tumque ultimis
laetus trophaeis nobili fato cades!
Sed differendus aestuantis impetus
pectoris in hostem. Natus occurret meus?   255
Theodorus: Ignosce lento. Trahere tempestas moras
subita coegit; ocius nunc exsequar,
quod imperasti. *Victor*: Protinus tecum redux

240–86 I.5. Victor continues his imaginary sword fight on stage, while fellow
converts Leo and Quirinus watch from the side and laugh at this vain exercise.
They intercept Theodorus, who is being dispatched again to summon
Andreas, and learn from him the reason for Victor's sudden agitation. In
contrast to Victor, Leo and Quirinus face the prospect of persecution calmly
and strengthen each other's resolve to undergo martyrdom without resistance.

    Victor in this scene combines elements of the ancient comic *senex iratus*
and *miles gloriosus*. For these character types in Graeco-Roman comedy see
e.g. Barsby 1999: 157, 264–5. See also Introduction 1.2 for classical reception
in Jesuit school drama.

I.5

The Christians Leo and Quirinus laugh at the old man exercising his arms,
  and fortify themselves for martyrdom.
Victor, Theodorus, Leo, Quirinus.
Victor: [*Continuing his imaginary battle*] Come, minion! I am here.
  Swing your sword!   240
My hard-working right hand will parry your blows.
Come! See how my old age, in full possession of itself,
triumphs. *Leo*: [*Observing Victor from one side of the stage*] What
  madness enraptures the old man?
Quirinus: [*Also on the side of the stage, speaking to Leo*] He is like a
  lunatic. *Victor*: Your guilty head, split by my sword
will open up thus. *Leo*: As I see, he, being of unsound mind,   245
fancies his own battles. *Victor*: I shall chop off heads expertly, thus,
as well as guilty hands. Innards will be torn apart,
cut open by this blow. *Quirinus*: He thunders threats
and does slaughter with his speech. *Victor*: Thus, a way will open up
  through battle lines
and dense formations. *Quirinus*: The madman attacks   250
an imaginary enemy. *Victor*: Victor, you will see limbs
awash with their own blood, and then, happy in your last trophies
you will fall in a noble death!
But the impetus of my boiling heart against our enemy
must wait. Will my son come?   255
Theodorus: [*Enters stage*] Excuse my tardiness. A sudden storm forced
  me
to be delayed; I shall now perform in a hurry
what you commanded. *Victor*: Make sure that my son is here right away

---

Leo ('lion') and Quirinus ('true Roman') are appropriately named, generic
local believers standing in for unnamed spectators of Ogasawara Ginsei's
mock sword fight in the original accounts (see Yūki 1994: 90, Scioli 2013: 306).

244 *entheat* is back formation from *entheatus* which is attested in classical
Latin.

245 *furenti similis* recalls *similis furenti* in Sen. *Hercules Oetaeus* 240.

248 *reculsa. Quirinus: Ore*: There is a hiatus (lack of elision), perhaps
occasioned by the change in speaker. On hiatus in Senecan tragedy see e.g.
Fitch 2004: 219.

fac adsit. *Theodorus*: Aderit protinus, ut optas, here.
Quirinus: Theodore, quonam rapitur iratus senex?   260
Quid aestuanti pectore tonat? *Leo*: Num potis
est mentis? *Theodorus*: Iram stimulat exortus furor
in Christianos. *Leo*: Cadere decrepitis pavet
gravatus annis? *Theodorus*: Cadere, sed vindex necis
exoptat ultro ac hostium malo. Morae   265
nescius herilis imperia iussi exsequor.
Quirinus: Vah! Christiani roboris animum senis
inopem, profanus miles auspiciis agit
Martis profani et fortitudinis sacrae
expers pudendis pascitur victoriis   270
laurosque spirat nomine indignas suo.
Leo: Senis inhibete, caelites, rabidas manus!
Haec arma Victor ponat, auspiciis legat
trophaea vestris. *Quirinus*: Hic facile sidet calor.
Verum quis animus tibi, Leo? *Leo*: gaudio mihi   275
liquescit animus, illa quod venit dies,
quae nos beatos martyres sistet deo.
Quirinus: Et mihi animosum pectus insolito salit
ardore; iungam socius unanimes gradus;
sequar aut praeibo, quo sitis palmae vocat;   280
nec fugio, quidquid armet in meos furor
artus tyranni. *Leo*: Macte! Nil, Christo auspice,
nobis timendum est; misceant terram inferis,
nocere nequeunt; quidquid elicient mali,
id dissipabit Christus. *Quirinus*: Hoc tuti duce   285
sumus . Incohatam pergimus caeli viam.

269–70 *fortitudinis sacrae/expers*: Victor's armed resistance is here explicitly said to be lacking in sacred fortitude which is the very theme of the play.

275 *gaudio* is scanned as two syllables, with synizesis of -io-. Cf. also note to 206.

returning with you. *Theodorus*: He will be here right away as you wish,
master.
Quirinus: [*To Theodorus, who is leaving stage*] Theodorus, where is the
angry old man rushing to?   260
Why is he emitting thunder from his boiling breast? *Leo*: Is he of sound
mind? *Theodorus*: The furor that has arisen against the Christians
is stirring up his anger. *Leo*: Is he afraid that he is going to die,
weighed down by his old age? *Theodorus*: He wishes to die, but as
an avenger of murder, of his own accord and while doing harm to his
enemies. Tarrying   265
no more, I will fulfil my master's command. [*Leaves stage*]
Quirinus: Alas! The old man has become a completely profane soldier
in his mind,
a mind which is deficient in Christian strength. He is under the auspices
of profane Mars, and lacking in sacred fortitude,
he gorges himself with shameful victories   270
and aspires for laurels which are unworthy of their name.
Leo: Heavenly beings, hold back the rabid hands of the old man!
May Victor put down these arms, may he choose trophies
under your auspices. *Quirinus*: This heat will easily subside.
But of what mind are you, Leo? *Leo*: My mind   275
melts with joy, since that day has come,
which will place us before God as martyrs.
Quirinus: My courageous heart also throbs
with unusual ardour; as your companion, I will go with you in one mind;
I will go after you, or ahead of you, where the thirst for victory-palm
summons us;   280
nor do I recuse myself, whatever the tyrant's madness prepares against
my limbs. *Leo*: Bravo! Under the protection of Christ,
we must fear nothing; let them mix this world up with the underworld,
they cannot harm us; whatever the evil people attempt,
Christ will dissipate it. *Quirinus*: With him as leader, we go   285
safely. We continue on the path to heaven, on which we have begun.

---

278 *insolito*: Emended from *in solito* (two words) in the manuscript.

286 *sumus*: The manuscript has *imus* which also suits the sense but not the
metre, hence the emendation.

I.Chorus

Docet, quae vera sit fortitudo
Ecclesia, Fortitudo Sacra, Fortitudo Profana.
Ecclesia: Quam turbo truces agitat nubes!
Furor insanos in nostra citat
fata tyrannos. Animae fortes,
quas sacra trahit palma, venite,   290
vos bella manent, vos sacra vocat
palma, venite!
Fortitudines 2: Adsumus, adsumus animae fortes;
quae bella manent? Quae palma vocat?
Ecclesia: Styx vipereis concita furiis   295
in bella citat dira tyrannos.
Fortitudines 2: Bella auspiciis his, diva, pete;
bella auspiciis his victa cadent.
Fortitudo Profana: Arma, arma ferox rapio; totum
in bella paro Liparae chalybem.   300
Fortitudo Sacra: Erras! Erras! Quemcumque deus
armat in hostes, hunc palma manet.
Fortitudo Profana: Quodcumque tegunt haec arma latus
immune patet; nil penetrabit.
Fortitudo Sacra: Quemcumque tegit pietas, extra   305
ictum iaculi est; nil penetrabit.
Ecclesia: Animae fortes, properate, vocat
gloria palmae. *Fortitudo Profana*: Propero; galea
vertice stabit; nil penetrabit.
Fortitudo Sacra: Sacra salutis melius galea   310
vertice stabit; nil penetrabit.
Fortitudo Profana: Pectora clipeus munita teget.
Fortitudo Sacra: Est mihi clipeus fidei scutum;
hoc sub clipeo secura ruo;

287–330 I Chorus. The personified figures Church, Sacred Fortitude, and Profane Fortitude give an allegorical interpretation of the preceding scenes. Church announces the onset of persecution which calls for struggle to maintain true faith. While Sacred Fortitude vows to uphold faith with spiritual means, Profane Fortitude resorts to earthly arms. Finally, Church and Sacred Fortitude chant in unison against the still recalcitrant Profane Fortitude. The chorus also foreshadows the argument between Victor, the representative of Profane Fortitude, and his son Andrea, who stands for Sacred Fortitude, which takes place in the following scene. The metre is anapestic dimeter.

I.Chorus

The chorus teaches what true fortitude is.
Church, Sacred Fortitude, Profane Fortitude.
Church: What dire clouds does the storm churn up!
Its furor stirs up tyrants raging
for our death. Strong souls,
drawn together by the sacred victory-palm, come,   290
war awaits you, the sacred victory-palm
calls you, come!
2 Fortitudes: We are here, we, the brave souls, are here;
what war awaits us? What victory-palm calls us?
Church: Hell, churning with snake-girded furies,   295
stirs up tyrants for dire war.
2 Fortitudes: Divine lady, seek war under these auspices;
the war will end, overcome under these auspices.
Profane Fortitude: I angrily snatch up arms, arms; I prepare
all the steel of Lipari for wars.   300
Sacred Fortitude: You err! You err! Whomever God
arms against enemies, that one does the victory-palm await.
Profane Fortitude: Whatever flank these arms defend
will be left unharmed; nothing will penetrate it.
Sacred Fortitude: Whomever piety defends is   305
outside the range of missiles; nothing will pierce that one.
Church: Brave souls, hurry, the glory of victory-palm
calls you. *Profane Fortitude*: I hurry; my helmet
will stand on my crown; nothing will penetrate it.
Sacred Fortitude: The sacred helmet of salvation will stand   310
better on my crown; nothing will penetrate it.
Profane Fortitude: My shield will defend my guarded breast.
Sacred Fortitude: My shield is the shield of faith;
I charge securely under this shield,

---

300 *Liparae*: A learned reference to the island of Lipari near Sicily, which in
antiquity had an active volcano and was associated with the furnace of the
Cyclopes producing metal implements for the Olympian gods; see e.g. Virg.
Aen. 8.416–25.

310–4 The list of sacred arms recalls the metaphorical divine weaponry
that protects the faithful in biblical language; cf. *Ps.* 28.7, *1 Thess.* 5.8, *Eph.*
6.11.

nil penetrabit. *Ecclesia*: Properate, sacra   315
vos bella vocant. *Fortitudo Profana*: Propero, medios
tendo per hostes; agmina gladio
prostrata cadent.
Fortitudo Sacra: Erras! Erras! Gladius domini
conteret hostes. *Fortitudo Sacra et Ecclesia*: Erras! Erras!   320
procul hinc dextrae, quas nobilitant
arma profana! *Fortitudo Profana*: Haec arma tuentur.
Fortitudo Sacra et Ecclesia: Erras! Erras! *Fortitudo Profana*: Ista minantur.
Fortitudo Sacra et Ecclesia: Erras! Erras! *Fortitudo Profana*: Propero,
    propero.
Concita medios tendo per hostes.   325
Fortitudo Sacra et Ecclesia: Erras, erras, cui ficta placet
laudis adorea! Gloria palmae
Marte vel armis haud parta venit.
Haec magnanimos semper alumnos
gloria poscit.   330

II.1

Andreas filius Victori parenti suadet, ut arma reponat, sed non persuadet.
Victor, Andreas, Theodorus.
Victor: Iterum furori reddor et motus graves
herous agitat animus. Obvius ferar
in fata certus gloriae vindex meae.
Faustum calorem pectoris superi exitu
pari beabunt. Cara progenies, ades?   335

---

323 *Ista minantur*: The manuscript gives these words to Profane Fortitude, a reading which the current edition and translation follow. It may however also make sense to give them to Sacred Fortitude and Church, to make *Ista* contrast with *Haec* in 322.

331–424 II.1. Theodorus comes back with Andreas, whom he had been sent to summon. Victor and Andreas begin to speak amicably, but their

nothing will penetrate it. *Church*: Hurry on, sacred 315
war calls you. *Profane Fortitude*: I hurry, I go
in the midst of enemies; their army, cut down
by my sword, shall fall.
Sacred Fortitude: You err! You err! The sword of the Lord
shall vanquish our enemies. *Sacred Fortitude and Church*: You err!
    You err! 320
Let hands, which profane arms ennoble,
be far away from me! *Profane Fortitude*: These arms defend.
Sacred Fortitude and Church: You err! You err! *Profane Fortitude*:
    Those arms threaten.
Sacred Fortitude and Church: You err! You err! *Profane Fortitude*: I
    hurry, I hurry.
Excitedly I go through the midst of enemies. 325
Sacred Fortitude and Church: You err, you err, you, for whom the false
    reward
of glory is pleasing. The glory of victory-palm
hardly comes from Mars or from arms.
This glory always requires
high-spirited pupils. 330

II.1

Victor's son Andreas tries to persuade his father to put down his arms
    but fails.
Victor, Andreas, Theodorus.
Victor: Rage again takes hold of me and my heroic mind
plans momentous steps. I shall rush head-on to my doom,
as an avenger, certain of my glory.
The angels will bless the happy heat of my breast
with a good end. [*To Andreas, who enters stage*] Dear progeny, are you
    here? 335

---

conversation soon breaks down into a shouting match as the father insists on
armed resistance against persecution, while the son tries to teach him that the
correct Christian way is to meekly submit to martyrdom and not return evil
for evil. Victor orders Andreas, whom he now regards as a coward unworthy
of his illustrious lineage, to leave him and the son obeys sadly. Together with
Theodorus, who professes his readiness to follow his master to the bitter end,
Victor remains steadfast in his warlike resolve.

Andreas: Adsum, verende genitor. O curae meae
pars prima, salve! *Victor*: Nate, solamen meae,
salve, senectae! *Andreas*: Gemmeos soles age
aevumque faustum. *Victor*: Ut luce recreor tua!
Andreas: Quid video, genitor? Ense quid, genitor, latus   340
senile cingis? *Victor*: Martius rediit calor;
parens in hostem, O nate, iam redit tuus
necesque versat. *Andreas*: Quas senex verset neces
annisque fractus? *Victor*: Hostium insidias manu
forti refellam, militem ut fortem decet.   345
Andreas: Exue furores Martios; abest procul
hinc, genitor, hostis. *Victor*: Imminet senio prope
meo cruentus. *Andreas*: Hostis? *Victor*: Hostis, et gravis.
Andreas: Hostis? Quis ille? *Victor*: Regio iussu ferox,
qui Christianis vincula, catastas , rogos   350
et mille clades fraudibus struit malis.
Andreas: Hos Christiani non pavent hostes. Metum
curasque, genitor, pone. *Victor*: Non ponit metum
pectus pavoris nescium. *Andreas*: Si non paves,
quid arma gestas? *Victor*: Fortis animi sunt nota   355
haec, non paventis. Fata quem trepidum movent,
manu reponit arma, quae fortis rapit.
Andreas: Est fortis animi ferre fortiter necem
nec vindicare. *Victor*: Vindicare necem nota
est fortioris indolis dignae viro.   360
Andreas: Sed militari. *Victor*: Miles est genitor tuus.
Andreas: Sed Christianus. *Victor*: Fortiter agere indolis
est Christianae. *Andreas*: Fortiter pati indolis
est Christianae. *Victor*: Fortiter agere et pati,
novi voloque. *Andreas*: Fortiter agit is satis,   365
qui fata patitur fortiter. *Victor*: Votum est mori;
haec sparsa canis tempora in testes voco,
sed morte tali, quae impios mecum pari
dabit ruinae. *Andreas*: Christiano non licet
quemquam ruinae dare. *Victor*: Nisi hostem. *Andreas*: Nec licet   370
hostem. *Victor*: Sed hostem, damna qui cumulat, licet
perdere. *Andreas*: Nec hostem, qui eripit vitam, licet

Andreas: I am here, venerable progenitor. O the foremost
of my cares, greetings! *Victor*: Son, solace of my
old age, greetings! *Andreas*: I command you to spend bejewelled days
and a blessed life. *Victor*: How am I refreshed by your splendour!
Andreas: What do I see, father? Why, father, do you gird your aged flank   340
with a sword? *Victor*: My martial heat has returned,
your parent has now come back, O son, against the enemy
and is practising slaughter. *Andreas*: What slaughter should an old man,
     and one
broken with old age, practice? *Victor*: With my strong hand, I shall repel
the plots of our enemies as befits a brave soldier.   345
Andreas: Shake off your martial rage; the enemy is far away
from here, father. *Victor*: He cruelly threatens my old age
from nearby. *Andreas*: The enemy? *Victor*: And the enemy is a serious one.
Andreas: The enemy? Who is he? *Victor*: The one who is rabid by regal
     command,
who prepares with his evil trickery chains, gallows, funeral-pyres   350
and a thousand calamities against the Christians.
Andreas: The Christians are not afraid of these enemies. Forget
your fear and worries, father. *Victor*: My breast, ignorant
of cowardice, needs not forget fear. *Andreas*: If you do not fear,
why do you carry arms? *Victor*: These are signs   355
of a courageous soul, not a cowardly one. The coward, shaken by doom,
is the one who puts down arms, arms which a courageous fellow snatches up.
Andreas: It is the sign of a courageous soul to endure death bravely
and to exact no revenge. *Victor*: To avenge murder is a sign
of a stronger character, one that befits a man.   360
Andreas: But a military man. *Victor*: Your father is a soldier.
Andreas: But a Christian. *Victor*: To act bravely is a Christian
characteristic. *Andreas*: To endure bravely is a Christian
characteristic. *Victor*: I know how to act and endure bravely
and am willing to do so. *Andreas*: The one who endures doom bravely   365
acts bravely enough. *Victor*: It is my wish to die;
I call to witness these temples of my head, sprinkled with white hair;
but I wish to die such a death as will hand over the impious ones to a
     ruinous end equal
with mine. *Andreas*: A Christian is not permitted to hand over anyone
to a ruinous end. *Victor*: Except an enemy. *Andreas*: He may not do so   370
even to an enemy. *Victor*: But one is permitted to destroy an enemy
who piles up destruction. *Andreas*: One may not destroy an enemy even
     when

perdere. Repone, genitor, arma! *Victor:* Mihi ultio
restat paranda. Non ego ulciscar? *Andreas:* Tenet
retrahitque pietas. *Victor:* Ergo pietatem putas?   375
Scelus est. *Andreas:* Genitor, O genitor, irae fac modum!
Hic Christianum dedecet pectus furor;
O genitor, arma pone! *Victor:* Ponam, at hostium
sanguine nocenti perlita. *Andreas:* Inhonora nece
claudes supremum genitor heu meus diem?   380
Victor: Inhonora non sunt fata, quae virtus parit.
Andreas: Virtutis umbra pectus heroum gravas.
Generosa virtus impetu ferri nequit
furoris. *Victor:* Ira quandoque rapitur (ut iubet
lex) in nocentes. *Andreas:* Nemini nocere imperat   385
lex Christiana, neminem perdit reum.
O parce, genitor, natus, O genitor, rogat;
miserere nati! *Victor:* Mitte, quas fundis preces
male ominatus? *Andreas:* Natus, en, supplex rogat;
miserere nati, genitor! *Victor:* Hoc nomen sile,   390
ignava suboles! Nescio insanam parens
subolem. Facesse! *Andreas:* Per deum supplex rogo;
miserere nati supplicantis per deum!
Victor: Deo exsecrandas perdere catervas vetat!
Facesse! *Andreas:* Parcit hostibus mitis deus.   395
Victor: Ultor scelestis imminet. *Andreas:* Numquam tamen
praeproperus urget supplicia. Crebro moras
trahendo differt. *Victor:* Damna si densat mora
maturus instat. *Andreas:* Perduelli distulit
mihi tibique lentus in poenas deus.   400
Compesce tandem pectoris, genitor, minas
et insolentis impetus animi doma.
Victor: Infanda blateras, patris O pudor tui

---

379 *nece*: corrected from *necem* in the manuscript.

394 This line, in which Andreas (who is present in front of Victor) is referred to in the third person, must be an aside addressed to the audience or to Theodorus.

he takes away one's life. Put down your arms, father! *Victor*: There remains
    revenge
for me to prepare. Shall I not exact revenge? *Andreas*: Piety takes hold of you
and drags you back. *Victor*: So you think this is piety? 375
This is a crime! *Andreas*: Father, O father, put a limit to your anger!
This rage is unbecoming of a Christian heart;
O father, put down your arms! *Victor*: I shall put them down, but after
    they have been
drenched with the sinful blood of our enemies. *Andreas*: Will you
    close your last days,
alas, my father, with dishonourable slaughter? 380
Victor: The doom which virtue begets is not dishonourable.
Andreas: You weigh down your heroic heart with what is a mere
    shadow of virtue.
Noble virtue cannot be carried away by the impetus
of rage. *Victor*: It is sometimes carried away by rage (as law
commands) against criminals. *Andreas*: Christian law commands one 385
to harm nobody, it condemns nobody as being guilty.
Be forgiving, O father; your son, O father, begs you;
take pity on your son! *Victor*: Abandon your prayers, which you pour out
under a bad omen. *Andreas*: Behold, your son asks you as a supplicant;
take pity on your son, father! *Victor*: Don't say that word, 390
you cowardly descendant! I, as a father, do not acknowledge an insane
descendant. Go away! *Andreas*: I ask you in the name of God as a supplicant;
take pity on your son, who begs you in the name of God!
Victor: [*Aside*] He forbids me to destroy crowds that are execrable to God!
Go away! *Andreas*: Gentle God forgives his enemies. 395
Victor: He threatens criminals as an avenger. *Andreas*: Yet he never
urges punishments over-hastily. Often he causes delay
by waiting. *Victor*: If delay makes calamities heavier,
he strikes at the right time. *Andreas*: When we were his enemies,
God was slow to punish us. 400
Hold back the threats of your heart at last, father,
and tame the impetus of your haughty breast.
Victor: You blabber unspeakable things, oh shame of your father

---

399–400 *Perduelli . . . deus*: Andreas's logic is that since God patiently waited
for him and Victor to convert voluntarily, so they must be equally patient and
forgiving toward their persecutors now.

aevique nostri dedecus! Novi satis,
quid militarem deceat animum. Proh! Pudet   405
spectare prolem milite indignam patre.
Procul facesse! Sanguinis probrum mei
grave est tueri. *Andreas*: Genitor, abeam? *Victor*: Abi! Patris
omitte nomen. Auribus grave est. Abi!
Vel perduellis primus hac manu cades.   410
Andreas: Rediturus abeo, dum patris sidat furor.
Victor: Abi! Statutum est. Sidet hic numquam furor.
Ergo tyrannos pariter involvam nece
et laureatus, quam dedit vitam deus
deo refundam. Fortiter patiar mihi   415
numquam pudendus. Fortiter similis mei
agam. *Theodorus*: Ergo sequar te socius ad mortem, O here,
seu fortiter agere aut pati tecum iubes.
Victor: Pectus animosum, filio magis sapis.
I, sequere fortis laureae consors meae!   420
Theodorus: Ibo libenter, ibo. Tibi comitem rigor
me nullus Orci facere dissimilem potest.
Victor: Praeeo. Stat animus, spiritum dum exhauriam,
hostem ferire. Sic mori volo lubens.

II.2

Andream parentis causa maestum amici solantur et sua opera eius animum
   mutandum promittunt.
Andreas, Secundus, Leo, Quirinus, Petrus.
Andreas: Heu, quam medullas rodit invisus dolor,   425
rapitque mentem sede deiectam sua!

---

406 *patre*: Corrected from *parte* in the manuscript.

413 *involvam*: Corrected from *incoluam* in the manuscript.

425–62 II.2. Andreas, grieving over his father's obstinacy, is joined by Leo
and Quirinus, the bystanders in I.5, as well as Secundus and Petrus, two other

and disgrace of my old age! I know well enough
what suits a soldier's heart. Alas, I am ashamed   405
to look on a child unworthy of a martial father.
Go far away! It is hard to look upon
the disgrace of my blood. *Andreas:* Shall I go away, father? *Victor:* Go
  away! Do not say
the word 'father'. It is harsh on my ears. Go away!
Otherwise you will fall first by my hand as my enemy.   410
Andreas: [*Starting to leave stage, as an aside*] I am going away, but I shall
  return, when my father's rage has subsided.
Victor: Go away! My mind is made up. This rage shall never subside.
So, I shall cut down the tyrants together in slaughter,
and, crowned with victory, shall pour my life back to God,
the life which God gave me. I shall endure bravely, never an object of
  shame   415
to myself. I shall act bravely, true
to myself. *Theodorus:* So will I follow you as your companion to death,
  O master,
whether you command me to act or to endure bravely with you.
Victor: Brave heart, you are wiser than my son.
Go! Follow me as a brave companion of my laurel!   420
Theodorus: I shall go willingly, I shall go. No fear of the underworld
can turn me into a companion unequal to you.
Victor: I go first. For me it is a fixed decision, as long as I draw my breath,
to strike the enemy. Thus I want to die of my own accord. [*Victor and
  Theodorus exit*]

II.2

Friends console Andreas, who is sad on account of his parent, and promise
  that they will make him change his mind with their help.
Andreas, Secundus, Leo, Quirinus, Petrus.
Andreas: Alas, how much does hateful grief eat away at my marrows   425
and take hold of my mind, which has been unseated from its place!

---

local believers. These fellow faithful offer their help in Andreas's attempt to
calm Victor down and teach him the correct way of martyrdom. Like Leo and
Quirinus, so Secundus and Petrus are generic characters with no identifiable
historical models.

Heu, genitor, ultro pergis annosis gravis
artubus in hostem Christianae nescius
felicitatis? Caelites, caecos senis
inhibete motus! Gaudia, heu, miscet viae   430
nec patitur aequis fluere laetitiam rotis
aestus parentis. Martyr excipiam necem.
Gaudeo! Sed ingens gaudium expungit dolor.
Genitor profanae laureae fuco satur
palma carebit martyrum? Superi, malum   435
prohibete! Liceat ah, mihi liceat mori
et pro parente! Moriar ah, moriar libens!
Sed en, Secundus omine secundo venit.
Secunde, salve! Vosque salvete, et modum
meo dolori ponite. *Secundus*: Absorptum dolor   440
quis pectus agitat? *Andreas*: Heu, dolor acerbus animi,
animi molestus gaudio inserpit dolor.
Secundus: Quis, fare, dubiis fluctuat vicibus dolor
obiectus animi gaudio? *Leo*: Mentem explica!
Andreas: Heu, genitor aestus anxios nato creat.   445
Secundus: Aetate fessum summa fors hora evocat?
Andreas: Ah, evocasset! Cura tangeret minor
prolem parentis. *Secundus*: Fare; qua causa creat
genitor dolores? *Andreas*: Percitum gravis furor
agitavit oestro, fluctuat, spirat neces   450
cladesque. *Quirinus*: Nondum cessit hic animo furor?
Andreas: Heu, gravis ardet. *Quirinus*: Tempore abscedet suo.
Moderare luctum! *Andreas*: Crescet, heu, crescet magis
exulcerato. *Quirinus*: Ratio cum vincat, furor
cito sopietur. *Andreas*: Obstinatus cum negat   455

---

438 *Secundus omine secundo*: A pun on the proper name Secundus, homonymous with the adjective meaning 'favourable'.

446 *Aetate*: The manuscript has *Aestate*, but the word is emended here since the action is set in winter (see line 64 and Introduction 3.1). Victor's old age is also repeatedly mentioned elsewhere (cf. e.g. 46–7).

Alas, father, do you continue on your way, weighed down by your aged
    limbs,
against your enemy, ignorant of Christian
felicity? Heavenly beings, hold back the blind motions
of the old man! Alas, the passion of my parent confounds   430
the joys of my path, nor does it allow my happiness
to coast along on balanced wheels. I shall accept death as a martyr;
I rejoice! But this huge grief expunges my joy.
Shall my father, full of the pretence of a profane laurel,
be without the victory-palm of martyrs? Heavenly beings, prohibit   435
this evil! O let me die and let me die
for my parent! O I shall die, I shall die willingly! [*Sees Secundus and his
    friends enter*]
But look, Secundus comes in a fortunate omen.
Secundus, greetings! And greetings to you all, now please put an end
to my grief. *Secundus*: What grief agitates your engrossed   440
heart? *Andreas*: Alas, a harsh grief of the mind,
a bothersome grief of the mind creeps into my joy.
Secundus: Speak, what grief, thrown against the joy of your mind,
fluctuates with uncertain motions? *Leo*: Explain your thoughts!
Andreas: Alas, my parent creates anxious worries for me, his son.   445
Secundus: Is his last hour perhaps pulling him away, as he has been
    fatigued by his age?
Andreas: Oh, I wish it were so! Then, a smaller worry for my father
    would have laid hold
Upon me, the son. *Secundus*: Speak; why does your father cause
grief? *Andreas*: A heavy rage has stirred him up,
excited with frenzy, he is restless, he spews out slaughter   450
and destruction. *Quirinus*: Has this rage not left his mind yet?
Andreas: Alas, it burns on heavily. *Quirinus*: It will go away in its own time.
Control your grief! *Andreas*: It will grow, alas, it will grow more
as my wound grows. *Quirinus*: When reason triumphs, rage
will soon be put to rest. *Andreas*: As he obstinately refuses to give   455

---

452 *Heu*: metrically, two syllables are required in this position. *Heu* is usually
a monosyllable but here it may be taken as a dissyllable by diaeresis, or the
scribe may have mistakenly written *eheu* as *heu*.

455 *Obstinatus cum negat*: Since a causal relationship is implied with the
next phrase, the subjunctive *neget* would be somewhat better, but the reading
of the manuscript is kept here.

aures, ratio nil efficit. *Secundus*: Novi senem;
consilia numquam respuet, rabies cadet.
Petrus: Dolorem acerbum mitiga; evincent preces.
Andreas: Ni concitabunt. *Petrus*: Sit silex, precibus fluet,
ut cera mollis. *Leo*: Ecce, fert contra gradus.   460
Andreas: Ut saevus ira tumuit! *Secundus*: An cedat tumor,
libet experiri.

II.3

Victor ab amicis persuasus arma abicit.
Victor, Andreas, Secundus, Leo, Quirinus, Petrus, Theodorus.
    Secundus: O Christiani fax gregis
decusque, salve! Vive felices dies!
Victor: Et vos, beati vivite! *Andreas*: Et natus iubet
salvere patrem. *Victor*: Natus hoc dignus patre,   465
si patris animos induat. *Secundus*: Natus senis
lumen et imago patris ac morum aemulus.
Leo: Alterque Victor. *Quirinus*: Natus, ut parens, probus.
Petrus: Et Christiani nominis honor, ut pater.
Victor: Sed meticulosus. *Andreas*: Nullus hunc animum metus   470
subivit umquam. *Victor*: Fata qui cavet, pavor
hunc arguit. *Andreas*: Quem nuntius mortis movet,
illum pavores arguunt. *Victor*: Me non movet;
moriar libenter. *Leo*: Hostium insidiis tamen
obstare pergis. *Quirinus*: Fortis est ultro necem   475
expetere. *Victor*: Mortem fessus hic animus diu

462–520 II.3. When Victor returns on stage, he is met not only by Andreas but also by his fellow believers Leo, Quirinus, Secundus and Petrus. The latter four, as promised, pile on Victor in order to reconcile him to his son and to make him lay down his arms, arguing that true Christian fortitude is manifested in passive submission to persecution. Victor reluctantly agrees and Theodorus likewise abandons the plan for armed resistance.

his ears, reason is of no effect. *Secundus*: I know the old man;
he will never reject advice; his madness will subside.
Petrus: Mitigate your harsh grief; our prayers will win him over.
Andreas: Unless they egg him on. *Petrus*: Even if he is made of flint-
stone, he will melt with prayers
like soft wax. *Leo*: [*Seeing Victor returning on stage*] Look, he comes
this way.   460
Andreas: How savagely does he swell with anger! *Secundus*: I want to
try and see
if this swelling subsides.

II.3

Victor, persuaded by his friends, throws down his arms.
Victor, Andreas, Secundus, Leo, Quirinus, Petrus, Theodorus.
          Secundus: O torch of the Christian flock
and its grace, greetings! Live through your happy days.
Victor: And all of you, live happily. *Andreas*: Also your son
wishes his father to be well. *Victor*: A son is worthy of his father for
this reason,   465
namely if he adopts his spirit. *Secundus*: The son is the splendour
of the father, his very image and a rival of his morals.
Leo: And another Victor. *Quirinus*: This son is upright like his parent.
Petrus: And an honour to Christianity like his father.
Victor: But he is timid. *Andreas*: [Pointing at his breast] No fear ever
came close   470
to this, my heart. *Victor*: He who guards against his doom,
clearly has fear. *Andreas*: He whom the message of death moves,
he clearly has fears. *Victor*: It does not move me;
I shall die willingly. *Leo*: Nonetheless, you keep on standing in the way
of the plots of our enemies. *Quirinus*: It is the sign of a brave man   475
to seek death of one's own accord. *Victor*: This exhausted heart has long
wished

The usage of *persuasus* as a past passive participle in the scene outline is
rare but classical; see e.g. Cic. *Ad Familiares* 6.7.2.

470 *animum*: Emended from *animus* in the manuscript.

optavit. Ultro moriar, at vindex calor
animum fatigat, urget, ultrices manus
in arma cogit. *Quirinus*: Victor, heu, praeceps abis?
Secundus: Meliora, Victor! Comprime effrenem impetum 480
gliscentis odii, corque populantem doma
flammam furoris! *Victor*: Fusus hostium cruor
solum domabit, laureis fetus cruor.
Secundus: Heu, Victor, heu! Ignobilis lauri expetis
decus profanum. *Victor*: Laurus est sat nobilis 485
et non profana, sternere nocentes viros,
ut innocentum hac strage redimatur salus.
Secundus: Maius periclum pariet incautus furor.
Victor: Maiorque crescet gloriae seges. *Leo*: Preme,
preme, Victor, iram mentis. *Victor*: Impatiens premi 490
tumet ira. *Leo*: Legem Christianam respice,
an deceat hoc te. *Victor*: Christiana lex docet,
fidem tueri fortiter. *Quirinus*: Cuncti fidem
pariter tuemur nec tamen ferrum manu
stringimus in hostis fata. *Secundus*: Quod cuncti probant, 495
cur refugis unus? *Victor*: Arma militem decent.
Secundus: Haec Christianus abnuit miles. *Victor*: Sacra
propugnat armis. Laureis obicem facis.
Secundus: Te mente ab ista revocet exemplum patrum.
Victor: Id destinatum facinus accelerat magis 500
et concitatum pectus urget. *Secundus*: Non patres
sic agitat ultrix furia; sed beneficiis
armantur hosti. *Andreas*: Te tui hortentur patres;
hos aemulare. *Petrus*: Suadet hoc pietas patrum
suadetque pietas martyrum. *Andreas*: Hos sequere, O pater! 505

---

499 In the manuscript, no change of speaker is indicated. But context requires that this line be given to Secundus or at least to some character other than Victor or Theodorus.

499–505 The *patres* whose example and teaching Victor is here urged to follow are the Catholic missionary priests. The Martyrdom of Twenty-Six Saints which forms the backdrop of this story started when Franciscan as

for death. I shall die of my own account, but the ardour for revenge
drives on, eggs on my heart, and forces my avenging hands
to take up arms. *Quirinus*: Alas, Victor, are you rushing away headlong?
Secundus: You should do better, Victor! Hold back the unbridled
    impetus   480
of your blazing hatred, and tame the flame of rage which
is ravaging your heart! *Victor*: The blood of the enemy, when it is shed,
will alone tame it, the blood that is rich in laurels.
Secundus: Alas, Victor, alas! You seek out the profane honour
of an ignoble laurel. *Victor*: To defeat harmful fellows   485
is a sufficiently noble, and not profane, laurel,
so that the safety of the innocent may be guaranteed by their destruction.
Secundus: Incautious rage begets greater danger.
Victor: But the harvest of glory shall grow greater. *Leo*: Repress,
repress, Victor, the anger of your mind. *Victor*: My anger swells,   490
impatient at being repressed. *Leo*: Take a good look at Christian law,
to see if this befits you. *Victor*: Christian law teaches us
to defend our faith bravely. *Quirinus:* We all equally
defend our faith, nonetheless we do not draw the sword
with our hands for the enemy's doom. *Secundus*: Why do you alone
    refuse   495
what everyone approves of? *Victor*: Arms are fitting for a soldier.
Secundus: A Christian soldier renounces them. *Victor*: With arms
he defends the sacred rites. You hinder my laurels.
Secundus: May the example of the priests call you away from that mindset.
Victor: It rather adds haste to my resolved purpose   500
and urges on my excited heart. *Secundus*: Avenging fury
does not agitate the priests in this way; but they are armed against the
    enemy
with good deeds. *Andreas*: Let your priests exhort you;
emulate them. *Petrus*: The piety of the priests counsels thus
and the piety of the martyrs too. *Andreas*: Follow them, oh father!   505

---

well as Jesuit priests and missionaries were rounded up by the local authorities
(see Introduction 1.1 and 3.1).

502 *furia*: Emended from *furiae* in the manuscript for the sake of metre.
furia in the singular, while rare, is classically attested (see e.g. Cic. *Pro Sestio*
33). Cf. also note to *JM* 55.

Victor: Ponere iubetis arma militem? *Petrus*: Iubent
id monita Christi. *Andreas*: Sequere praeeuntem deum
pietate forti! *Victor*: Vincor! Invitum trahunt
haec monita pectus. *Vincor!* *Theodorus*: Here, facinus pie
semel incohatum deseris? *Victor*: Vincor! Prece   510
extinctus ardor friget; ingrata mihi
pietate coepta desero. *Theodorus*: Arma, si praeis,
reicio, Victor. *Victor*: Sequere, reicio. *Theodorus*: Sequor.
Victor: Ut placeo, nate? *Andreas*: Perge, sic belle places;
Sic perge! *Victor:* Pergam. *Andreas*: Quanta mihi, genitor, paris   515
gaudia! Recedit tristitia animo et prior
menti recurrit languidae serenitas.
O sacra turba! Digna, quam caelum suo
beet favore; debitas vobis vices
superi rependant; redditis nato patrem.   520

II.4

Victor, nuntio de captis patribus accepto, arma abiecta repetit nec flecti
    amplius potest.
Victor, Andreas, Secundus, Iustus, Leo, Quirinus, Petrus, Theodorus.
Iustus: Heu, dura fata! Heu, fata! *Secundus*: Quae fata ingemit?
Iustus: Heu, dura nimium fata! *Andreas*: Iuste, quid gemis?
Quae fata luges? *Iustus*: Quae dolor loqui vetat,
amor tacere. Heu, Christiani! *Andreas*: Proh! Malum
quod Christianos urget? *Iustus*: Heu patres! *Victor*: Mali,   525

---

510 *Prece*: Emended from *Preae* in the manuscript.

521–57 II.4. Iustus, another local believer, rushes in with the news that some
Catholics, including priests, have been arrested and imprisoned in accordance
with the anti-Christian decree. The news reignites Victor's fury who decides
to take up arms again together with Theodorus. Iustus, Andreas and other
fellow believers try to dissuade him in vain.

Victor: Do you order a soldier to put his arms down? *Petrus*: The laws
of Christ order this. *Andreas*: Follow God as your leader
with your brave piety. *Victor*: I am defeated! These precepts take hold
of my unwilling heart. I am defeated! *Theodorus*: Master! Do you abandon
the deed which you piously initiated? *Victor*: I am defeated! My ardour,   510
extinguished with prayer, grows cold; I desert
my plans due to piety, which is bitter to me. *Theodorus*: If you go ahead, I
    throw down
my arms, Victor. *Victor*: Follow me, I throw them down. *Theodorus*: I
    follow. [*Victor and Theodorus lay down their weapons*]
Victor: How am I to your liking, son? *Andreas*: Go on, thus you are very
    pleasing;
go on thus. *Victor*: I shall go on. *Andreas*: Father, what great joy do you
    beget   515
for me! Sadness leaves my mind, and former
serenity returns to my languid soul.
[*To his friends*] O sacred group! You are worthy of being blessed by heaven
with its favour; may the heavenly ones grant you
your deserts; you give back a father to his son.   520

II.4

Victor, having heard the news about the capture of the priests, seeks his
    arms again and cannot be dissuaded any more.
Victor, Andreas, Secundus, Iustus, Leo, Quirinus, Petrus, Theodorus.
Iustus: [*Rushing onto stage*] Alas, harsh fate! Alas, fate! *Secundus*: What
    fate does he bemoan?
Iustus: Alas, too harsh a fate! *Andreas*: Iustus, why do you moan?
What fate do you grieve over? *Iustus*: My grief forbids me to say it
but my love forbids me to keep silent. Alas, Christians! *Andreas*: Alas!
    What evil
eggs on the Christians? *Iustus*: Alas, the priests! *Victor*: Speak out,   525

The new character Iustus is likely to be identified with Iustus Takayama
Ukon, probably the most famous of the *kirishitan daimyō* and hero of several
Jesuit plays, including one performed in the same Munich academy in 1663
(see Introduction 1.1 and 3.2). Ukon is reported to have been active in the
Kyoto-Osaka area around this time (see e.g. Yūki 1994: 92–3, Scioli 2013:
309).

dic, quicquid est. *Iustus*: Ut multa paucis eloquar,
heu, Christianos carcere et patres tenet
rabidus satelles. *Andreas*: O duces sancti! O patres!
O Christiani! *Iustus*: Nosque protinus pari
feritate quaerunt. *Secundus*: Gaudium impar vix capit   530
animus. Favete caelites! Summa evocant
nos decora. Gaude! Christianorum cohors
veneranda, gaude! Martyrum palma imminet.
Andreas: Utinam latentem corde spectetis meo
flammam. Moriar et ad necem, O pater, patres   535
comitabor! *Petrus*: Et nos aemulus honor abripit.
Victor: Ergo hoc supinus sorbeam nefas? Patres,
patres inultus patiar ad caedem rapi?
Abominandum facinus! Hoc patiar probrum?
Mihi reddor iterum. *Theodorus*: Rapimur ulturi scelus.   540
Victor: Redde arma, rapior! Arma mihi amor in patres
repetere suadet. Rapimur! *Theodorus*: Here! Fortis sequar.
Andreas: Heu, genitor, iterum temet in furias agis?
Sine mente pergis? *Victor*: Victimas rursus feror
in destinatas. *Andreas*: Heu! Novus plagam dolor   545
exulceravit. *Victor*: Rursus iratum furor
animum occupavit. Perimere mente mihi sedet.
Andreas: Meliora, genitor! *Victor*: Consilia patris iuva,
ignava proles! *Andreas*: Mitte, quas animo coquis,
O genitor, iras! Mitte! Te supplex rogo.   550
Victor: Absiste! *Iustus*: Iustus, Victor, en supplex rogat.
Victor: Absiste! *Omnes*: Victor, respice preces supplicum!
Victor: Absiste! Mihi maior increvit furor,
en, se renatus. *Andreas*: Mitte! *Victor*: Mitte istas preces!
Deliberatum est. Sancta si patris negas   555

---

529 *Christiani*: Emended from *Christianis* in the manuscript.

553 *Absiste! Mihi*: To save the metre, a syllable must be inserted before or
after *Mihi*. Possibiities include *iam, nunc, -que, -met*.

whatever the evil is. *Iustus*: To say many things with few words,
alas, the raging minion holds Christians
and the priests imprisoned. *Andreas*: O sacred leaders, O our priests,
O Christians! *Iustus*: And they are seeking us out urgently
with the same ferocity. *Secundus*: My mind, unequal to the great joy,
    can hardly   530
grasp hold of it. Heavenly beings, support us! The highest honours
invite us. [*To his friends*] Rejoice! Venerable cohort
of Christians, rejoice! The victory-palm of martyrs comes close.
Andreas: I wish you could all see the flame that is hidden
in my heart. I shall die, and I shall accompany our priests, O father,   535
to death! *Petrus*: A rival sense of honour also takes hold of us.
Victor: So, should I passively take on this disgrace? Shall I let the priests,
the priests be snatched away to slaughter unavenged?
Abominable deed! Am I to endure this disgrace?
I am given back to myself, again. *Theodorus*: We rush on to avenge the
    crime.   540
Victor: Give back my arms, I rush on! Love of the priests persuades me
to take back my arms. We rush on! *Theodorus*: Master, I shall follow
    you bravely.
Andreas: Alas, father, do you drive yourself to fury again?
Do you go on senselessly? *Victor*: I am being carried away again against
    my destined
victims. *Andreas*: Alas! A new grief has opened up   545
my wound. *Victor:* Again, rage has occupied
my angry heart. My mind is resolved on destruction.
Andreas: Do better, father! *Victor*: Help your father's plans,
cowardly descendant! *Andreas*: Abandon the anger, which you
are cooking up in your mind, O father! Abandon it! I beg you as a
    supplicant.   550
Victor: Go away! *Iustus*: Look, Iustus begs you as a supplicant.
Victor: Go away! *All*: Victor! Respect the prayers of supplicants!
Victor: Go away! My anger grows greater,
look, than itself, born anew. *Andreas*: Abandon it! *Victor*: Abandon your
    prayers!
It has been decided. If you refuse to follow bravely   555

---

555 *Sancta*: Emended from *Sanctis* in the manuscript.

decreta fortis exsequi, noli tamen
tardare patiens, quod amor exigit patrum!

II.5

Christiani Andreae lugenti parentem fusis precibus animum flectendum
  promittunt.
Andreas, Secundus, Iustus, Leo, Quirinus, Petrus.
Andreas: Eheu, dolores obiacent semper meae
beatitati, gaudia aestibus novus
dolor inquietat et animo metum ingerit.   560
Heu, genitor iterum rapitur. Infreni tumet
iterum furore durus, intractabilis.
Heu, Christiani generis infamem notam
aevique cani dedecus et ingens probrum
spectare cogor! Siccine annosus senex   565
consilia sana et supplicum spernis preces?
Leges, amicos, filium, patres, deum
avidus cruoris reicis? Nihil est super,
heu, quod dolorem mitiget. Dolor, heu, ferus
nimium reliquias vocis absorbes, dolor.   570
Iustus: Nimium dolorem supprime et luctum exue!
Andreas: Premere dolorem nescio impotens mei.
Iustus: Supprime ferendo fortiter! *Andreas*: Iterum redit.
Iustus: Preme redeuntem! *Secundus*: Casibus duris quati
animoque frangi est in malo duplex malum.   575
Andreas: Lamenta patris memoria revocat; O pater,
male ominatis pergis auspiciis, pater!
Leo: Bene ominatis redeat auspiciis pater.
Quirinus: Spera! Redibit Victor. Impetum senis
cohibebit aether mentium satis potens.   580

558–91 II.5. Andreas is despondent over his father's stubbornness. His five
faithful comrades remind him that where earthly means fail, prayer must be
the next resort.

the sacred decrees of your father, do not, to add insult to injury,
delay with your pacifism what my love for the priests demands! [*Leaves
   stage*]

II.5

The Christians promise Andreas, who is mourning over his parent, that
   they will make the latter change his mind by pouring out prayers.
Andreas, Secundus, Iustus, Leo, Quirinus, Petrus.
Andreas: Alas, grief always stands in the way of my
happiness, a new pain disturbs my joy
with its passions and drives fear into my heart.   560
Alas, my parent rushes on again. Again he swells up angrily
with unbridled rage, intractable.
Alas, I am forced to watch this infamous blemish
of the Christian flock, the shame of white old age
and the huge disgrace! Do you, an aged old man   565
spurn the sane counsels and prayers of supplicants?
Do you reject laws, friends, your son, the priests and God,
and seek bloodshed? There is nothing left,
alas, which could mitigate my grief. Alas, grief, too ferociously
do you, grief, drink up the remnants of my voice.   570
Iustus: Suppress your excessive grief and stop mourning!
Andreas: I lack control of my own self and I know not how to suppress
   my grief.
Iustus: Suppress it by enduring bravely! *Andreas*: It comes back again.
Iustus: Suppress it when it returns! *Secundus*: To be shaken by harsh events
and to be heartbroken is a double evil in an evil situation.   575
Andreas: My father's memory brings back again my laments; O father,
father, you go on under auspices that were begun badly!
Leo: May he return under well-grounded auspices.
Quirinus: Keep on hoping! Victor will return. Heaven, having sufficient
   power over human minds,
will hold back the impetus of the old man.   580

---

565 *annosus*: Emended from *innosus* in the manuscript.

571 *supprime*: Emended from *supprimet* in the manuscript.

Andreas: Utinam secundet omen hoc aether mihi!
Quirinus: Precibus secundos sortietur exitus;
referet parentem pronus in preces polus.
Iustus: Libet adoriri, et luctui ut veniat tuo
medicina. *Petrus*: Fide; sopient rabiem senis   585
benigna terris astra. Supplicibus favent
suis amantque; nec pie effusas preces
surdis capessunt auribus. *Andreas*: Aliquid spei
affulget animo. Supplicis deo preces
iuvate iunctis precibus, ut numen cito   590
placetur. *Omnes*: Agimus. Pariter aggredimur polum.

II.Chorus

Precantur deum pro mutando senis animo, eo interim se cum Theodoro in
    hostem animante, qui demum ab eo recedit.
Priores omnes (chorus), Victor, Theodorus.
Chorus: O Christe, vena munerum
et aureus canalis,
sinus reclude viscerum
nec sperne supplicantes!   595
En, supplices prosternimur,
tuam tenemus aram.
En, lacrimarum flumine
preces inundat imber.
Qui mitis inter hostium,   600
ut agnus, is catervas
nec vindicas iniuriam,
cum tela sunt parata,
O Christe, mentis impetus
compesce vindicantes!   605

---

583 *parentem*: Emended from *parentum* in the manuscript.

592–664 II chorus. Andreas and his five friends pray to heaven for Victor's
conversion. As a result Victor's ardour seems reduced, although he is short of
abandoning his stubborn resolve. The prayer however has a greater effect on
Theodorus, who suddenly loses his fighting spirit and leaves his protesting
master.

Andreas: May heaven support your omen on my behalf!
Quirinus: It will allot favourable outcomes to prayers;
heaven, favourably disposed to prayer, will bring back your parent.
Iustus: Let us begin, so that for your grief, too, a solution
will arise. *Petrus*: Believe; heaven, which is favourable to earth,   585
will put the old man's rage to rest. They favour and love those
who supplicate them; nor do they close up their ears to
prayers that are piously poured out. *Andreas*: A measure of hope
shines on my mind. Help my prayer, as I supplicate God,
with your joint prayers, so that divine power may soon   590
become favourable. *All*: We do so. We are soliciting heaven together.

II.Chorus

They pray to God for a change in the old man's heart, while he stirs up his
    mind against the enemy together with Theodorus, who leaves him in
    the end.
Chorus (*Andreas, Secundus, Iustus, Leo, Quirinus, Petrus*), *Victor, Theodorus*.
Chorus: O Christ, vein of grace
and golden channel,
open up your innermost bosom
and do not spurn your supplicants.   595
Behold, we, the supplicants, lie prostrate
and we hold onto your altar.
Behold, a stream of tears,
like rain, drenches our prayers.
You, who go into the midst of an army   600
of enemies, mild as a lamb,
and do not avenge an injury
when arms stand ready,
O Christ, repress the urge
of the mind that is eager for revenge.   605

The metre is a combination of iambic trimetre spoken by Victor and
Theodorus and iambic dimetre/iambic dimetre catalectic chanted by Andreas
and his friends. The metrical scheme reinforces the pagan/Christian
dichotomy represented by the two groups on stage (see Introduction 3.4).

Nec irruat per hostium
Victor cruentus enses!
Victor: Adesto lictor! Vincula inice; pretium
tuo labori, quem vides, mucro dabit.
Chorus: Non Christus isto tramite   610
praeivit ad triumphum.
Qui vincla mitis excipis,
hunc mitiga furorem!
Victor: Adesto! Mille destina poenis caput
senile! Mille mihi modis votum est mori   615
pro Christianis patribus, fide et deo.
Chorus: Non Christus isto tramite
praeivit ad triumphum.
†Qui mille clades excipis,
da mille fata, temnat†.   620
Victor: Scelerata turba! Vulnere hoc pectus feri
non imparatum! Victor ingrediar polum;
sed tu praeibis, victima stygi debita.
Chorus: Non Christus isto tramite
praeivit ad triumphum.   625
Haec, Christe, vena, pectoris
hunc sopiat calorem!
Victor: Generosa dextra, roboris quicquid viget
collige! Patrumque vindica caedem sacra
pietate felix!   630
Chorus: Non Christus isto tramite
praeivit ad triumphum.
Per sacra dextrae vulnera
manum tene cruentam. *Victor*: Pergo; in hostiles volo
praeceps catervas. Ultimos, fracti pedes,   635
revocate nervos! Gloria suprema excitet.
Theodorus: Mihi pes hebescit, arma detrectat manus.
Chorus: Non Christus isto tramite
praeivit ad triumphum.
Per sacra calcis vulnera   640

619–20 The meaning of these two lines is obscure. Perhaps *excipis* (619)
should be emended to *excipit* and/or *temnat* (620) to *temnet*.

622 *Victor*: A rather bald pun on the speaker's name.

and may Victor not rush through
his enemies, holding his bloody sword.
Victor: Guardsman, come! Throw me into chains! The blade,
which you see, will repay you for your pains.
Chorus: Christ did not precede you to triumph   610
through that path.
You, who mildly let chains weigh on you,
mitigate this rage.
Victor: Come! Give over my old head to a thousand
punishments. It is my wish to die in a thousand ways   615
for our Christian priests, for faith, and for God.
Chorus: Christ did not precede you to triumph
through that path.
†You, who take on a thousand calamities,
give him a thousand deaths, he would despise them†.   620
Victor: Criminal crowd! Strike this breast with your blow,
my breast, which is fully prepared. I shall enter heaven as a victor.
But you will go ahead of me, you victim destined to hell.
Chorus: Christ did not precede you to triumph
through that path.   625
May this channel, Christ, put to rest
this heat of the breast.
Victor: Noble right hand! Whatever strength abounds in you,
gather it, and happy in sacred piety, avenge
the murder of priests.   630
Chorus: Christ did not precede you to triumph
through that path.
By the sacred wounds of your right hand
hold back the bloody hand. *Victor*: I go on; I fly headlong into
the hostile crowd. My broken legs, summon back   635
your last remaining strength. Let the final glory incite you.
Theodorus: My foot grows numb; my hand drops its arms.
Chorus: Christ did not precede you to triumph
through that path.
By the sacred wounds of your foot   640

630–4 *pietate felix . . . pergo*: Victor's words, though separated by four lines
given to the chorus of his friends, still manage to form one line of iambic
trimetre.

pedes tene ruentes!
Victor: Heu, quis medullis torpor inserpit meis?
Theodorus: Mihique friget animus expers roboris
et abire suadet. Vincor! *Victor*: Instabilis vices,
Theodore, mentis abice. Ubi primus vigor,   645
Theodore? Consta! *Theodorus*: Vincor, heu, vincor. Novus
me vincit ardor. *Victor*: Mollis es nimium, puer.
Consta, anime! Consta! *Theodorus*: Christianorum globo
me iungo. Longas trahere quid moras iuvat?
Hinc abeo, Victor! Propero, quo pietas vocat.   650
Victor: Ignave, propera, trepida quo pietas vocat!
Nil agere possum genere non dignum meo.
Ibo, ibo solus. Turpiter nequeo mori.
Chorus: Non Christus isto tramite
praeivit ad triumphum.   655
Qui mitis alto stipite
ab hostibus triumphas,
da, Christe, Victor aemulus
sequatur ad triumphos.
Lamenta, Christe, supplicum   660
precesque mitis audi.
Per te, deus, rogantium
preces benignus audi.

III.1

Victor languentem animum ad vindictam excitat.
Victor.
Victor: Et mihi pavores viscera obruunt pigri
ferrumque lentus horreo. Extincto riget   665
calore pectus. Ultionem animus fugit
imbellis. Abeunt odia nolenti quoque.
Negat mucronem segnior manus. Quid hoc?
Sic tibi pudendus redderis, Victor? Tibi
dispar abhorres caede? Trepidus deseris   670

664–84 III.1. Victor speaking alone admits to a decrease in his fighting spirit but reminds himself of the shame of deserting the priests. He

hold back the rushing feet.
Victor: Alas! What numbness crawls into my bones?
Theodorus: And my powerless heart grows cold
and persuades me to go away. I am defeated! *Victor*: Theodorus, abandon
the unstable turn of your mind. Where is your pristine strength,   645
Theodorus? Stand firm! *Theodorus*: I am defeated, alas, I am defeated!
    A new
ardour defeats me. *Victor*: You are a boy, too soft.
Stand firm, my heart, stand firm! *Theodorus*: I join myself
to the Christian crowd. What profit is there in tarrying long?
I am going away from here, Victor! I hurry off to where piety calls me.   650
Victor: Coward! Hurry off to where cowardly piety calls you.
I can do nothing unworthy of my lineage.
I will go, I will go alone. I cannot die shamefully.
Chorus: Christ did not precede you to triumph
through that path.   655
You, who triumph over your enemies
mercifully from your tall cross,
Christ, grant that Victor, as your rival, would
follow you to triumph.
Mercifully, Christ, listen to the laments   660
and prayers of your supplicants.
Mercifully, God, listen to the prayers
of those asking in your name. [*Everyone leaves stage except Victor*]

III.1

Victor stirs up his mind for revenge.
Victor.
Victor: Slovenly fear takes hold also of my inner self,
and reluctantly do I fear the sword. My heart grows cold   665
with its heat gone. My cowardly breast turns away
from revenge. Hatred leaves me, even as I am unwilling to let go of it.
My hand is lazier and refuses the sword. What is this?
Victor, do you thus become shameful to yourself? Dissimilar
to your own self, do you abhor slaughter? Do you, coward, desert   670

---

reanimates himself with thoughts of military glory and appears ready to take
up arms again.

pie auspicatum facinus? O iners manus,
elumbe pectus, qualis in regni prius
fueras tyrannos ultor, heu, talem piget
pro patribus esse? O pudor gravis, heu, scelus
abominandum! Victor, age! Similem tibi   675
te redde, Victor, esse si melior negas!
Consta, anime, consta fortis! In apertum ruat
vindicta callem. Roscidos necdum suo
artus cruore cernis? O probrum! Patres
deseris, ut hostis vivat? Hoc scelus feres,   680
inultus ut sis? Militi, heu, dirus pudor!
Aude, anime fortis! Primus increscat calor;
Aude, anime, perge, nobili victoria
hoc laureatus infer in caelum caput!

III.2

Modesti nepotis sui intrepido ad martyrium animo Victor recreatur.
Victor, Modestus.
Modestus: O me beatum gaudio! O quanto exsilit   685
amore pectus! Gaudii modum capit
vix animus impar. Vena laetitiae micat
omnis. *Victor*: Modeste, fare; quis animum tenet
insuetus ardor? *Modestus*: Martyrum, O ave, imminet
mihi corona. Gaudeo! *Victor*: O avo nepos   690
avoque tali digne! Vincula et necem
non extimescis? *Modestus*: Quid necem timeam, O ave?
Victor: Necis metum natura cunctis indidit.
Modestus: Non ego miselli spiritus sic sum tenax,
ut fata timeam. Moriar! O cito accidat   695

---

675 *pro patribus esse? O pudor*: As these words stand, the elision between *esse* and *O* makes the line unmetrical. The metre could be saved by changing *esse* to *fieri*, with no difference in overall meaning.

685–707 III.2. Victor's appropriately named grandson Modestus ('modest') appears on stage, rejoicing in the imminent prospect of martyrdom. Victor,

a deed that was begun piously? O my lazy hand!
My spineless heart! You were an avenger for the tyrants of the realm
before; do you refuse to be such an avenger
for the priests? O heavy shame, alas, abominable
crime! Come, Victor! Become like 675
your own self, Victor, if you refuse to become better!
Stay, my mind, stay strong! Let revenge rush onto
its open path. Do you not yet see the limbs
dripping with their own blood? Oh disgrace! Do you desert
the priests, so that the enemy may stay alive? Do you allow this crime 680
and not exact revenge? O dire shame for a soldier!
Dare, my brave mind! Let my pristine ardour increase;
dare, my mind! Go on! Raise this head up
into heaven, crowned with noble victory.

II.2

Victor is refreshed by the resolve of Modestus, his grandson, who is
   fearless in the face of martyrdom.
Victor, Modestus.
Modestus: [*Enters stage*] O how blessed am I with happiness! Oh, with
   how much love 685
does my breast exult! My mind, unequal to the quantity of the
   happiness it feels
can hardly take stock of it. Every strain of joy
sparkles forth. *Victor:* Speak, Modestus; what unaccustomed ardour
takes hold of your mind? *Modestus:* O grandfather, the crown of martyrs
comes close to me. I rejoice! *Victor:* O grandson worthy 690
of your grandfather, and of such a grandfather! Are you not afraid
of chains and of death? *Modestus:* Why should I fear death, O grandfather?
Victor: Nature endowed everyone with the fear of death.
Modestus: I am not so greedy of my miserable earthly life
as to fear death. Let me die! O may this happen to me 695

---

witnessing Modestus's readiness to die (not yet knowing that the youngster
intends to submit meekly to persecution), rejoices and praises him as a child
worthy of his gallant grandfather.

mihi! *Victor*: O senectae grande solamen meae!
Sic fata nosti temnere et mori expetis!
Modestus: Quid fata timeam? Laureas spondet deus
vitamque spero morte defunctus pia
nec longioris opto mihi vitae moram.   700
Maturus aevi est, qui mori potest deo.
Victor: Mature nimium laureae puer sacrae!
Sic perge fortis; ducet ad vitam necis
contemptus iste. Perge! *Modestus*: Sat terris diu,
cum nascar astris, sat, ave, vixi, nec mori   705
recuso.

III.3

Victor Narcissi et Modesti nepotum pietate victus arma abicit.
Victor, Modestus, Narcissus.
        Victor: Proh! Quae turbidis sedet genis,
Narcisse, nubes? *Modestus*: Fratris, heu, vultu dolor
inusitatus gaudium expulit. Quid hoc,
frater? Tyranni supplicia trepidus gemis?
Narcissus: Non sunt gemenda. Pectus in mortem affero   710
non imparatum. *Victor*: Macte generosa puer
virtute! Consta fortiter! Sed quid gemis?
Modestus: Expelle luctum, frater! Hic fleri nequit,
qui nos triumphus evocat. Luctum exue!
Narcissus: Iterum recurrens gaudia expellit dolor,   715

---

701 See note to *JM* 1463.

706–77 III.3. Another appropriately named grandson, Narcissus (the name
most famously of the beautiful and narcissistic young man in Greek
mythology, see e.g. Ov. *Met.* 3.346–493), joins the two on stage. Unlike
Modestus, Narcissus appears sad; not because he fears martyrdom, but
because his grandfather is not ready to die peacefully as befits a Christian
martyr. Victor is initially offended at the suggestion that armed resistance to
persecution is impious, but the two boys together manage to convince their

quickly! *Victor:* O grand solace of my old age!
You know how to despise doom and seek to die in such a way!
Modestus: Why should I fear death? God promises me laurels
and I hope for life after I piously go through death,
nor do I wish to wait and live longer.   700
The one who can die for God is mature in age.
Victor: You boy of sacred laurel, so very mature!
Go on bravely in this way; that contempt of death
will bring you to life. Go on! *Modestus:* I have lived on earth for long
    enough,
since I am born for heaven, grandfather, nor do I refuse   705
to die.

III.3

Victor, overcome by the piety of his grandsons Narcissus and Modestus,
    throws down his arms.
Victor, Modestus, Narcissus.
        Victor: [*Seeing his other grandson entering stage*] Alas! What
        cloud sits on your saddened
face, Narcissus? *Modestus:* Alas, the unusual signs of grief
on my brother's face have erased my joy. What is this,
brother? Do you tremble and groan over the punishment expected
    from the tyrant?
Narcissus: This is not what I groan over. I bear a heart not unprepared   710
for death. *Victor:* Bravo, boy of noble
virtue! Stand firm, with courage! But why do you groan?
Modestus: Drive out your grief, brother! This triumph which calls us
should not be grieved over. Let go of your grief!
Narcissus: The returning grief again erases my joy   715

---

grandfather that they are right by acting out how they would verbally provoke
an imaginary executioner into chopping them up and thereby demonstrating
that one can display great fortitude even as one is being executed. Victor is
finally convinced that peaceful submission to martyrdom is the most correct
as well as glorious path, and puts on some devotional article, probably a
rosary, on his neck in a gesture showing that he is now ready to follow his
grandson and the rest of his faithful clan.

711 *Macte:* Emended from *Marte* in the manuscript.

sine laude sancti nominis quod abnuat
avus mori; mortemque tardare appetat.
Victor: Erras, animula sancta! Non mortem appeto
tardare. Tecum moriar invictus; cadam
tecum beatus. *Narcissus*: Attamen munis latus   720
hostemque metuis. *Victor*: Metuere hostes haud scio;
sed ultor illos funeri iungam meo.
Narcissus: Non vindicare Christiani est, O ave!
Moritur inultus. *Modestus*: Martyr ad palmam evolat
et provocare novit imminens malum.   725
Victor: Animosa suboles! Pone sollicitos metus;
vos ad coronam fortis antevolo et necem
provoco. Nepotes sancti, avi exemplum sequi
discite! *Modestus*: Sequemur impigre. *Narcissus*: Haec arma abice,
ave, ut verendam martyrum palmam feras.   730
Victor: Et vos iubetis impie in patres avum
agere, catenis Christianos ut feram
vinctos inultus? *Narcissus*: Christianum non decet
vindicta. *Modestus*: Cessa polluere frustra pias
manus cruore. *Narcissus*: Martyrum serva decus   735
intaminatum. *Modestus*: Sanguine, invitis, ave,
vis taminari, patribus? *Narcissus*: Nos, nos, ave,
ad fata promptos sequere! Sine telis neci
occurrimus; nos sequere. *Victor*: Capularis senex
pueros tenellos et nepotes avus, avus   740
senex sequatur consilia? *Modestus*: Ferrum impiger
abicio cupidus gloriae sacrae, deus
quam liberalis spondet. *Narcissus*: Exemplum pii
sequere nepotis, morte qui digna occidet.
Victor: O sancta prolis pectora! O fortes viri!   745
Tenella pectus indoles rapit et docet
fortia patrare. *Narcissus*: Pectus intrepidum fero,
cruenta rabies quidquid in caput struat.

---

724 *Non vindicare Christiani est*: Cf. e.g. *Rom.*12.19 on the advice to Christians not to seek vengeance for themselves but to leave retribution to God.

since my grandfather, who lacks the fame of sacred honour,
refuses to die; and he seeks to delay death.
Victor: You are wrong, dear little soul! I do not seek to delay
death. I shall die invincible, with you; I shall fall
blessed, with you. *Narcissus*: And yet you guard your flank   720
and fear your enemy. *Victor*: I do not know any fear of enemy;
but as an avenger, I shall join their death to mine.
Narcissus: It is the sign of a Christian not to exact revenge, O grandfather!
A Christian dies unavenged. *Modestus*: A martyr rushes to the victory-palm
and is able to challenge the evil which threatens him.   725
Victor: A lineage full of bravery! Let go of your fearful anxiety;
I am flying ahead of you to the prize and am challenging
death. Sacred grandsons, learn to follow
your grandfather's example! *Modestus*: We shall follow you promptly.
    Narcissus: Throw away these weapons,
grandfather, so that you may win the venerable victory-palm of martyrs.   730
Victor: You, too, order your grandfather to act impiously
toward the priests, so that I should let Christians be bound
in chains unavenged? *Narcissus*: Revenge is not suitable
for a Christian. *Modestus*: Stop polluting in vain your pious
hands with bloodshed. *Narcissus*: Preserve the honour of martyrs   735
uncontaminated. *Modestus*: Do you want to be contaminated with
    blood, grandfather,
though the priests be unwilling? *Narcissus*: Follow us, us, grandfather,
promptly to our death! We are meeting death
without weapons; follow us. *Victor*: Must an old man, close to his grave
follow tender little boys, must a grandfather, an aged grandfather   740
follow a grandson's advice? *Modestus*: I promptly throw away
my sword, wishing for sacred glory, which God
generously promises. *Narcissus*: Follow the example of your pious
grandson, who will die a worthy death.
Victor: O sacred hearts of my descendants! O courageous men!   745
Their young, tender nature takes hold of their hearts and teaches them
to perform courageous deeds. *Narcissus*: I keep my heart intrepid,
whatever cruel madness prepares against my own self.

738–9 *Sine telis neci/occurrimus*: The manuscript has *Sine telis necis/ occurrimus*, which may make sense if translated as 'We have come up (perfect tense) to you without weapons of death'. But the current emendation seems to make better sense.

Adesset utinam lictor et vinclis meos
obrueret artus; obvios ferrem pedes   750
non imparatus. Sequere praeeuntem, O ave!
Victor: Animula fortis! Melior, O suboles, calor
senile pectus incitat. *Modestus*: Ferrum abice!
Feri, satelles, viscera! En, ferro viam
pronus recludo. *Narcissus*: Praesto sum. Iugulum mete!   755
Modestus: Effunde vitam; sanguinis teneri sinus
rimare cunctos; lauream celera improbe!
Victor: O celsa mentis, O viro digna indoles!
Narcissus: In mille partes disseca! *Modestus*: Lania! *Narcissus*: Fode!
Modestus: Discerpe plagis! Corpus, en, sponte offero,   760
donec supremum spiritum eliciat furor.
Victor: Sancti nepotes! Gloria parentum et decus,
avoque melior degenere! Quo me rapis
ardore sacrae mentis? Ulceror! Comes
quo vos praeitis insequor, pugiles sacri.   765
Narcissus: Frustra sequeris, haec arma ni abicis, O ave,
minasque ponis. *Victor*: Abicio. *Narcissus*: Sic martyrum
simul ad coronas ferimur, et victoriae
lauros paramus. *Modestus*: Ferimur; armati sacrae
fidei sat armis, terimus in caelum viam.   770
Victor: O mihi nepotum nomen, O blandum nimis!
Ibo, ibo, sacrae Christus erit auspex viae.
Narcissus: Haec arma collo Christiani innectimus.
Modestus: His gloriosi martyres tuti satis
excipimus enses hostium. *Victor*: Et meo insero   775
sacra arma collo. Stabo pro causa dei
defensus istis fortis, invictus, pius.

---

754 In the manuscript the speaker's name (*Mod.*) is erroneously repeated at
the beginning of this line.

757 *lauream*: Emended from *laveam* in the manuscript.

I wish the guardsman were here, and were loading my limbs
with chains; I would move forward my steps 750
not unprepared. Follow our lead, O grandfather!
Victor: Courageous little soul! O my offspring, a better ardour
heats up my senile breast. *Modestus*: Throw away your sword!
[*Speaking to an imaginary executioner*] Strike, minion, my innards! [*Lies
    down, as if ready to be killed*] Behold, I open the path for your sword
lying prone. *Narcissus*: [*Stretching out his neck to an imaginary
    executioner*] I am here, slash my neck! 755
Modestus: Let my life-force flow out; open up every channel
of my youthful blood; make haste for my laurel, you wicked one!
Victor: O superb mental nature, worthy of a grown-up man!
Narcissus: Chop me up into a thousand pieces! *Modestus*: Mangle me!
    Narcissus: Stab me!
Modestus: Dismember me with cuts! Look, I offer my body of my own
    accord, 760
until your rage should draw out my last breath.
Victor: Sacred grandsons! Glory and honour of your parents,
better than your degenerate grandfather! Where are you taking me
with the ardour of your sacred mind? I am in pain! Sacred pugilists,
I am following you, whither you lead me. 765
Narcissus: [*Pointing to Victor's weapons*] You shall follow us in vain,
    unless you throw away these arms, O grandfather,
and unless you let go of your threats. *Victor*: I let them go. *Narcissus*:
    Thus we proceed
together to the prizes of martyrdom, and prepare
the laurels of victory. *Modestus*: We rush on; sufficiently armed
with the weapons of sacred faith, we march on our way to heaven. 770
Victor: O my grandsons, excessively sweet names to me!
I shall go, I shall go, Christ will be my guide on my sacred pathway.
Narcissus: [*Putting a rosary around Victor's neck*] We bind the neck of a
    Christian with this weapon.
Modestus: We, as glorious martyrs, sufficiently guarded with this,
take on the sword of our enemies. *Victor*: I, too, put on my neck 775
the sacred weapon. I shall stand for the cause of God
defended by this, brave, invincible, pious.

---

773 *Haec arma collo*: The 'arms' mentioned here may very well be a rosary.
Jesuit accounts on Japan often mention the *kirishitan* carrying rosaries
around their necks (see e.g. Trigault 1623: 58 and 122).

III.4

Andreas cum Christianis in Victorem et nepotes incidens gaudio
   perfunditur, et simul inermes ad martyrium pergunt.
Victor, Andreas, Modestus, Narcissus, Secundus, Iustus, Leo, Quirinus, Petrus,
   Theodorus.
Victor: O nate, lumen unicum patris!
O sacra turba, columen afflicti senis
et Christiani gloria populi, redis?   780
Andreas: O genitor! Oculus, genitor, O nati unicus!
Secundus: O quanta, Victor, cura nos tangit tui!
Andreas: Quis, genitor, armis efferum subito latus
distinuit? Ut me recreas! Salve, O pater!
Victor: Ignosce, fili; vosque, lux casti gregis,   785
ignoscite senio. †*Fran.*†: Excidit animo tumor
avidus cruoris? *Victor*: Excidit studium ferox.
Andreas: Totus revixi, genitor! O genitor, tua
pietate vivo; solida iam redit quies.
Quis efferati pectoris domuit minas?   790
Victor: Pietas pudicae prolis et sinus tui
viro invidenda germina, nepotes avo
meliore digni. *Andreas*: O macta progenies! *Modestus*: Pater,
Narcissus: Adest, pater, qui martyres caelo inserat
hostis. *Leo*: Beatum prole tam sancta patrem!   795
Andreas: O filiorum nomen, O blandum patri!
Victor: Avo nepotum blandius! *Andreas*: Sic, sic pii
esse in parentes pergite, O genus meum
meusque sanguis! *Quirinus*: Gratior numquam dies

778–824 III.4. Andreas, Secundus and other fellow Catholics come to join
Victor and his grandsons and congratulate him on his conversion. As one of
the persecutors silently appears on one side of the stage (794), the celebratory
group gets ready to march off to their glorious martyrdom.

778 *O nate, lumen unicum patris!*: The line is unmetrical as it stands. It may
be emended if one inserts *salve* after *nate*.

III.4

Andreas, chancing upon Victor and his grandsons together with the
Christians, is overcome with joy, and together they all proceed to
martyrdom unarmed.

*Victor, Andreas, Modestus, Narcissus, Secundus, Iustus, Leo, Quirinus, Petrus,
Theorodus.*

Victor: [*To Andreas and the rest of his fellow-believers, who return on stage*]
O son, sole splendour of me, your father!
O sacred crowd, bulwark of this afflicted old man
and glory of the Christian people, are you coming back? 780
Andreas: O father, O father, the only ornament of your son!
Secundus: O how much do we care about you, Victor!
Andreas: Who, father, suddenly removed the savage arms from
your flank? You give me such relief! Greetings, O father!
Victor: Forgive me, son; [*Turning to others*] and you all, splendour of
chaste flock, 790
forgive my old age. †*Fran.*†: Has anger, which was thirsting for blood,
left your soul? *Victor:* The savage zeal has left.
Andreas: I have wholly come back to life, father! O father, because of your
piety, I feel alive; now, solid peace returns to my mind.
Who tamed the threats of your angry heart? 790
Victor: The piety of my chaste offspring, the outgrowth
of your love who are worthy of a man's envy, grandsons worthy
of a better grandfather. *Andreas:* O my fine progeny! *Modestus:* [*Noticing
the persecutors approaching*] Father,
Narcissus: father, the enemy intent on sending martyrs to heaven
is here. *Leo:* O father blessed with such sacred progeny! 795
Andreas: O sons, appellation sweet to me your father!
Victor: And one sweeter to the grandfather, that of grandsons! *Andreas:*
Thus, thus
continue to be pious toward your parents, O my stock
and my blood! *Quirinus:* Never has a more pleasant day,

---

786 †*Fran.*†: The manuscript clearly has these letters, but there is no
character potentially matching such an abbreviation. Presumably this is an
error for another name, perhaps Andreas.

magis ominato Christianis sidere   800
refulsit ista. *Petrus*: O diem laetum! Diem
bene auspicatum, quo reviviscit gregis
pars Christiani! *Andreas*: Quo redit proli pater.
Modestus et Narcissus: Nepotibus avus. *Victor*: Parcite; gravia haec mihi
sunt immerenti nomina. Vocate impium,   805
sontem, ferocem, perfidum, consortio
tali pudendum, Christianorum probrum.
Andreas: O quantus isthaec viscera affectus tenet!
Agnosco numen, quod ratas voluit preces;
agnosco; largus munerum precantibus,   810
deus, es canalis. Quas tuis beneficiis
vices feremus ? *Iustus*: Summa contigimus spei
nihilque nobis restat optandum super.
Modestus: Imus! Trophaea legimus! *Narcissus*: Imus, o ave!
Victor: O sancta pectora! Imus auspiciis tuis,   815
O Christe; vitae vincula perosi necem
oppetimus ultro. *Modestus*: Christe, nos socia tuo
favore castis martyrum choris! *Narcissus*: Preces
ne sperne, Christe! *Andreas*: Gradimur in caelum viam;
vix, genitor, quid agam, gaudii impotens scio.   820
Amore tremulis sanguis in venis salit.
Victor: Cohors beata, prole cum sancta iuvat
praeire. Sequere. *Theodorus*: Rursus, O Victor, tibi
me iungo comitem. *Narcissus*: Pergimus. *Modestus*: O ave, pergimus.

---

802 *ista. Petrus: O diem*: The elision between *ista* and *O* would make the line
unmetrical. Other than assuming a hiatus, the change of *ista* to the alternate
form *istac* would fix the metre without causing any difference in meaning
(see L&S *istic* s.v.).

with a star more favourable to Christians,   800
shone forth than this one. *Petrus*: O happy day! Day
with a favourable omen, on which a part of the Christian flock
comes back to life! *Andreas*: On which a father has come back to his
    offspring.
Modestus and Narcissus: A grandfather to grandsons. *Victor*: Let go; to
    me, these appellations,
since I am unworthy, are painful. Call me impious,   805
guilty, savage, perfidious, worthy of shame
for such a group, the opprobrium of Christians.
Andreas: O what great affection takes hold of my innermost self!
I recognize the spirit of God, which wished our prayers to come true;
I recognize it; God, you are a generous source   810
of grace to those who pray. What return shall we offer
for your good deeds? *Iustus*: We have come to the pinnacle of our hope
and nothing more is left for us to wish.
Modestus: Off we go! We grasp our trophies! *Narcissus*: O grandfather,
    off we go!
Victor: O sacred hearts! We are going under your auspices,   815
O Christ; in hatred of the fetters of life, of our own accord
we seek death. *Modestus*: Christ, with your favour, make us join
the chaste troupes of martyrs! *Narcissus*: Do not spurn
our prayers, Christ! *Andreas*: We go on our way to heaven;
dizzy with joy, father, I hardly know what I am doing.   820
My blood dances with love in my vibrant veins.
Victor: Blessed cohort, it is a joy to go ahead
with my sacred progeny. Follow me! *Theodorus*: I join myself, O Victor,
as your companion again. *Narcissus*: We go on. *Modestus*: O grandfather,
    we go on. [*With Victor in the lead they begin to march off to meet the*
    persecutors, while they sing or chant the following hymn]

---

812 *vices feremus*: The manuscript has *feremus vices*, but a simple reversal of
the order corrects the metre.

819–21 *gradimur . . . salit*: These words are erroneously given to Victor in the
manuscript, but the speaker must be Andreas (cf. *genitor*: 820).

III.Chorus

Adhortatio brevis ad martyrium.
Andreas, Iustus, Secundus, Leo, Quirinus, Petrus.
Andreas: Pergite, carae, pergite, suboles,   825
haec stelliferos ducit ad axes,
generose parens, semita, perge.
Omnes: Hoc Christus iter, pergite, monstrat;
hac heroae virtute manus,
hac ad superos casibus ipsis   830
animae fortes ivere via.
Incluta palmae manet intrepidas
gloria mentes, quando tyranni
furor indomitus per membra rota
saevit et ense.   835
Sic martyrii sublime decus,
invicta cohors, perge, paramus.
Hoc, qui palma victrice calens
clarus in aevum vivere gestis,
tramite perge.   840

825–40 III chorus. In a concluding hymn, Andreas and others declare that
the path they have chosen is the one that leads to true Christian victory and
to heaven. The metre is anapestic dimetre.

III.Chorus

A brief exhortation to martyrdom.
Andreas, Iustus, Secundus, Leo, Quirinus, Petrus.
Andreas: [*To Modestus and Narcissus*] Go on, go on, my dear children,   825
this way leads to star-studded heaven,
[*To Victor*] noble parent, go on.
All: Go on, Christ shows us this path;
on this path, the bands heroic in virtue,
on this path, the souls made strong   830
by their very calamities, have gone.
The famed glory of the palm-wreath awaits intrepid
souls, as the tyrant's
untamed furor rages through the limbs with the wheel
and the sword.   835
In this way we prepare the sublime honour
of martyrdom; invincible cohort, go on.
You who, burning with the victorious palm-wreath
wish to live in fame through the ages,
go on this path.   840

---

832 *manet*: Emended from *manent* in the manuscript.

Bibliography

Latin Lexical Aids

DMLBS=The Dictionary of Medieval Latin from British Sources, in ΛΟΓΕΙΟΝ
  https://logeion.uchicago.edu (accessed 6 September 2021).
Forcellini=Forcellini, E. (1858–79), *Totius Latinitatis lexicon I-X*, Prato.
L&S=Lewis and Short's Latin-English Lexicon, in ΛΟΓΕΙΟΝ (see under
  DMLBS).
NLW=Johann Ramminger neulateinische Wortliste http://nlw.
  renaissancestrudier.org (accessed 6 September 2021).

Manuscripts

Archive der Zentraleuropäischen Provinz der Jesuiten (AZPJ), Signatur 41–6
  Abt. 4 (*Annales collegii Monacensis*).
Bayerische Staatsbibliothek (BSB), CLM 1550–3 (*Diarium Gymnasii et Collegii
  S.J. Monachii*), 1554 (*VJ, FE*).
Historisches Archiv Köln (KS), Best. 223 A684 (*Acta Sodalitatis B.V.
  Annuntiatae Confluentianae*), A 685 (*Annales Gymnasii Confluentini*).
Landeshauptarchiv Koblenz (LHA), Bestand 117 no. 706 (*JM A*), no. 716 (*JM
  B*), nos. 722 and 723 (*I&X*), no. 727 (*CB*).

Early Prints (–1800)

Besold, C. (1620), *De bombardis, ac item de typographia*, Tübingen.
Bidermann, J. (1666), *Ludi theatrales sacri sive opera comica posthuma*, Munich.
Caussin, N. (1621), *Tragoediae sacrae*, Cologne.
Erasmus, D. (1703), *Desiderii Erasmi Roterodami opera omnia emendatiora et
  auctiora II*, Leiden.
Fróis, L. (1599), *De rebus Iaponicis historica relatio*, Mainz.
Hontheim, J. N. von (1750), *Historia Trevirensis diplomatica et pragmatica III*,
  Augsburg.
Jesuits (1600), *Ratio atque institutio studiorum Societatis Iesu*, Dillingen.
Jesuits (1604), *Litterae societatis Iesu duorum annorum MDXCIIII et MDXCV,
  ad patres et fratres eiusdem sodietatis*, Naples.
Jesuits (1634), *Selectae Pp. soc. Iesu tragoediae*, Antwerp.
Kircher, A. (1665), *Mundus subterraneus, in XII libros digestus*, Amsterdam.

Locre, Ferry de (1608), *Maria Augusta virgo Deipara in septem libros tributa*, Arras.

Monte Simoncelli, B. (1614), *Laudatio in funere Francisci Medicei*, Florence.

Morejon, P. (1616), *Relacion de la persecucion que vuo en la yglesia de Iapon y de los insignes Martyres*, Mexico.

Pontanus, J. (1600), *Poeticarum institutionum libri III*, Ingolstadt.

Reusner, E. (1600), *Isagoges historicae libri duo*. Jena.

Rhay, T. (1665), *Amica lis, d.i. Streit ohne Streit*, Cologne.

Sacchini, F. (1652), *Historiae Societatis Iesu pars quarta sive Everardus*, Rome.

Sande, Duarte de (1590), *De missione legatorum Iaponensium ad Romanam curiam*, Macao.

Strigel, V. (1565), Ὑπομνήματα *in omnes epistolas Pauli et aliorum apostolorum et Apocalypsin*, Leipzig.

Tixier de Ravisi, J. (1615), *Ioan. Ravisii Textoris Nivernensis dialogi aliquot*, Basel.

Tixier de Ravisi, J. (1616), *Epitheta Ioannis Ravisii Textoris Nivernensis*, Lyon.

Torsellini, O. (1596), *De vita Francisci Xaverii*, Antwerp.

Trigault, N. (1623), *De Christianis apud Iaponios triumphis*, Munich.

Weyer, J. (1577), *De praestigiis daemonum et incantationibus ac veneficiis libri sex*, Basel.

Modern Sources (1801–)

Abele. A., ed. (2019), *Jeremias Drexel SJ: Iulianus Apostata Tragoedia*, Berlin.

Abmeier, K. (1986), *Der Trierer Kurfürst Philipp Christoph von Sötern und der Westfälische Friede*, Münster.

Bahlmann, P. (1896), *Die Jesuitendramen der niederrheinischen Ordensprovinz*, Leipzig.

Barbosa, M. J. de and S. T. de Pinho (eds), (2011), *Luís da Cruz: Teatro: Tomo II Vida Humana*, Coimbra.

Barea, J. P. (2013), 'Neo-Latin Drama in Spain, Portugal and Latin-America', in J. Bloemendal and H. B. Norland (eds), *Neo-Latin Drama and Theatre in Early Modern Europe,* 545–631, Leiden.

Barsby, J., ed., (1999), *Terence Eunuchus*, Cambridge.

Bauer, B. and J. Leonhardt (eds), (2000), *Triumphus divi Michaelis archangeli Bavarici*, Regensburg.

Becker, P. C. (1982), 'Die Entwicklung der Koblenzer Jesuitenschule (1580–1773) bis zur Übernahme durch Preussen (1815)', in Stadt Koblenz Presse-und Informationsamt, ed., *400 Jahre Gymnasium Confluentinum: Görres-Gymnasium Koblenz 1582–1982*, 10–13, Koblenz.

Becker, W. J. (1919), *Gesammelte Beiträge zur Literatur- und Theatergeschichte von Coblenz*, Koblenz.

Bellinghausen, F. (1973), *2000 Jahre Koblenz: Geschichte der Stadt an Rhein und Mosel*, Koblenz.

Boge, B. (2001), *Die Drucke der Offizin Haenlin in Dillingen und Ingolstadt von 1610 bis 1668. Eine kommentierte Bibliographie*, Wiesbaden.

Boxer, C. R. (1951), *The Christian Century in Japan 1549–1650*, Berkeley CA.

Büttner, M., ed. (2004), *Ludovicus Crucius: Sedecias: Die lateinische Tragödie von Luís da Cruz S. J.*, Frankfurt.

Chaplin Child, G. (1868), *Benedicite; or, Song of the Three Children*, London.

Chevalier, J. -F. (2013A), 'Contextualizing Nicolas Caussin's *Tragoediae Sacrae* (1620)', in J. Bloemendal, P. G. F. Eversmann and E. Streitman (eds), *Drama Performance and Debate: Theatre and Public Opinion in the Early Modern Period*, 253–68, Leiden.

Chevalier, J. -F. (2013B), 'Jesuit Neo-Latin Tragedy in France', in J. Bloemendal and H. B. Norland (eds), *Neo-Latin Drama and Theatre in Early Modern Europe*, 415–69, Leiden.

Chevalier, J. -F. (2013C), 'Neo-Latin Theatre in Italy', in J. Bloemendal and H. B. Norland (eds), *Neo-Latin Drama and Theatre in Early Modern Europe*, 25–101, Leiden.

Cieslik, H and T. Sakuma (eds and trans), (1974), *Pedouro Morehon: Nihon junkyōroku*, Tokyo.

Cieslik, H. (2004), *Kirishitan jidaino Nihonjin shisai*, Tokyo.

Clements, J. (2016), *Christ's Samurai: The True Story of the Shimabara Rebellion*, London.

Clulow, A. (2013), *The Company and the Shogun: The Dutch Encounter with Tokugawa Japan*, New York NY.

Collani, C. von (2005), 'Jesuitisches Schrifttum als Quellenfundus der China-Japan-Dramen', in A. Hsia and R. Wimmer (eds), *Mission und Theater: Japan und China auf den Bühnen der Gesellschaft Iesu*, 259–88, Regensburg.

Cooper, M. (2005), *The Japanese Mission to Europe, 1582–1590: The Journey of Four Samurai Boys Through Portugal, Spain and Italy*, Folkestone.

Csapo. E. (2014), 'Performing Comedy in the Fifth through Early Third Centuries', in M. Fontaine and A. Scafuro (eds), *The Oxford Handbook of Greek and Roman Comedy*, 50–69, Oxford.

Dietrich, M. (2000), 'Aufführung und Dramaturgie', in W. Pass and F. Niiyama-Kalicki (eds), *Johann Berhanrdt Staudt (1654–1712): Mulier Fortis: Drama des Wiener Jesuitenkollegium*, xvii–xxi, Graz.

Dillinger J. (2008), *Die politische Repräsentation der Landbevölkerung: Neuengland und Europa in der Frühen Neuzeit*, Stuttgart.

Ding. W. (2006), 'Remnants of Christianity from Chinese Central Asia in Medieval Ages', in R. Malek and P. Hofrichter (eds), *Jingiao: The Church of the East in China and Central Asia*, 149–62, Sankt Augustin.

Döpfert, M. (2017), 'Miles Iaponus et Christianus: Japanische Märtyrer auf der Jesuitenbühne', in A. Aurnhammer and B. Korte (eds), *Fremde Helden auf Europäischen Bühnen (1600–1900)*, 49–70, Würzburg.

Duhr, B. (1907–28), *Geschichte der Jesuiten in den Ländern deutscher Zunge I–IV*, Freiburg/Munich.

Dyck, A. R., ed. (2008), *Cicero: Catilinarians*, Cambridge.

Eckert, D. (2012), *Von Wilden un Wahrhaft Wilden: Wahrnehmungen der 'Neuen Welt' in ausgewählten europäischen Reiseberichten un Chroniken des 16. Jahuhunderts*, Hamburg.

Fernandes, R. M. R. and J. M. de Castro (eds), (1989), *Luís da Cruz: O pródigo v.1–2*, Lisbon.

Ferrand, M. (2014), 'Neo-Latin Literature-France: The Sixteenth Century: Literature', in P. Ford, J. Bloemendal and C. Fantazzi (eds), *Brill's Encyclopaedia of the Neo-Latin World: Micropedia*, 1068–71, Leiden.

Fitch, J. G. (2004), *Annaeana Tragica: Notes on the Text of Seneca's Tragedies*, Leiden.

Frèches, C. -H. (1964), *Le théâtre neo-latin au Portugal (1550–1745)*, Paris.

Garrod. R. (2019), 'Senecan Catharsis in Nicolas Caussin's Felicitas (1620): A Case Study in Jesuit Reconfiguration of Affects', in Y. Haskell and R. Garrod (eds), *Changing Hearts: Performing Jesuit Emotions between Europe, Asia and the Americas*, 23–42, Leiden.

Giraldez, A. (2015), *The Age of Trade: The Manila Galleons and the Dawn of the Global Economy*, Lanham.

Gonoi. T., ed. (2021), *Hidden Kirishitan of Japan Illustrated*, Kamakura.

Green, R. (2014), 'Poetic Psalm Paraphrases', in P. Ford, J. Bloemendal and C. Fantazzi (eds), *Brill's Encyclopaedia of the Neo-Latin World: Macropedia*, 461–9, Leiden.

Griffin, N. (2017), 'Drama', in V. Moul, ed., *A Guide to Neo-Latin Literature*, 221–34, Cambridge.

Grund. G. (2015), 'Tragedy', in S. Knight and S. Tilg (eds), *The Oxford Handbook of Neo-Latin*, 103–17, Oxford.

Gunderson, E. (2015), *Sublime Seneca: Ethics, Literature, Metaphysics*, Cambridge.

Haas, H. A. (1977), 'Erstausgabe eines lateinischen Jesuitendramas. Ein Unterrichtsversuch in der Studienstufe', *Der altsprachliche Unterricht*, 1977(5): 42–57.

Haas, H. A. (1982), 'Jodocus: Editio princeps der Handschrift 117 Nr. 725 im Landeshauptarchiv Koblenz', in Stadt Koblenz Presse-und Informationsamt, ed., *400 Jahre Gymnasium Confluentinum: Görres-Gymnasium Koblenz 1582–1982*, 124–32, Koblenz.

Haga, T. (2021), *Pax Tokugawana: The Cultural Flowering of Japan, 1603–1853*, trans. J. W. Carpenter, Tokyo.

Haskell, Y. (2014), 'The Passion(s) of Jesuit Latin', in P. Ford, J. Bloemendal and C. Fantazzi (eds), *Brill's Encyclopaedia of the Neo-Latin World: Macropedia*, 775–88, Leiden.

Helander, H. (2014), 'On Neologisms in Neo-Latin', in P. Ford, J. Bloemendal and C. Fantazzi (eds), *Brill's Encyclopaedia of the Neo-Latin World: Macropedia*, 37–54, Leiden.

Hesselink, R. H. (2016), *The Dream of Christian Nagasaki: World Trade and the Clash of Cultures, 1560–1640*, Jefferson, NC.

Henshall, K. (2013), *Historical Dictionary of Japan to 1945*, Lanham, MD.

Hocking, G. D. (1943), *A Study of the Tragoediae Sacrae of Father Caussin (1583–1651)*, Baltimore, MD.

Huber, G. (1954), *Kreuze über Nagasaki: Den sechsundzwanzig Erstlingsmartyrern Japans zum Gedächtnis*, Werl.

Immoos, T. (1981), 'Japanische Helden des europäischen Barocktheaters', *Maske und Kothurn* 27.1: 36–56

Immoos, T. (2005A), 'Fürstenspiegel in Japandramen', in A. Hsia and R. Wimmer (eds), *Mission und Theater: Japan und China auf den Bühnen der Gesellschaft Iesu*, 355–72, Regensburg.

Immoos, T. (2005B), 'Gratia Hosokawa, Heroine of an Opera in Vienna 1698', in A. Hsia and R. Wimmer (eds), *Mission und Theater: Japan und China auf den Bühnen der Gesellschaft Iesu*, 373–8, Regensburg.

Jontes, G. (1984), '"Japonenses Martyres": Japanische Stoffe im Grazer Jesuitentheater des 17. und 18. Jahrhunderts', *Historisches Jahrbuch der Stadt Graz* 15: 27–52.

Jowett, B. (trans.), (1892), *The Dialogues of Plato Translated into English II.* Oxford.

Kapitza, P. (1990), *Japan in Europa: Texte und Bilddokumente zur europäischen Japankenntnis von Marco Polo bis Wilhelm von Humboldt I*, Munich.

Kaminski, N. (1995), *Nicodemus Frischlin: Hildegardis Magna. Dido. Venus. Helvetiogermani: Historisch-kritische Edition. Band II: Überblicks- und Stellenkommentare*, Bern.

Kataoka, Y. (2010), *Nihon kirishitan junkyōshi*, Tokyo.

Keener, A. S. (2021), 'Japan Dramas and Shakespeare at St. Omers Jesuit English College', *Renaissance Quarterly* 74: 876–917.

Kishimoto, E. (2006), 'The Process of Translation in *Dictionarium Latino Lusitanicum, ac Iaponicum*', *Journal of Asian and African Studies* 72: 17–26.

Korenjak, M. (2016), *Geschichte der Neulateinischen Literatur: Vom Humanismus bis zur Gegenwart*, Munich.

Kunnert, H. (1963), 'Franz Fugger und der Türkenkrieg 1664', *Südostforschungen* 22: 299–311.

Leuchtenberger, J. C. (2013), *Conquering Demons: The 'Kirishitan', Japan, and the World in Early Modern Japanese Literature*, Ann Arbor, MI.

Lindauer, T. (2012), *But I thought all witches were wicked: Hexen und Zauberer in der phantastischen Kinder- und Jugendliteratur in England und Deutschland*, Marburg

Logan, A. M. and L. M. Brockey (2003), 'Nicolas Trigault, SJ: A Portrait by Peter Paul Rubens', *Metropolitan Museum Journal*, 38: 157–67.

Mahoney, A. (2001), *Allen and Greenough's New Latin Grammar*, Newburyport MA.

Manuwald, G. (2011), *Roman Republican Theatre*, Cambridge.

Matsuo, K. (2007), *A History of Japanese Buddhism*, Folkestone.

McCabe, W. H. (1983), *An Introduction to Jesuit Theater*, St. Louis MO.

Michel, F. (1919), 'Das ehemalige Jesuitenkolleg und seine Bauten. Beitrag zur Baugeschichte der Stadt Koblenz', *Trierisches Archiv*, 28/29: 81–144.

Minkova, M. (2015), 'Conversational Latin: 1650 to the Present', in P. Ford, J. Bloemendal and C. Fantazzi (eds), *Brill's Encyclopaedia of the Neo-Latin World: Macropedia*, 83–6, Leiden.

Miyake, H. (1956), 'Nagasaki bugyō Hasegawa Sahyōe ronkō: kinsei gaikōseisakuno ichikōsatsu', *Shien*, 69: 75–97.

Mizobe, O. (1990), 'Ogasawara Genyano junkyō', *Bulletin for the Association for the Study of Kirishitan Culture*, 96: 13–30.

Money, D. (2015), 'Neo-Latin Verse in the Twilight Years (1700–Present)', in P. Ford, J. Bloemendal and C. Fantazzi (eds), *Brill's Encyclopaedia of the Neo-Latin World: Macropedia*, 865–78, Leiden.

Moran, J. F. (1993), *The Japanese and the Jesuits: Alessandro Valignano in Sixteenth Century Japan*, London.

Mortimer, G. (2015), *The Origins of the Thirty Years War and the Revolt in Bohemia, 1618*, Basingstoke.

Oba, H. (2016), 'kinseinai Ōsutoriano kyojōtoshi Gurātsuni okeru Iezusukaigekito Higo·Yatsushirono junkyōsha – 'Nihongeki'no hikaku kōsatsuno tameni –', *Hikakutoshikenkyū* 35.1: 43–58.

Oda, Z. (1986), *Makaoni nemuru Kirishitan junkyōsha*, Tokyo.

Ogasawara, K. (2020), *Dignity in Silence: Secrets to Mastering the Undefeatable Presence of a Samurai*, Chigasaki.

O'Malley, J. W. (1993), *The First Jesuits*, Cambridge MA.

O'Malley, J. W. (2010), *A History of the Popes: From Peter to the Present*, Lanham, MD.

Omata, R. H. (2020), 'Iezusukaino kōtekijunkyōkanwo *Iezusukaino hyakunenzō* (1640) kara himotoku: Nipponno daihyōtekina junkyōshatoshiteno Spinorazō', *Bulletin for the Association for the Study of Kirishitan Culture*, 155: 1–44.

Parente, J. (1987), *Religious Drama and the Humanist Tradition: Christian Theater in Germany and in the Netherlands, 1500–1680*, Leiden.

Parente, J. (1996), 'Tragoedia Politica: Strasbourg School Drama and the Early Modern State, 1583–1621', *Colloquia Germanica*, 29: 1–11.

Pass, W. and N. F. Kalicki (eds), (2000), *Mulier fortis: Drama des Wiener Jesuitenkollegium*, Graz.

Pavone, S. (2005), *The Wily Jesuits and the Monita secreta: The Forged Secret Instructions of the Jesuits: Myth and Reality*, trans. J. P. Murphy, St. Louis, MO.

Plechl, H. (1972), *Orbis latinus: Lexikon lateinischer geographischer Namen des Mittelalters und der Neuzeit, I A–D*, Budapest.

Pöhlmann, E. (2020), *Ancient Music in Antiquity and Beyond*, Berlin.

Proot, G. and J. Verberckmoes (2002), '*Japonica* in the Jesuit Drama of the Southern Netherlands', *Bulletin of Portuguese – Japanese Studies* 5: 27–47.

Rädle, F. (1979), 'Das Jesuitentheater in der Pflicht der Gegenreformation', *Daphnis* 8.3: 167–99.

Rädle, F. (2013), 'Jesuit Theatre in Germany, Austria and Switzerland', in J. Bloemendal and H. B. Norland (eds), *Neo-Latin Drama and Theatre in Early Modern Europe*, 185–292, Leiden.

Rasch, R. (2014), 'Latin Words to Music', in P. Ford, J. Bloemendal and C. Fantazzi (eds), *Brill's Encyclopaedia of the Neo-Latin World: Macropedia*, 519–36, Leiden.

Reff. D. T., R. K. Danford, and R. D. Gill (eds), (2014), *The First European Description of Japan, 1585*, London.

Retana, W. E. (1910), *Noticias histórico-bibliográficas del teatro en Filipinas desde sus orígenes hasta 1898*, Madrid.

Rohrschneider, M. (2016), 'Französisch-habsburgische Kooperation im Jahrhundert vor dem „renversement des alliances": Die Schlacht von Mogersdorf/St. Gotthard 1664', in K. Sperl, M. Scheutz and A. Strohmeyer (eds), *Die Schlacht von Mogersdorf/St. Gotthard und der Friede von Eisenburg/Vasvár*, 101–20, Eisenstadt.

Roldán-Figueroa, R. (2021), *The Martyrs of Japan: Publication History and Catholic Missions in the Spanish World (Spain, New Spain, and the Philippines, 1597–1700)*, Leiden.

Rosenstatter, J. (2010), *Dramenstoffe aus Karibik und Fernost im lateinischen Barocktheater der Alma Mater Benedictina zu Salzburg*, Frankfurt.

Rubiés, J.- P. (2020), 'From Idolatry to Religions: The Missionary Discourses on Hinduism and Buddhism and the Invention of Monotheistic Confucianism, 1550–1700', *Journal of Early Modern History* 24: 499–536.

Schmid, A. (2001), 'Das Jesuitenkolleg St. Michael zu München in der frühen Neuzeit', in J. Oswald and Rita Haub (eds), *Jesuitica. Forschungen zur frühen Geschichte des Jesuitenordens in Bayern bis zur Aufhebung 1773*, 115–54, Munich.

Schwemmer, P. (2022), 'Found in Translation: The Jesuit Japan Letters as a Source of Early Modern European Images of Japan', in H. Oba, F. Schaffenrath and A. Watanabe (eds), *Japan on the Jesuit Stage: Transmissions, Receptions, and Regional Contexts*, 35–56, Leiden.

Scioli, S., ed. (2013), *Daniello Bartoli: Il Giappone, Edizione critica*, University of Bologna Ph.D. dissertation.

Selbmann, R. (1996), *Vom Jesuitenkolleg zum humanistischen Gymnasium: Zur Geschichte des Deutschunterrichts in Bayern zwischen Gegenreformation und Gegenwart am Wilhelmsgymnasium München*, Frankfurt.

Sidwell, K. (2015), 'Classical Latin-Medieval Latin-Neo-Latin', in S. Knight and S. Tilg (eds), *The Oxford Handbook of Neo-Latin*, 13–26, Oxford.

Sidwell, K. (2017), 'Editing Neo-Latin Literature', in V. Moul, ed., *A Guide to Neo-Latin Literature*, 394–407, Cambridge.

Shimizu, K. (1975), 'Kinsei shotō Nagasaki daikanno ichi yakuwarini tsuite: tokuni Hasegawa Fujihirowo chūshinto shite', *Nagasaki teidan* 58: 50–70.

Shimizu, Y. (2012), *Kinsei Nihonto Ruson*, Tokyo.

Smutny, Y. (2016), *Chanoyuto Iezusukai senkyōshi*, Kyoto.

Staud, G. (1994), *A magyarországi jezsuita iskolai színjátékok forrásai IV*, Budapest.

Strasser, U. (2015), 'Copies with Souls: The Late Seventeenth-century Marianas Martyrs, Francis Xavier, and the Question of Clerical Reproduction', *Journal of Jesuit Studies* 2: 558–85.

Szarota, E. M. (1980–7), *Das Jesuitendrama im deutschen Sprachgebiet: eine Periochen-Edition I–IV*, Munich.

Takao, M. (2019), '"In what storms of blood from Christ's flock is Japan swimming?": Gratia Hosokawa and the Performative Representation of Japanese Martyrdom in *Mulier fortis* (1698)', in Y. Haskell and R. Garrod (eds), *Changing Hearts: Performing Jesuit Emotions between Europe, Asia and the Americas*, 87–120, Leiden.

Takenaka, M. and C. Burnett (eds), (1995), *Jesuit Plays on Japan and English Recusancy*, Tokyo.

Tilg, S., ed. (2005), *Die Hl. Katharina von Alexandria auf der Jesuitenbühne: Drei Innsbrucker Dramen aus den Jahren 1576, 1577 und 1606*, Berlin.

Toifl, L. (2016), 'Die Schlacht von Mogersdorf/St. Gotthard am 1. August 1664', in K. Sperl, M. Scheutz and A. Strohmeyer (eds), *Die Schlacht von Mogersdorf/ St. Gotthard und der Friede von Eisenburg/Vasvár*, 151–72, Eisenstadt.

Torino, A., ed. (2007), *Bernardinus Stephonius S. J.: Crispus: Tragoedia*, Rome.

Tunberg, T. (2014), 'Conversational Latin up to 1650', in P. Ford, J. Bloemendal and C. Fantazzi (eds), *Brill's Encyclopaedia of the Neo-Latin World: Macropedia*, 75–82, Leiden.

Urbano, C. M. (2005), 'The Paciecidos by Bartolomeu Pereira S. J. – An Epic Interpretation of Evangelisation and Martyrdom in 17th century Japan', *Bulletin of Portuguese-Japanese Studies*, 11: 61–95.

Valentin, J. M. (1983–4), *Le théâtre des jésuites dans les pays de langue allemande. Répertoire chronologique des pièces représentées et des documents conservés (1555–1773) I–II*, Stuttgart.

Washizuka, H. and R. Goepper (1997), *Enlightenment Embodied: The Art of the Japanese Buddhist Sculptor (7th–14th Centuries)*, New York.

Watanabe, A. (2018), '*mirum videri non debet, si Iapones Romano nonnumquam vestitu induantur* – Romanization of the Japanese in Jesuit Neo-Latin', *Bulletin of Portuguese-Japanese Studies*, 4: 101–16.

Watanabe, A. (2020), 'Catholicism, Early Modern Japan, and the Greco-Roman Classics', *Itineraria*, 19: 197–213.

Weber, D. (1997), *Japanische Märtyrer auf der Bühne des Jesuitentheaters*, Vienna.

Weber, H. (1969), *Frankreich, Kutrier, der Rhein und das Reich 1623–1635*, Bonn.

Wiley, T. (2002), *Original Sin: Origins, Developments, Contemporary Meanings*, New York, NY.

Wilson, P. H. (2009), *Europe's Tragedy: A History of the Thirty Years War*, London.

Wimmer, R. (2005), 'Japan und China auf den Jesuitenbühnen des deutschen Sprachgebietes', in R. Wimmer and A. Hsia (eds), *Mission und Theater: China und Japan auf den deutschen Bühnen der Gesellschaft Jesu*, 17–58, Regensburg.

Yamada, R. (2003), 'The Myth of Zen in the Art of Archery', in T. A. Green and J. R. Smith (eds), *Martial Arts in the Modern World*, 71–92, Westport, CT.

Yanitelli, V. R. (1949), 'Jesuit Education and the Jesuit Theatre', *Jesuit Educational Quarterly* XI.3: 133–45.

Yilmaz, Y. (2016), 'Grand Vizieral Authority Revisited: Köprülüs' Legacy and Kara Mustafa Paşa', *Mediterranean Historical Review* 31.1: 21–42.

Yūki, R., ed. (1994), *Nihon nijyūrokuseijin jyunkyōki*, Nagasaki.

Zuber, K. H. (2016), *Koblenz erleben: Die 25 schönsten Entdeckungen*, Erfurt.

Index of Names

This index includes the names of ancient and early modern authors and biblical books referred to as inspirations and precedents, and of the historical figures which the early modern texts mention, as well as selected Buddhist appellations which may be less familiar to Western readers; it covers the Introduction and Commentaries.